Ninth Workshop on NLP for Similar Languages, Varities and Dialects (VarDial 2022)

Gyeongju, South Korea
16 October 2022

ISBN: 978-1-7138-6199-7

Printed from e-media with permission by:

Curran Associates, Inc.
57 Morehouse Lane
Red Hook, NY 12571

Some format issues inherent in the e-media version may also appear in this print version.

Association for Computational Linguistics
209 N. Eighth Street
Stroudsburg, Pennsylvania 18360

Phone: 1-570-476-8006
Fax: 1-570-476-0860

acl@aclweb.org

Additional copies of this publication are available from:

Curran Associates, Inc.
57 Morehouse Lane
Red Hook, NY 12571 USA
Phone: 845-758-0400
Fax: 845-758-2633
Email: curran@proceedings.com
Web: www.proceedings.com

COLING

Volume 29 (2022), No. 19

Proceedings of the Ninth Workshop on NLP for Similar Languages, Varieties and Dialects (VarDial 2022)

The 29th International Conference on Computational Linguistics

October 12 - 17, 2022
Gyeongju, Republic of Korea

Preface

These proceedings include the 13 papers presented at the Ninth Workshop on NLP for Similar Languages, Varieties and Dialects (VarDial), co-located with the 29th International Conference on Computational Linguistics (COLING). Both COLING and VarDial were held in Gyeongju, South Korea, in a hybrid format, allowing all participants to either be present on-site or join virtually.

VarDial has now reached its ninth edition and continues serving the community as the main venue for researchers interested in the computational processing of diatopic language variation. The papers accepted this year address a wide range of NLP tasks such as corpus building, part-of-speech tagging and machine translation, but also address more theoretical questions related to micro-scale variation, cognate detection, mutual intelligibility and dialectometry. We are happy to see such a diverse set of research papers advancing the state of the art of NLP for dialects, low-resource languages, and language varieties.

As in previous years, the evaluation campaign continues to be an essential part of the VarDial workshop. This year, three shared tasks were proposed: Identification of Languages and Dialects of Italy (ITDI), French Cross-Domain Dialect Identification (FDI), and Dialectal Extractive Question Answering (DialQA). All three tasks address important issues in dialect and language identification. This volume includes five system description papers prepared by the participating teams, as well as a report summarizing the results and findings of the evaluation campaign.

Finally, we would like to take this opportunity to thank the shared task organizers and the participants of the evaluation campaign for their hard work. We further thank our amazing VarDial program committee members for their thorough reviews. They have been a very important part of the workshop's success in the past years.

The VarDial workshop organizers:

Yves Scherrer, Tommi Jauhiainen, Nikola Ljubešić, Preslav Nakov, Jörg Tiedemann, and Marcos Zampieri

`http://sites.google.com/view/vardial-2022/`

Organizers:

Yves Scherrer - University of Helsinki (Finland)
Tommi Jauhiainen - University of Helsinki (Finland)
Nikola Ljubešić - Jožef Stefan Institute (Slovenia) and University of Zagreb (Croatia)
Preslav Nakov - Qatar Computing Research Institute, HBKU (Qatar)
Jörg Tiedemann - University of Helsinki (Finland)
Marcos Zampieri - George Mason University (USA)

Program Committee:

Željko Agić (Corti, Denmark)
César Aguilar (Universidad Veracruzana, Mexico)
Laura Alonso y Alemany (University of Cordoba, Argentina)
Eric Atwell (University of Leeds, United Kingdom)
Jorge Baptista (University of Algarve and INESC-ID, Portugal)
Eckhard Bick (University of Southern Denmark, Denmark)
Johannes Bjerva (University of Copenhagen, Denmark)
Francis Bond (Nanyang Technological University, Singapore)
Aoife Cahill (Educational Testing Service, United States)
David Chiang (University of Notre Dame, United States)
Paul Cook (University of New Brunswick, Canada)
Çağrı Çöltekin (University of Tübingen)
Jon Dehdari (Think Big Analytics, United States)
Liviu Dinu (University of Bucharest, Romania)
Stefanie Dipper (Ruhr University Bochum, Germany)
Sascha Diwersy (University of Montpellier, France)
Mark Dras (Macquarie University, Australia)
Tomaž Erjavec (Jožef Stefan Institute, Slovenia)
Pablo Gamallo (University of Santiago de Compostela, Spain)
Cyril Goutte (National Research Council, Canada)
Nizar Habash (New York University Abu Dhabi, UAE)
Chu-Ren Huang (Hong Kong Polytechnic University, Hong Kong)
Radu Ionescu (University of Bucharest, Romania)
Surafel Melaku Lakew (FBK , Italy)
Ekaterina Lapshinova-Koltunski (Saarland University, Germany)
Lung-Hao Lee (National Central University, Taiwan)
John Nerbonne (University of Groningen, Netherlands and University of Freiburg, Germany)
Kemal Oflazer (Carnegie-Mellon University in Qatar, Qatar)
Maciej Ogrodniczuk (IPAN, Polish Academy of Sciences, Poland)
Petya Osenova (Bulgarian Academy of Sciences, Bulgaria)
Santanu Pal (Saarland University, Germany)
Barbara Plank (LMU Munich, Germany and ITU Copenhagen, Denmark)
Taraka Rama (University of North Texas, United States)
Francisco Rangel (Autoritas Consulting, Spain)
Reinhard Rapp (University of Mainz, Germany and University of Aix-Marseille, France)
Paolo Rosso (Technical University of Valencia, Spain)
Rachel Edita O. Roxas (National University, Phillipines)

Fatiha Sadat (Université du Québec à Montréal (UQAM), Canada)
Tanja Samardžić (University of Zurich, Switzerland)
Kevin Scannell (Saint Louis University, United States)
Serge Sharoff (University of Leeds, United Kingdom)
Miikka Silfverberg (University of British Columbia, Canada)
Kiril Simov (Bulgarian Academy of Sciences, Bulgaria)
Milena Slavcheva (Bulgarian Academy of Sciences, Bulgaria)
Marco Tadić (University of Zagreb, Croatia)
Liling Tan (Rakuten Institute of Technology, Singapore)
Joel Tetreault (Dataminr, United States)
Francis Tyers (Indiana University, United States)
Pidong Wang (Google Inc., United States)
Taro Watanabe (Google Inc., Japan)

Table of Contents

Conference Program

Sunday, October 20, 2022

10:00–10:10 ***Opening Session***

10:10–10:30 *Findings of the VarDial Evaluation Campaign 2022*
Noëmi Aepli, Antonios Anastasopoulos, Adrian-Gabriel Chifu, William Domingues, Fahim Faisal, Mihaela Gaman, Radu Tudor Ionescu and Yves Scherrer

10:30–10:45 *Transfer Learning Improves French Cross-Domain Dialect Identification: NRC @ VarDial 2022*
Gabriel Bernier-Colborne, Serge Leger and Cyril Goutte

10:45–11:00 *Is Encoder-Decoder Transformer the Shiny Hammer?*
Nat Gillin

11:00–11:30 ***Coffee break***

11:30–11:45 *Italian Language and Dialect Identification and Regional French Variety Detection using Adaptive Naive Bayes*
Tommi Jauhiainen, Heidi Jauhiainen and Krister Lindén

11:45–12:00 *The Curious Case of Logistic Regression for Italian Languages and Dialects Identification*
Giacomo Camposampiero, Quynh Anh Nguyen and Francesco Di Stefano

12:00–12:15 *Neural Networks for Cross-domain Language Identification. Phlyers @Vardial 2022*
Andrea Ceolin

12:15–13:15 ***Invited Talk by Tanja Samardžić (University of Zurich)***

13:15–14:30 ***Lunch break***

Phonetic, Semantic, and Articulatory Features in Assamese-Bengali Cognate Detection
14:30–15:00 Abhijnan Nath, Rahul Ghosh and Nikhil Krishnaswamy

15:00-15:15 *Annotating Norwegian language varieties on Twitter for Part-of-speech*
Petter Mæhlum, Andre Kåsen, Samia Touileb and Jeremy Barnes

15:15–15:45 *OcWikiDisc: a Corpus of Wikipedia Talk Pages in Occitan*
Aleksandra Miletic and Yves Scherrer

Sunday, October 20, 2022

15:45–16:00 *Low-Resource Neural Machine Translation: A Case Study of Cantonese*
Evelyn Kai-Yan Liu

16:00–16:30 ***Coffee break***

16:30–17:00 *Mapping Phonology to Semantics: A Computational Model of Cross-Lingual Spoken-Word Recognition*
Iuliia Zaitova, Badr Abdullah and Dietrich Klakow

17:00–17:15 *Social Context and User Profiles of Linguistic Variation on a Micro Scale*
Olga Kellert and Nicholas Hill Matlis

17:15–17:45 *dialectR: Doing Dialectometry in R*
Ryan Soh-Eun Shim and John Nerbonne

17:45–18:45 ***Invited Talk by Dong Nguyen (Utrecht University)***

18:45–19:00 ***Closing Remarks***

Findings of the VarDial Evaluation Campaign 2022

Noëmi Aepli[1 · ITDI], Antonios Anastasopoulos[2 · DialQA], Adrian Chifu[3 · FDI], William Domingues[3 · FDI], Fahim Faisal[2 · DialQA], Mihaela Găman[4 · FDI], Radu Tudor Ionescu[4 · FDI], Yves Scherrer[5 · ITDI]

[1]University of Zurich, [2]George Mason University, [3]Aix-Marseille Université, [4]University of Bucharest, [5]University of Helsinki

Abstract

This report presents the results of the shared tasks organized as part of the VarDial Evaluation Campaign 2022. The campaign is part of the ninth workshop on Natural Language Processing (NLP) for Similar Languages, Varieties and Dialects (VarDial), co-located with COLING 2022. Three separate shared tasks were included this year: Identification of Languages and Dialects of Italy (ITDI), French Cross-Domain Dialect Identification (FDI), and Dialectal Extractive Question Answering (DialQA). All three tasks were organized for the first time this year.

1 Introduction

The workshop series on *NLP for Similar Languages, Varieties and Dialects* (VarDial), traditionally co-located with international conferences, has reached its ninth edition. Since the first edition, VarDial has hosted shared tasks on various topics such as language and dialect identification, morphosyntactic tagging, question answering, and cross-lingual dependency parsing. The shared tasks have featured many languages and dialects from different families and data from various sources, genres, and domains (Chakravarthi et al., 2021; Gaman et al., 2020; Zampieri et al., 2019, 2018, 2017; Malmasi et al., 2016; Zampieri et al., 2015, 2014).

We offered three shared tasks as part of the VarDial Evaluation Campaign 2022, which we present in this paper: Identification of Languages and Dialects of Italy (ITDI), French Cross-Domain Dialect Identification (FDI), and Dialectal Extractive Question Answering (DialQA).

This overview paper is structured as follows: in Section 2, we briefly introduce the three shared tasks. Section 3 presents the teams that submitted systems to the shared tasks. Each task is then discussed in detail, focusing on the data, the participants' approaches, and the obtained results. Section 4 is dedicated to ITDI, Section 5 to FDI, and Section 6 to DialQA.

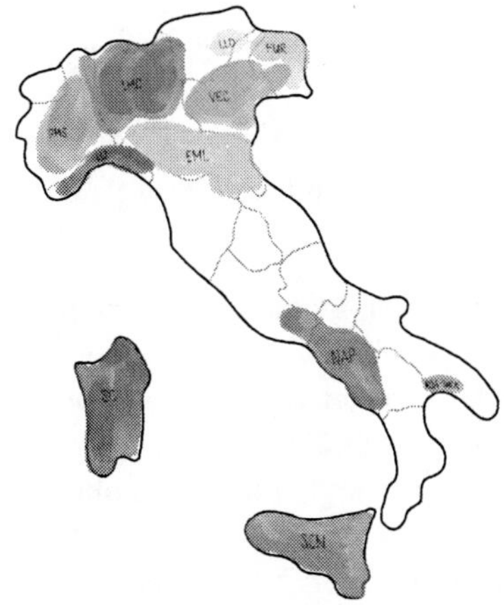

Figure 1: Rough regions where the eleven considered languages and dialects of Italy are spoken. magenta: Italo-Dalmatian; turquoise: Gallo-Italian; yellow: Gallo-Rhaetian; red: Sardinian. The map is vague; the situation is more complex. However, it gives an idea of where in Italy to locate the varieties.

2 Shared Tasks at VarDial 2022

2.1 Identification of Languages and Dialects of Italy (ITDI)

Italy features a rich linguistic diversity with numerous local and regional language varieties. Many of the varieties form a continuum, but some others are very distinct. The ITDI shared task focuses on eleven language varieties that belong to the Romance language branch (like Italy's official language, Italian) and have their own Wikipedia.[1] Figure 2 displays the relations of the eleven language varieties according to the classification by Ethnologue (Eberhard et al., 2022), and Figure 1 shows the approximate regions where they are mainly spoken.

[1]by March 2022, when we created the shared task.

Proceedings of the Ninth Workshop on NLP for Similar Languages, Varieties and Dialects, pages 1–13
October 16, 2022. ©2022 Association for Computational Linguistics

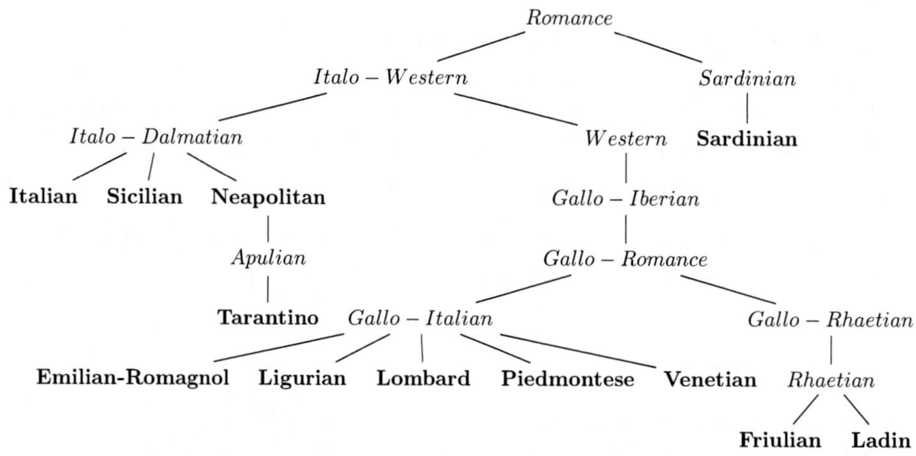

Figure 2: Relations between the eleven considered languages and dialects of Italy, according to Ethnologue.

ken.[2] More fine-grained classifications within dialects are possible. We must remember that classification into categories is imprecise for a continuum as we work with distinct rather than continuous values. Depending on the availability of data, all the data splits (training, development, test) may contain one or several sub-varieties of the category predetermined by the Wikipedia dumps. Furthermore, we rely on the categorization by the authors of the texts, which might not be the one every native speaker agrees upon.

To the best of our knowledge, no previous language identification research focuses exclusively on Italy's languages and dialects. However, some of the language varieties featured in our shared task have been part of other research related to language identification. Jauhiainen et al. (2022) present a detailed overview. More generally, Ramponi (2022) reviews recent work on NLP for the language varieties of Italy and identifies the most pressing challenges for their computational processing.

The ITDI task is a cross-domain classification task in which the model is required to discriminate between eleven languages and dialects of Italy. The setting is similar to a real-world problem because the training data consists only of Wikipedia dumps, i.e., careful pre-processing is part of the task. Furthermore, the data is not balanced in any of the data splits. Finally, development and test splits only contain sentences of distinct subsets of the eleven languages and dialects and come from different sources and domains (see Appendix A.1 for details). The submission format is closed, meaning that participants cannot use additional data to train their models – exceptions are off-the-shelf pre-trained language models, which only one team made use of.

2.2 French Cross-Domain Dialect Identification (FDI)

For the 2022 French Cross-Domain Dialect Identification (FDI) shared task, participants had to train a model on news samples collected from a set of publication sources and evaluate it on news samples collected from a different set of publication sources. To ensure that dialect identification models do not rely on features such as author style or text topic, the publication sources and the topics are different across splits. Therefore, participants had to build a model for a cross-domain four-way classification by dialect task, in which a classification method is required to discriminate between the French (FR), Swiss (CH), Belgian (BE), and Canadian (CA) dialects observed in news samples. For the shared task, we provided participants with the French Cross-Domain Dialect dataset (Găman et al., 2022), which contains French, Swiss, Belgian, and Canadian samples of text collected from the news domain. The corpus is divided into training, validation and test, such that the training set contains 358,787 samples, the development set 18,002 samples, and the test set 36,733 samples.

Participants are evaluated in two separate scenarios: open and closed. In the closed format, participants are not allowed to use pre-trained models or external data to train their models. In the open

[2]We created this map according to `https://upload.wikimedia.org/wikipedia/commons/3/32/Dialetti_e_lingue_in_Italia.png` (Antonio Ciccolella via Wikimedia Commons, 2015).

Team	ITDI	FDI	DialQA	System Description Paper
DCT		✓		Gillin (2022)
ETHZ	✓			Camposampiero et al. (2022)
NRC		✓		Bernier-Colborne et al. (2022)
Phlyers	✓			Ceolin (2022)
SUKI	✓	✓		Jauhiainen et al. (2022)

Table 1: The teams that participated in the VarDial Evaluation Campaign 2022.

format, participants are allowed to use external resources such as unlabeled corpora, lexicons, and pre-trained embeddings (e.g. CamemBERT (Martin et al., 2020)), but the use of additional labeled data is still not allowed.

2.3 Dialectal Extractive Question Answering (DialQA)

Question Answering (QA) systems are capable of answering human prompts with or without context. With the advancement of query-based smartphone assistants (eg. Google Assistant, Amazon Alexa, or Apple Siri), the use-case scenarios of such systems have already reached a global scale. However, in most cases, the traditional text-based extractive QA systems still follow the training routine on error-free written text, whereas the real-world scenario contains error-prone interfaces.

This year we introduced the DialQA shared task to build QA systems that are robust to dialectal variation. To make extractive QA systems more representative of real-world scenarios, we prepared an evaluation dataset based on the existing TyDi-QA (Clark et al., 2020) dataset with two additional dimensions. First, the augmented question text contains dialectal and/or geographical language variations. Second, we provide these questions in spoken form to match the scenario of users querying virtual assistants for information. The participants could either (a) use the baseline automatic speech recognition outputs for each dialect to make a robust text-based QA system, or (b) they may use the provided audio recordings of the questions to make a dialect-robust ASR system which can be then evaluated with a baseline QA system, or (c) both of the above. The shared task was based on the SD-QA (Faisal et al., 2021) development and test datasets for English, Arabic, and Kiswahili varieties, as well as code for training text-based baseline extractive QA systems based on TyDi-QA.

3 Participating Teams

A total of five teams submitted runs to the ITDI and FDI shared tasks. Unfortunately, we did not receive any submissions for DialQA. In Table 1, we list the teams that participated in the shared tasks, including references to the system description papers which are published as parts of the VarDial workshop proceedings. Detailed information about the submissions is included in the task-specific sections below.

4 Identification of Languages and Dialects of Italy

4.1 Dataset

The training set consists of eleven Wikipedia dumps:[3] Emilian-Romagnol (EML), Friulian (FUR), Ladin (LLD), Ligurian (LIJ), Lombard (LMO), Neapolitan (NAP), Piedmontese (PMS), Sardinian (SC), Sicilian (SCN), Tarantino (ROA_TARA) and Venetian (VEC). We provided the participants with a script to download and extract the dumps on the basis of WikiExtractor (Attardi, 2015).

The development and test sets come from several online sources.[4] We only included sentences with a minimum length of five and a maximum of 35 tokens. Table 2 shows the number of articles (training set) and sentences (development and test set) of the data splits. The released test set contains 11,090 lines.[5]

4.2 Participants and Approaches

ETHZ: The predictions submitted by the ETHZ team (Camposampiero et al., 2022) were produced by a logistic regression (using a sag solver and

[3] `pages-articles-multistream.xml.bz2`, from 01.03.2022, now available on GitHub: `https://github.com/noe-eva/ITDI_2022`.

[4] See Appendix A.1 and for more information.

[5] Including three empty lines, which we deleted for the evaluation.

Language	Tag	Train articles	Dev sentences	Test sentences
Emilian-Romagnol	EML	12,996	–	825
Friulian	FUR	3,750	676	1,323
Ladin	LLD	11,981	–	2,200
Ligurian	LIJ	10,912	617	2,282
Lombard	LMO	50,518	1,231	689
Neapolitan	NAP	14,789	–	2,026
Piedmontese	PMS	66,268	1,191	–
Sardinian	SC	7,419	477	–
Sicilian	SCN	26,464	1,371	–
Tarantino	ROA_TARA	9,322	–	603
Venetian	VEC	68,955	1,236	1,139
Total		283,374	6,799	11,087

Table 2: Number of articles (train) and sentences (dev/test) in the ITDI data set.

class weights) and a BERT model built on the `dbmdz-xxl-cased`[6] model. The logistic regression model ended up in fifth place. The team improved the model by a better choice of class weights but it was not considered in the ranking because it was a late submission. The BERT model brought up the rear of the team submissions.

Phlyers: The Phlyers (Ceolin, 2022) submitted three runs based on deep feedforward neural networks (DNN). The team mainly used the development data for training where possible and Wikipedia data only for the language varieties not present in the development set. For the first submission, the team re-trained the DNN, excluding PMS and ROA_TARA. The second and third submissions were similar but re-trained using the label/sentences from the test set for which the predicted label was associated with a high likelihood (with different thresholds for the two submissions), following a language model adaptation strategy.

SUKI: The SUKI team (Jauhiainen et al., 2022) applied the system they used for the FDI shared task (see Section 5.2), which is also the system they used in their winning submission of the 2021 edition of Romanian Dialect Identification (Jauhiainen et al., 2021). It is a Naïve Bayes-based method using the observed relative frequencies of multiple size character n-grams as probabilities. The system uses an adaptation technique to learn from the test data. The three submissions mainly differ in the training data used. The first submission used combined training and development data, and the second just the training data. The third system combined the training and development data, leaving out the data for PMS and SC because the number of instances did not meet their threshold.

For the ITDI shared task, the SUKI team used their own method to extract the training data from the dumps and performed extensive filtering and pre-processing, making use of their extensive experience with Wikipedia data.

Baselines: We created three baselines. The weakest one (Baseline 1) with a weighted F1-score of 0.1322 shows the results of applying an off-the-shelf tool for language identification: `FastText`[7] (Joulin et al., 2016b,a). Note that this model has been trained on earlier Wikipedia dumps and only supports seven of our eleven languages but not Friulian, Ladin, Ligurian, and Tarantino. We created this baseline by considering the ten best predictions for each sentence and took the first prediction that was one of the eight remaining varieties.

For the two other baselines (Baseline 2 and Baseline 3), we trained Support Vector Machines (SVM) with TF-IDF features using the `scikit-learn` toolkit (Pedregosa et al., 2011). We used the training data as is, i.e., no pre-processing was done after extracting the dumps except splitting the text at the line breaks (`\n`) produced by the extraction script. Baseline 2 was trained with character unigrams. It was mainly intended to see whether some individual characters are specific to certain

[6] https://huggingface.co/dbmdz/bert-base-italian-xxl-cased

[7] https://dl.fbaipublicfiles.com/fasttext/supervised-models/lid.176.bin

Team rank	Submission rank	Team	Run	Weighted-F1	Macro-F1
1	1	**SUKI**	2	0.9007	0.6729
	2	SUKI	1	0.8983	0.6714
	3	SUKI	3	0.8982	0.7458
	–	Organizers	Baseline 3	0.7726	0.5193
	*	ETHZ		0.7058	0.4885
2	4	**Phlyers**	3	0.6943	0.5379
3	5	**ETHZ**	2	0.6880	0.4828
	6	Phlyers	1	0.6631	0.5188
	7	Phlyers	2	0.6365	0.5094
	8	ETHZ	1	0.5760	0.4224
	–	Organizers	Baseline 2	0.4899	0.3424
	–	Organizers	Baseline 1	0.1322	0.1004

Table 3: Ranking of the teams and submissions according to the weighted average F1-score. The * marks a late submission by team ETHZ, which is not ranked. The baselines were created by the shared task organizers.

language varieties. It resulted in a weighted F1-score of 0.4899 and was beaten by all the submissions. The second SVM was trained on character 1-to-4-grams. It reached a weighted F1-score of 0.7726 and was only outperformed by the three submissions of team SUKI.

4.3 Results

The submissions were ranked according to the weighted average F1-score. Table 3 presents the ranking of the submissions and baselines. For comparison, we also report the macro-averaged F1-scores. We got one late submission which is marked by * in the table.

With three top-ranked submissions, team SUKI is a clear winner with their Naïve Bayes-based method using an adaptation technique. The team in the second place is Phlyers with one of their DNN models, closely followed by the logistic regression system by the ETHZ team in the third place.

One salient result was a very low recall for Ligurian by team Phlyers, which came with the cost of a few percentage points in the F1-score because Ligurian was heavily weighted with many sentences in the test set. This underprediction is due to their strategy to use mainly the development set for the varieties included in the development data, which did not work out well for this setting because apparently, the Wikipedia training data was closer to the one Wikisource book of the test set than the other Wikisource books in the development set.

The gap between the first team and the other submissions is quite big. The reason seems to be the sum of different optimal choices, like a more extensive pre-processing and the use of adaptive language models. The fourth-ranked system by Phlyers also used adaptive language models but had a different data strategy, while the third baseline ranking in between them was created without any pre-processing of the data.

Figure 3 displays the confusion matrices of the three baselines. Tarantino is the dialect with which all the systems struggled. In the best baseline (Figure 3c) and all the team submissions, it mostly gets confused with Neapolitan and Sicilian, which makes sense considering the relations in Figure 2 where Tarantino is a sub-dialect of Neapolitan further down in the language tree. Furthermore, looking at the best baseline, Neapolitan was often classified as Sicilian; Emilian-Romagnol and Venetian as Lombard; and Ladin as Venetian. The first two pairs are in the same subgroup (Gallo-Italian), while the latter pair is not so closely related in the language tree but geographically close, which might explain overlapping features of some kind in the used data set. In addition, most of the development and test data comes from Wikisource and websites, both of which have specific features; older texts for the former and texts most likely written by several and younger users for the latter. The Friulian data comes from a book (dev) and a newspaper (test) which can be considered as "controlled" in the aforementioned aspects.

Looking at Figure 3a, we have to keep in mind that FastText does not include Friulian, Ladin, Ligurian, or Tarantino. Lombard, Neapolitan, and Emilian-Romagnol seem the easiest to classify, while Friulian gets mostly misclassified with one other variety that is linguistically unrelated. The other varieties have very high entropy and were often classified as unk, i.e., something other than the eight included language varieties.

4.4 Summary

We proposed a closed cross-domain classification task for the Identification of Languages and Dialects of Italy shared task. We received a total of nine submissions[8] coming from three different teams. The results of the submissions are distributed over a wide range from 0.5760 to 0.9007 weighted F1-score, with two baselines even worse.

Furthermore, the differences between the results of the eleven language varieties are enormous, probably for several reasons. As data used in this shared task comes from many different sources, there are several factors to consider: different genres, domains, writing styles, average sentence length, number of authors (each with their own style), and year of publication, to name but a few.

Unsurprisingly, an off-the-shelf system like FastText performs quite poorly for language varieties, even those included in its training data. However, a shallow machine learning system like Naïve Bayes, support vector machine, or logistic regression can achieve good performance for most language varieties included in this task.

Along with this shared task, we release a newly collected and annotated data set for language identification featuring the previously mentioned eleven languages and dialects of Italy. The shared task and data are available on GitHub: https://github.com/noe-eva/ITDI_2022.

5 French Cross-Domain Dialect Identification

5.1 Dataset

The French Cross-Domain (FreCDo) corpus (Găman et al., 2022) contains plain text excerpts from news samples collected from public news websites in France, Switzerland, Belgium, and Canada. The corpus is divided into training, validation, and test, such that the publication sources and topics are distinct across splits. The corpus evaluates the models' ability to solve a cross-domain four-way dialect classification task. The text samples are pre-processed to hide named entities, thus eliminating country-specific clues. The named entities

[8]one of which was a late submission

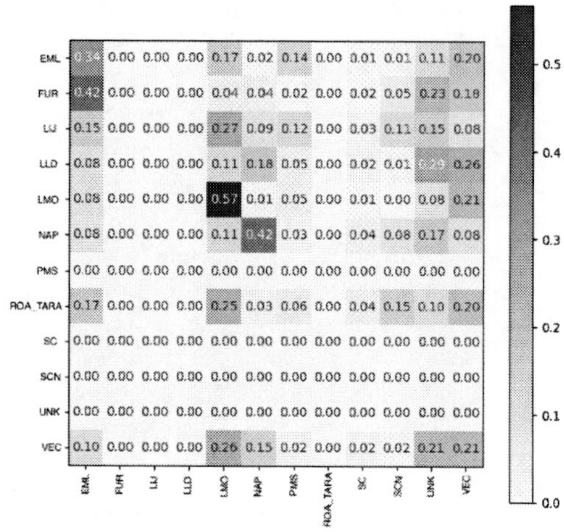

(a) Baseline 1: FastText

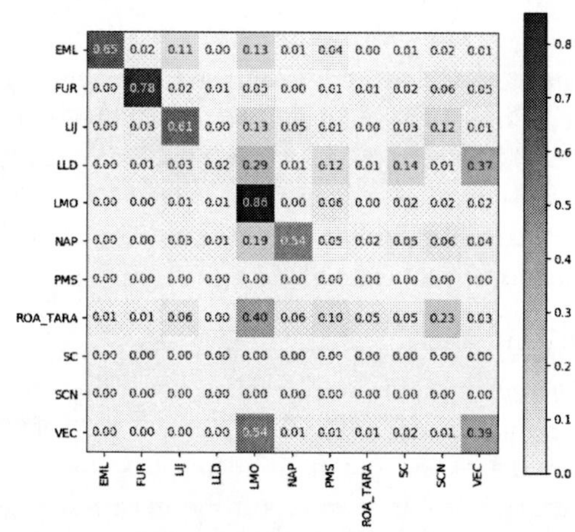

(b) Baseline 2: Unigram SVM

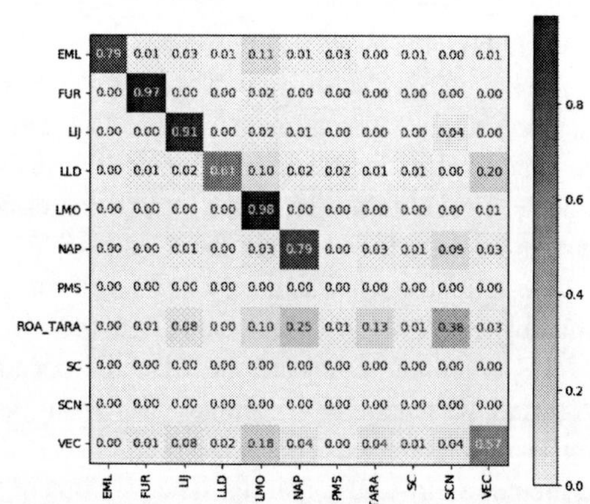

(c) N-Gram SVM

Figure 3: Confusion matrices of the three baselines (see Section 4.2). The numbers indicate the counts normalized over the true conditions of the test set (i.e. no instances of PMS, SC, and SCN in the gold standard). True labels on the y-axis, predicted on the x-axis.

Split	Country	# Samples	# Tokens
Train	BE	121,746	11,619,874
	CA	34,003	2,505,254
	CH	141,261	12,719,203
	FR	61,777	6,397,943
	Total:	358,787	33,242,274
Dev	BE	7,723	824,871
	CA	171	17,061
	CH	5,244	476,338
	FR	4,864	434,547
	Total:	18,002	1,752,817
Test	BE	15,235	1,227,263
	CA	944	86,724
	CH	9,824	910,700
	FR	10,730	848,845
	Total:	36,733	3,073,532

Table 4: The FreCDo corpus is composed of about 400K data samples, containing a total of 38M tokens.

were identified using Spacy,[9] then replaced with the special token `$NE$`. Some statistics about the FreCDo corpus are presented in Table 4.

5.2 Participants and Approaches

Don't classify, translate (DCT): Instead of approaching dialect identification as a classification task, Gillin (2022) treated French variety identification as a translation task where the input text is the source, and the language labels are the target. To simplify the vocabulary used in the encoder-decoder model, the authors set FR, BE, CH, and CA as reserved symbols and allowed the vocabulary to be shared for both encoder and decoder. They employed a model inspired by Li et al. (2018), using slightly modified scripts from Susanto et al. (2019) to train the model. The DCT team submitted two closed runs with different architectures. The first run is based on an encoder with 6 layers, a decoder with 2 layers, and 8 attention heads. There are three models trained with different random seeds, which are combined into an ensemble. The second run is based on a similar ensemble, but the architecture is shallower, being formed of an encoder with 1 layer, a decoder with 1 layer, and 1 attention head. For cases in which the translation model fails (e.g. when returning blank labels), the authors fall back to the FR label.

NRC: The NRC team (Bernier-Colborne et al., 2022) submitted three closed runs and three open runs. They constructed a majority vote ensemble for the first closed run based on five multi-class SVMs trained on the joint training and development data, using different data processing and feature sets. The differences between the models involve the usage of word tokenization, the removal of redundant NE tokens, the filtering of training data using a minimum text length threshold, and the usage of n-grams as features. Three of the models used only word bigrams as features, while the other two used word unigrams and bigrams, as well as character trigrams and 4-grams. The authors carried out a greedy search among a dozen SVM models, looking at the results on the development set to select the best subset of models. For the second closed run, the authors employed a probabilistic classifier similar to Naïve Bayes, trained on the concatenation of the training and development data, as well as the pseudo-labeled test data, where the test labels are those predicted by the SVM ensemble used for their first run. The feature set used by this classifier includes only word bigrams. The third closed run is based on a single multi-class SVM classifier, providing the best development data results. This model was trained on the concatenation of the training and development data, using only word bigrams as features.

The open runs submitted by the NRC team are all based on variants of CamemBERT (Martin et al., 2020). The first open run is based on a majority vote ensemble of 3 pre-trained CamemBERT models, which were fine-tuned on the concatenation of the training and development data, starting with the pre-trained encoder weights and tokenizer. The authors performed model selection based on the scores obtained on the development data. The differences between the three models involve the batch size (8 or 16), the learning rate schedule (constant or linear decay), and the number of encoder layers that were fine-tuned (either just the last layer or the last two layers). For the second open run, the NRC team relied on their best single CamemBERT model according to the results on the development set, fine-tuned on the joint training and development data. This model was fine-tuned with a batch size of 8 and a constant learning rate for 3 epochs. Only the last 2 layers of the encoder were fine-tuned. For the third open run, the team employed

[9] `https://spacy.io`

Rank	Team	Run	Macro-F1	Micro-F1
1	NRC	2	0.3437	0.4936
2	NRC	1	0.3266	0.4642
3	NRC	3	0.3149	0.4530
4	SUKI	3	0.2661	0.3918
5	DCT	1	0.2627	0.3914
6	SUKI	1	0.2603	0.3984
7	DCT	2	0.1905	0.3421
8	SUKI	2	0.1383	0.2339

Table 5: F1-scores attained by the teams participating in the 2022 FDI **closed** shared task.

Rank	Team	Run	Macro-F1	Micro-F1
1	NRC	1	0.4299	0.5243
2	NRC	3	0.4145	0.4936
3	NRC	2	0.4108	0.5067
–	Organizers	Baseline	0.3967	0.5584

Table 6: F1-scores attained by the teams participating in the 2022 FDI **open** shared task.

their second-best single CamemBERT model. The last 2 layers of this model were fine-tuned using a batch size of 16 for 5 epochs with linear learning rate decay.

SUKI: Jauhiainen et al. (2022) employed a custom-coded language identifier using the product of relative frequencies of character n-grams. The model is essentially a Naïve Bayes classifier using the relative frequencies as probabilities, being inspired by Jauhiainen et al. (2019). The authors only applied pre-processing to replace number-characters with '1'. The length of the character n-grams is set to 8. Instead of multiplying the relative frequencies, the authors summed up their negative logarithms. As a smoothing value, they used the negative logarithm of an n-gram appearing only once multiplied by a penalty modifier. The penalty modifier is set to 1.26. In addition, the SUKI team used the same language model adaptation technique as in their previous work (Jauhiainen et al., 2018). The adaptation to the test data is performed for 3 epochs, following Jauhiainen et al. (2019). In the end, the system is identical to the one used to win the RDI shared task 2021 (Chakravarthi et al., 2021), with some slight differences in pre-processing only (Jauhiainen et al., 2021). The SUKI team submitted three runs. The first run is based on considering the training data as training material, the second run uses the development data as training material, and the third run takes both the training and development data as training material. All runs are closed.

Baseline: Găman et al. (2022) introduced a CamemBERT model as baseline for the FreCDo corpus. The text is first tokenized with the CamemBERT tokenizer, obtaining 768-dimensional embedding vectors. Each sequence is then represented as a Continuous Bag-of-Words (CBOW) via appending a global average pooling layer. The final predictions are given by a Softmax classification layer. The whole model is fine-tuned for 30 epochs on mini-batches of 32 samples, using the AdamW optimizer (Loshchilov and Hutter, 2019).

5.3 Results

Evaluation measure: With the release of the test set, the participants were announced that the macro-averaged F1-score would be used to rank the submitted runs. For completeness, we also report the micro-averaged F1-score (which is equivalent to accuracy).

Closed: Table 5 presents the results for the 2022 FDI closed shared task. The NRC team's probabilistic model achieves the best score, closely followed by the SVM ensemble that was used to convey pseudo-labels for the test set to the top scoring model. The NCR team's best single SVM model ranked third. Interestingly, the SUKI team also pro-

Language	Dialect		F1	Exact Match		# Dev Questions	# Test Questions
Arabic	Algeria (DZA)		71.72	56.17		324	921
	Egypt (EGY)		72.39	56.39		324	921
	Jordan (JOR)		73.27	57.41		324	921
	Tunisia (TUN)		73.55	57.71		324	921
		Avg.	71.72	56.17	*Total*	1296	3684
English	Australia (AUS)		73.67	59.52		494	440
	India-South (IND-S)		72.22	58.10		494	440
	Nigeria (NGA)		73.36	58.70		494	440
	Philippines (PHI)		73.76	59.11		494	440
	USA-Southeast (USA-SE)		74.35	59.31		494	440
		Avg.	73.47	58.95	*Total*	2470	2200
Kiswahili	Kenya (KEN)		72.12	63.1		1000	472
	Tanzania (TZN)		70.74	61.7		1000	463
		Avg.	72.60	59.71	*Total*	2000	935

Table 7: DialQA baseline results (development set) on Answer Selection task.

posed a probabilistic model, but their results seem considerably lower. The main difference between the two probabilistic models, the one submitted by NRC and the other submitted by SUKI, seems to be the use of word n-grams in favor of character n-grams. Although character n-grams have been found useful in dialect identification in other languages, e.g. Arabic (Ionescu and Butnaru, 2017) or Romanian (Găman and Ionescu, 2022; Jauhiainen et al., 2021), it appears that word n-grams are more discriminative for French dialect identification on FreCDo. Perhaps using an entire range of character n-grams would have been a better choice for the SUKI team than just character 8-grams. The model employed by DCT stands out due to its unusual approach based on translation. Unfortunately, applying a translation model to the dialect identification task did not seem to pay off for the DCT team. Their models landed in ranks five and seven.

Open: NRC was the only team to submit runs for the 2022 FDI open shared task. The corresponding results are shown in Table 6. Here, the ensemble of CamemBERT models yielded the top score, but the individual CamemBERT models (second and third runs) also attained very good results. Comparing the open runs with the closed ones, it becomes clear that pre-trained language models benefit a lot from the large-scale corpora used to train the respective models, even if pre-training is carried out in a self-supervised manner.

5.4 Summary

For the French Dialect Identification shared task, we proposed a cross-domain four-way classification task. We received a total of eight closed submissions and three open submissions coming from three different teams. Each team submitted between two and six runs. Considering the results of the shared task participants and those attained by the baseline proposed with the dataset (Găman et al., 2022), we conclude that the cross-domain four-way FDI task remains very challenging, leaving sufficient room for future exploration. Basic machine learning models, e.g., Naïve Bayes or SVM, attained the strongest results in the closed setting. In the open scenario, we observed that using pre-trained language models is beneficial.

6 Dialectal Extractive Question Answering (DialQA)

6.1 Dataset

The task builds on the existing QA benchmarks TyDi-QA (Clark et al., 2020) and SD-QA (Faisal et al., 2021): specifically, it uses portions of the SD-QA dataset, which recorded dialectal variations of TyDi-QA questions. The original SD-QA dataset includes more than 68k audio prompts in 24 dialects from 255 annotators. In DialQA, we include development and test data for five varieties of English (Nigeria, USA, South India, Australia, Philippines), four varieties of Arabic (Algeria, Egypt, Jordan, Tunisia), and two varieties of Kiswahili (Kenya, Tanzania). The recorded and transcribed questions are highly parallel across the dialects within a language.

6.2 Approach and Baselines

Answer Selection Task: In the first part, we provide a text-based extractive QA baseline. Here, we fine-tune mBERT (Devlin et al., 2019) on a modified TyDi-QA training dataset so that, given the question and a single passage, the system returns the start and end byte indices of the minimal span that answers the question (Alberti et al., 2019). The baseline is prepared within the constraints of SQuAD (Rajpurkar et al., 2016) Question Answering settings. So all the unanswerable questions are discarded beforehand while preparing the DialQA dev and test set.

Automatic Speech Recognition (ASR) Task: This second part is an open task defined over the utterances of the different language varieties. Given the audio file of the utterance, the model has to produce an accurate transcription to be provided as input to the text-based QA system.

6.3 Discussion

Table 7 presents the baseline scores (development set) for the Answer Selection part. We calculate both dialect and language level F1 and exact match scores. The F1-score varies from 70.7 to 74.4, with USA-Southeast English being the best performing variety. The difference in performance can largely be attributed to the dialect-level differences induced as transcription noise. For the second task, no baseline is provided. However, the difference across dialectal audios and their corresponding transcription could be considered to design an ASR module. Another possibility could be designing an end-to-end speech-to-text extractive QA system capable of taking the dialectal audios as input.

6.4 Summary

We propose an extractive Dialectal Question Answering task that is open to both text and audio questions as the system input. Along with the task, we release the dialectal development and test datasets. The task is still open for submission and further development. The data and baselines are freely available on GitHub: `https://github.com/ffaisal93/DialQA`.

7 Conclusion

This paper presented an overview of the three shared tasks organized as part of the VarDial Evaluation Campaign 2022: Identification of Languages and Dialects of Italy (ITDI), French Cross-Domain Dialect Identification (FDI), and Dialect Extractive Question Answering (DialQA).

Participants of these shared tasks were provided with existing or new data sets made available to the community, which were discussed in detail in the respective sections. We furthermore included short descriptions of each team's systems, along with references to all system description papers published in the VarDial workshop proceedings (Table 1). We compared the participants' contributions with the organizer-provided baselines and found that participants were able to beat the latter both in ITDI and in the open FDI track.

For the ITDI task, we observed that shallow machine learning models outperformed deep learning models – even when using pre-trained language models for Italian. In contrast, pre-trained French language models provided much better performances than shallow models in the FDI task. It seems therefore that the optimal model choice for language and dialect identification tasks is largely task-dependent. This confirms the findings of previous editions of the VarDial campaign (Chakravarthi et al., 2021; Zampieri et al., 2020), where similar diverging trends were observed.

Acknowledgements

We thank all the participants for their interest in the shared tasks.

The work related to the ITDI shared task has received funding from the Swiss National Science Foundation (project no. 191934) and the Academy of Finland (project no. 1342859). The work related to the DialQA task was supported by the US National Science Foundation (project no. IIS-2125466).

References

Chris Alberti, Kenton Lee, and Michael Collins. 2019. A BERT baseline for the natural questions. *arXiv preprint arXiv:1901.08634*.

Antonio Ciccolella via Wikimedia Commons. 2015. Italiano: Mappa delle lingue e gruppi dialettali italiani. https://upload.wikimedia.org/wikipedia/commons/3/32/Dialetti_e_lingue_in_Italia.png.

Giuseppe Attardi. 2015. WikiExtractor. https://github.com/attardi/wikiextractor.

Gabriel Bernier-Colborne, Serge Leger, and Cyril Goutte. 2022. Transfer Learning Improves French Cross-Domain Dialect Identification: NRC @ VarDial 2022. In *Proceedings of the Ninth Workshop on NLP for Similar Languages, Varieties and Dialects*, Gyeongju, Republic of Korea. International Committee on Computational Linguistics (ICCL).

Giacomo Camposampiero, Quynh Anh Nguyen, and Francesco Di Stefano. 2022. The curious case of Logistic Regression for Italian Dialect Identification: ETHZ team at ITDI Vardial 2022 Shared Task. In *Proceedings of the Ninth Workshop on NLP for Similar Languages, Varieties and Dialects*, Gyeongju, Republic of Korea. International Committee on Computational Linguistics (ICCL).

Andrea Ceolin. 2022. Comparing the performance of CNNs and shallow models for language identification. In *Proceedings of the Ninth Workshop on NLP for Similar Languages, Varieties and Dialects*, Gyeongju, Republic of Korea. International Committee on Computational Linguistics (ICCL).

Bharathi Raja Chakravarthi, Gaman Mihaela, Radu Tudor Ionescu, Heidi Jauhiainen, Tommi Jauhiainen, Krister Lindén, Nikola Ljubešić, Niko Partanen, Ruba Priyadharshini, Christoph Purschke, Eswari Rajagopal, Yves Scherrer, and Marcos Zampieri. 2021. Findings of the VarDial evaluation campaign 2021. In *Proceedings of the Eighth Workshop on NLP for Similar Languages, Varieties and Dialects*, pages 1–11, Kyiv, Ukraine. Association for Computational Linguistics.

Jonathan H. Clark, Eunsol Choi, Michael Collins, Dan Garrette, Tom Kwiatkowski, Vitaly Nikolaev, and Jennimaria Palomaki. 2020. TyDi QA: A benchmark for information-seeking question answering in typologically diverse languages. *Transactions of the Association for Computational Linguistics*, 8:454–470.

Jacob Devlin, Ming-Wei Chang, Kenton Lee, and Kristina Toutanova. 2019. BERT: Pre-training of deep bidirectional transformers for language understanding. In *Proceedings of the 2019 Conference of the North American Chapter of the Association for Computational Linguistics: Human Language Technologies, Volume 1 (Long and Short Papers)*, pages 4171–4186, Minneapolis, Minnesota. Association for Computational Linguistics.

David M. Eberhard, Gary F. Simons, and Charles D. Fennig. 2022. Ethnologue: Languages of the world. twenty-fifth edition. http://www.ethnologue.com/. Dallas, Texas: SIL International.

Fahim Faisal, Sharlina Keshava, Md Mahfuz Ibn Alam, and Antonios Anastasopoulos. 2021. SD-QA: Spoken dialectal question answering for the real world. In *Findings of the Association for Computational Linguistics: EMNLP 2021*, pages 3296–3315, Punta Cana, Dominican Republic. Association for Computational Linguistics.

Mihaela Gaman, Dirk Hovy, Radu Tudor Ionescu, Heidi Jauhiainen, Tommi Jauhiainen, Krister Lindén, Nikola Ljubešić, Niko Partanen, Christoph Purschke, Yves Scherrer, and Marcos Zampieri. 2020. A report on the VarDial evaluation campaign 2020. In *Proceedings of the 7th Workshop on NLP for Similar Languages, Varieties and Dialects*, pages 1–14, Barcelona, Spain (Online). International Committee on Computational Linguistics (ICCL).

Nat Gillin. 2022. Is Encoder-Decoder Transformer the Shiny Hammer? In *Proceedings of the Ninth Workshop on NLP for Similar Languages, Varieties and Dialects*, Gyeongju, Republic of Korea. International Committee on Computational Linguistics (ICCL).

Mihaela Găman, Adrian Gabriel Chifu, William Domingues, and Radu Tudor Ionescu. 2022. FreCDo: A New Corpus for Large-Scale French Cross-Domain Dialect Identification. *(under review)*.

Mihaela Găman and Radu Tudor Ionescu. 2022. The Unreasonable Effectiveness of Machine Learning in Moldavian versus Romanian Dialect Identification. *International Journal of Intelligent Systems*, 37(8):4928–4966.

Radu Tudor Ionescu and Andrei Butnaru. 2017. Learning to identify arabic and german dialects using multiple kernels. In *Proceedings of the Fourth Workshop on NLP for Similar Languages, Varieties and Dialects (VarDial)*, pages 200–209, Valencia, Spain.

Tommi Jauhiainen, Heidi Jauhiainen, and Krister Lindén. 2018. HeLI-based experiments in Swiss German dialect identification. In *Proceedings of the Fifth Workshop on NLP for Similar Languages, Varieties and Dialects (VarDial 2018)*, pages 254–262, Santa Fe, New Mexico, USA. Association for Computational Linguistics.

Tommi Jauhiainen, Heidi Jauhiainen, and Krister Lindén. 2021. Naive Bayes-based experiments in Romanian dialect identification. In *Proceedings of the Eighth Workshop on NLP for Similar Languages, Varieties and Dialects*, pages 76–83, Kyiv, Ukraine. Association for Computational Linguistics.

Tommi Jauhiainen, Heidi Jauhiainen, and Krister Lindén. 2022. Italian Language and Dialect Identification and Regional French Variety Detection using Adaptive Naive Bayes. In *Proceedings of the Ninth Workshop on NLP for Similar Languages, Varieties and Dialects*, Gyeongju, Republic of Korea. International Committee on Computational Linguistics (ICCL).

Tommi Jauhiainen, Krister Lindén, and Heidi Jauhiainen. 2019. Discriminating between Mandarin Chinese and Swiss-German varieties using adaptive language models. In *Proceedings of the Sixth Workshop on NLP for Similar Languages, Varieties and Dialects*, pages 178–187, Ann Arbor, Michigan. Association for Computational Linguistics.

Armand Joulin, Edouard Grave, Piotr Bojanowski, Matthijs Douze, Hérve Jégou, and Tomas Mikolov. 2016a. Fasttext.zip: Compressing text classification models. *arXiv preprint arXiv:1612.03651*.

Armand Joulin, Edouard Grave, Piotr Bojanowski, and Tomas Mikolov. 2016b. Bag of tricks for efficient text classification. *arXiv preprint arXiv:1607.01759*.

Maggie Yundi Li, Stanley Kok, and Liling Tan. 2018. Don't classify, translate: Multi-level e-commerce product categorization via machine translation. *arXiv preprint arXiv:1812.05774*.

Ilya Loshchilov and Frank Hutter. 2019. Decoupled Weight Decay Regularization. In *Proceedings of ICLR*.

Shervin Malmasi, Marcos Zampieri, Nikola Ljubešić, Preslav Nakov, Ahmed Ali, and Jörg Tiedemann. 2016. Discriminating between similar languages and Arabic dialect identification: A report on the third DSL shared task. In *Proceedings of the Third Workshop on NLP for Similar Languages, Varieties and Dialects (VarDial3)*, pages 1–14, Osaka, Japan. The COLING 2016 Organizing Committee.

Louis Martin, Benjamin Muller, Pedro Javier Ortiz Suárez, Yoann Dupont, Laurent Romary, Éric de la Clergerie, Djamé Seddah, and Benoît Sagot. 2020. CamemBERT: a Tasty French Language Model. In *Proceedings of the 58th Annual Meeting of the Association for Computational Linguistics*, pages 7203–7219.

F. Pedregosa, G. Varoquaux, A. Gramfort, V. Michel, B. Thirion, O. Grisel, M. Blondel, P. Prettenhofer, R. Weiss, V. Dubourg, J. Vanderplas, A. Passos, D. Cournapeau, M. Brucher, M. Perrot, and E. Duchesnay. 2011. Scikit-learn: Machine learning in Python. *Journal of Machine Learning Research*, 12:2825–2830.

Pranav Rajpurkar, Jian Zhang, Konstantin Lopyrev, and Percy Liang. 2016. SQuAD: 100,000+ questions for machine comprehension of text. In *Proceedings of the 2016 Conference on Empirical Methods in Natural Language Processing*, pages 2383–2392, Austin, Texas. Association for Computational Linguistics.

Alan Ramponi. 2022. NLP for language varieties of Italy: Challenges and the path forward. *arXiv preprint arXiv:2209.09757*.

Raymond Hendy Susanto, Ohnmar Htun, and Liling Tan. 2019. Sarah's participation in WAT 2019. In *Proceedings of the 6th Workshop on Asian Translation*, pages 152–158, Hong Kong, China. Association for Computational Linguistics.

Marcos Zampieri, Shervin Malmasi, Nikola Ljubešić, Preslav Nakov, Ahmed Ali, Jörg Tiedemann, Yves Scherrer, and Noëmi Aepli. 2017. Findings of the VarDial evaluation campaign 2017. In *Proceedings of the Fourth Workshop on NLP for Similar Languages, Varieties and Dialects (VarDial)*, pages 1–15, Valencia, Spain. Association for Computational Linguistics.

Marcos Zampieri, Shervin Malmasi, Preslav Nakov, Ahmed Ali, Suwon Shon, James Glass, Yves Scherrer, Tanja Samardžić, Nikola Ljubešić, Jörg Tiedemann, Chris van der Lee, Stefan Grondelaers, Nelleke Oostdijk, Dirk Speelman, Antal van den Bosch, Ritesh Kumar, Bornini Lahiri, and Mayank Jain. 2018. Language identification and morphosyntactic tagging: The second VarDial evaluation campaign. In *Proceedings of the Fifth Workshop on NLP for Similar Languages, Varieties and Dialects (VarDial 2018)*, pages 1–17, Santa Fe, New Mexico, USA. Association for Computational Linguistics.

Marcos Zampieri, Shervin Malmasi, Yves Scherrer, Tanja Samardžić, Francis Tyers, Miikka Silfverberg, Natalia Klyueva, Tung-Le Pan, Chu-Ren Huang, Radu Tudor Ionescu, Andrei M. Butnaru, and Tommi Jauhiainen. 2019. A report on the third VarDial evaluation campaign. In *Proceedings of the Sixth Workshop on NLP for Similar Languages, Varieties and Dialects*, pages 1–16, Ann Arbor, Michigan. Association for Computational Linguistics.

Marcos Zampieri, Preslav Nakov, and Yves Scherrer. 2020. Natural language processing for similar languages, varieties, and dialects: A survey. *Natural Language Engineering*, 26(6):595–612.

Marcos Zampieri, Liling Tan, Nikola Ljubešić, and Jörg Tiedemann. 2014. A report on the DSL shared task 2014. In *Proceedings of the First Workshop on Applying NLP Tools to Similar Languages, Varieties and Dialects*, pages 58–67, Dublin, Ireland. Association for Computational Linguistics and Dublin City University.

Marcos Zampieri, Liling Tan, Nikola Ljubešić, Jörg Tiedemann, and Preslav Nakov. 2015. Overview of the DSL shared task 2015. In *Proceedings of the Joint Workshop on Language Technology for Closely Related Languages, Varieties and Dialects*, pages 1–9, Hissar, Bulgaria. Association for Computational Linguistics.

A Appendix

A.1 ITDI Data Sources

The development and test data come from the websites given below.

EML	https://www.bulgnais.com/libri.html
FUR	https://wikisource.org/wiki/Main_Page/Furlan
FUR	https://arlef.it/it/materiali
FUR	https://www.filologicafriulana.it/lenghe-e-culture
LLD	https://wikisource.org/wiki/Main_Page/Ladin
LLD	https://it.wikisource.org/wiki/Biancognee
LLD	https://www.istitutoladino.it
LIJ	https://lij.wikisource.org
LMO	https://wikisource.org/wiki/Main_Page/Lumbaart
LMO	https://www.lingualombarda.it/index.php/milanese.html
NAP	https://nap.wikisource.org
NAP	https://it.wikisource.org/wiki/Categoria:Testi_in_napoletano
PMS	https://pms.wikisource.org
SC	https://wikisource.org/wiki/Category:Sardu
SCN	https://wikisource.org/wiki/Category:Sicilianu
SCN	https://wikisource.org/wiki/Main_Page/Sicilianu
SCN	https://it.wikisource.org/wiki/Categoria:Testi_in_siciliano
SCN	http://www.linguasiciliana.org
SCN	http://www.salviamoilsiciliano.com/raccolte
SCN	http://www.museomirabilesicilia.it/folklore-siciliano.html
SCN	http://www.salviamoilsiciliano.com/raccolte
SCN	http://rapallosalvatore.blogspot.com/p/raccolta-poesie-in-dialetto-siciliano.html
ROA-TARA	http://www.tarantonostra.com
VEC	https://vec.wikisource.org
several	https://www.dialettando.com

Social Context and User Profiles of Linguistic Variation on a Micro Scale

Olga Kellert[1] and Nicholas H. Matlis[2]
[1]University of Göttingen, Germany
[2]Center for Free-Electron Laser Science CFEL, Deutsches Elektronen-Synchrotron DESY, Germany
olga.kellert@phil.uni-goettingen.de and nicholas.matlis@cfel.de

Abstract

This paper presents a new tweet-based approach in geolinguistic analysis which combines geolocation, user IDs and textual features in order to identify patterns of linguistic variation on a sub-city scale. Sub-city variations can be connected to social drivers and thus open new opportunities for understanding the mechanisms of language variation and change. However, measuring linguistic variation on these scales is challenging due to the lack of highly-spatially-resolved data as well as to the daily movement or users' "mobility" inside cities which can obscure the relation between the social context and linguistic variation. Here we demonstrate how combining geolocation with user IDs and textual analysis of tweets can yield information about the linguistic profiles of the users, the social context associated with specific locations and their connection to linguistic variation. We apply our methodology to analyze dialects in Buenos Aires and find evidence of socially-driven variation. Our methods will contribute to the identification of sociolinguistic patterns inside cities, which are valuable in social sciences and social services.

1 Introduction

Analysis of spatial patterns of linguistic variation is an important tool, not only for studying the dynamics of language change, but also as a probe of social dynamics which can be encoded in linguistic variation. The advent of social media and the growth of computational linguistic tools has created many opportunities for extending analysis of linguistic variation in new regimes. One in particular is the study of spatial or geographical patterns of linguistic varieties. Until now, most studies in this field have been limited to large scales of geographical analysis, from cities to countries (e.g., Eisenstein et al. 2010, Gonçalves & Sánchez 2016, Nguyen et al. 2016, Grieve et al. 2019, Hovy & Purschke 2020). However, urban dynamics, where social interaction and mixing occur, play an important role in language variation and also provide a window into linguistic variation on an urban scale (Abitbol-Levy et al. 2018, Kellert & Matlis 2022). Urban-scale analyses have been previously used to study the relation between urban location and language choice in multilingual cities (Mocanu et al. 2013, Kim et al. 2014). However, these studies focus on different languages and not on linguistic varieties of the same language.

Here we explore the use of Twitter data with precise geolocation information to map out patterns in the use of two linguistic variants (i.e., dialects) within the city of Buenos Aires, in order to get deeper insights into the relation between language use and urban structure. Our basic approach is to combine analysis of tweet metadata with analysis of tweet texts to first show that a large fraction of users in CABA is bi-dialectal (i.e., tweet in both variants) and then to determine how social context influences which dialect is used. Bi-dialectalism is established by exploiting the unique user ID metadata to perform linguistic profiling of the users, while the relevant geographical setting is extracted by using the precise GPS coordinates to pinpoint the location. The tweet texts then provide information on the associated topics of discussion which helps to complete the social-context picture.

Our work shows that combining social and geographical aspects of linguistic analysis, made possible by social-media data sources, opens new

Proceedings of the Ninth Workshop on NLP for Similar Languages, Varieties and Dialects, pages 14–19
October 16, 2022. ©2022 Association for Computational Linguistics

opportunities to illuminate the mechanisms driving linguistic variation, especially on urban scales. Our analysis also helps to establish how well dialect-use patterns in social media conform to those in standard linguistic sources and provides complementary information about the users not easily accessible by other means.

2 Identification of the Dialects

We selected two Spanish varieties: Argentinian Spanish (ArgSp) and Standard Spanish (PanSp). These varieties are marked by the variation in the 2nd person singular pronoun (i.e., *vos* 'you' in informal address in ArgSp and *tú* 'you' in PanSp) together with the corresponding verbs that agree with the pronoun (e.g., *vos podés* vs. *tú puedes* 'you can') (Fontanella de Weinberg 1999). We use geolocated tweets in Spanish limited to Greater Buenos Aires (CABA), i.e., the city of Buenos Aires and its close surroundings, from October 2017 to March 2021 (Kellert & Matlis 2022). The selection of this city is motivated in §3.

We use a token-based analysis method to extract the two linguistic variants (Gonçalves & Sánchez 2016, Grieve et al. 2019, Kellert & Matlis 2022). This method is a classical method in social dialectology (Labov 2006). For clarity, we here refer to the Spanish varieties ArgSp and PanSp as Spanish *dialects*. However, since these varieties can be used by the same group of people under different social circumstances, as we will show in §4, one can also refer to them as *sociolects*.

A priority was placed on ensuring accuracy of the dialect definitions. The token sets were designed to be balanced, so that for each token of ArgSp, there was a corresponding token with the same meaning in the set representing PanSp (Kellert & Matlis 2022). Our grammatical token set consists of the most frequent tokens used in Argentina according to the corpus *Corpus del Español*, which is one of the biggest Spanish corpora.[1] We excluded all ambiguous tokens (e.g., ArgSp *seguí* 'follow!', which corresponds to PanSp *sigue* 'follow!', but also to 'he/she/it follows' in both dialects). Finally, we take special measures to account for differences in how people use accents in social media and standard language (Nguyen et al. 2016). In particular, accents in Tweets are frequently omitted (Eisenstein et al. 2010). We therefore included both accented and unaccented versions of all verbs but excluded those verbs where eliminating the accent results in an ambiguity in assigning the dialect (e.g., ArgSp *sabés* vs. PanSp *sabes*). The remaining verbs were distinguishable by the verb stem (e.g., ArgSp *tenés* vs. PanSp *tienes*). Our final token list contained 235 tokens for ArgSp and 198 tokens for PanSp dialect (Kellert & Matlis 2022).

3 Background on the Dialects

A little background on the dialects will help us to evaluate the results. The dialects ArgSp and PanSp have well-known and distinct historical and socio-linguistic roles in CABA (Fontanella de Weinberg 1999). ArgSp is the most prominent and is also the standard dialect in Argentina, Paraguay, Uruguay and Central America (ibid.). PanSp, on the other hand, is a variety that is very prominent elsewhere in the Spanish-speaking world. This distinction between the two varieties has previously been reported on the basis of geolocated tweets collected in 2016 (Bland & Morgan 2021), and here we confirm it using our tweet corpus by mapping out the differential distribution of the two tweet varieties on the world scale (see Figure 1).

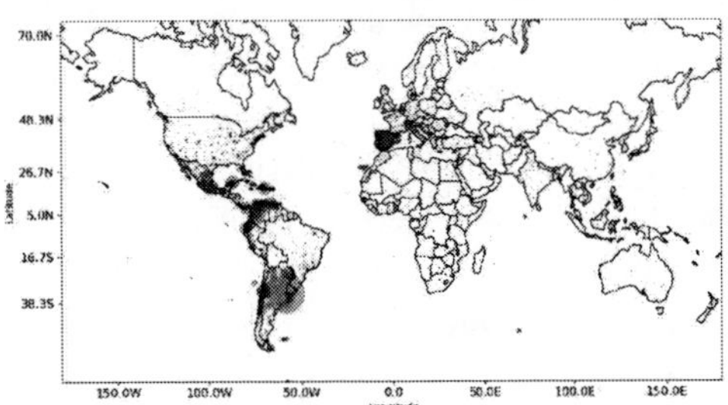

Figure 1: *ArgSp (red) and PanSp (blue) in the Twitter corpus collected from 2017-2021.* Map produced using *Cartopy*[2] on OpenStreetMap[3] data.

Despite the predominance of ArgSp in Argentina and CABA on the world scale, a closer inspection shows significant presence of both varieties within CABA (Kellert & Matlis 2022) which is to be expected for several reasons. First, PanSp is the Spanish variety that is used by Mass Media in Latin America and consequently also in CABA (Gonçalves & Sánchez 2016). Second, PanSp is used by tourists from PanSp speaking countries. And third, PanSp was long the standard variety in CABA and Argentina, before ArgSp took over this

[1] http:// www.corpusdelespanol.org/

[2] https://scitools.org.uk/cartopy/

[3] http://wiki.openstreetmap.org/wiki/Open_Database_License

role in the late 19th c. (Fontanella de Weinberg 1999). PanSp still exists in CABA as a substandard variety due to the region's history (ibid).

4 Detailed Methodology and Results

Our analysis, which is based on calculation of the spatial variations in the use of ArgSp and PanSp across the city, is done in three steps. First, the prevalence of the two dialects and the degree of bi-dialectalism are quantified. The presence of bi-dialectalism in CABA offers the opportunity to directly evaluate how social circumstances influence linguistic variation, since bi-dialectal users can choose when to use each variant. Second, regions where each dialect is most prominent are evaluated to look for correlations between social context and tweet content. And third, locations expected to have specific social functions (e.g., soccer stadiums) are evaluated to look for prominence of one or the other dialect.

4.1 ArgSp & PanSp vs Bi-Dialectalism

The observation in §3 that ArgSp is the predominant dialect of CABA is confirmed by the fact that ArgSp tweets outnumber PanSp tweets three to one (i.e., 18,731 vs 5,607 respectively). However, by using the unique user-ID metadata to associate multiple tweets to individual users, we found that a considerable number of CABA users (11%) are "bi-dialectal" in that they tweet using both dialects. Some users even mix the two dialects in a single tweet (e.g., *vos puedes* or *tú podés* 'you can'). The existence of bi-dialectal users and the existence of mixing dialects in a single tweet suggests that PanSp plays an important role in communication of CABA citizens and that it is not exclusively used by people of foreign background such as tourists or immigrants. However, ArgSp is a more important variety than PanSp because bi-dialectal users tweet twice as often in ArgSp as in PanSp (6,299 vs 3,040 respectively) and because there are more tweets posted by mono-dialectal users than by bi-dialectal users (14,999 vs. 9,339, respectively). The latter observation indicates that tweeting in both linguistic varieties is not the standard tweeting behavior of CABA citizens.

4.2 Analysis 2: Dialects in Geocontext

In this analysis, we focus on regions with the greatest prominence of each of the dialects to look for correspondences between dialect use and social context. The regions of prominence are determined by generating spatial distributions of each variant calculated by partitioning the city into small areas or "bins", corresponding roughly to the size of a city block, which define the spatial resolution of the maps (Schlosser et al. 2021, Kellert & Matlis 2022). We then selected five bins with the greatest prominence of each variant, based on the normalized difference in tweet counts (Kellert & Matlis 2022), and examined the associated geographical setting and tweet content (Figure 2).

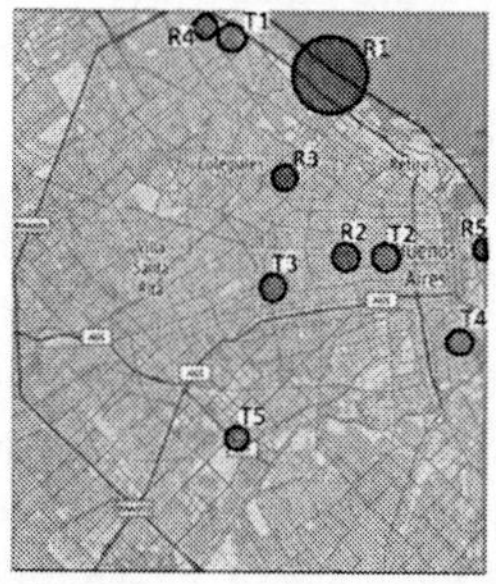

Bin	GPS Coordinates
T1:	-58.4130, -34.5570
T2:	-58.4068, -34.6113
T3:	-58.4298, -34.5879
T4:	-58.4598, -34.5428
T5:	-58.3556, -34.6088
R1:	-58.4501, -34.5461
R2:	-58.3918, -34.6113
R3:	-58.4342, -34.6205
R4:	-58.3644, -34.6364
R5:	-58.4474, -34.6657

Figure 2: *Left: Bins with the greatest representation of PanSp (blue) and ArgSp (red). Right: GPS coordinates of the bins.*

The geographical setting ("geocontext") was determined by using the GPS coordinates to identify buildings located within each bin, and the tweet-content was evaluated by performing uni-gram and bi-gram analyses of the tweet texts from each bin, using the software package NLTK, to determine the most frequent words and word pairs. (Bird et al. 2009). The results of the analysis for the most prominent bins of each type (bins T1 and R1 in Figure 2) are shown in Table 1.

Geocontext	Tweet-content features
PanSP Jorge Newbery International Airport	• location names mentioning CABA • Picture postings in CABA • Weekly horoscope • travel club postings • happy birthday wishes • good/happy day/night wishes
ArgSP Soccer stadium: Estadio "Monumental" Antonio V. Liberti	• location names mentioning the soccer stadium • reports about soccer matches • sentiments about soccer matches and players

Table 1: *Geographical context and tweet content features in most prominent bins for each dialect.*

The most prominent bin for PanSp covers the international airport in the northern part of the city (Figure 2, R1), and the associated tweets mention CABA in various forms (e.g., "Buenos Aires, BsAs") as well as picture postings and other references to travel. By contrast, the most prominent bin for ArgSp covers the famous soccer stadium River Plate (Figure 2, T1), and the associated tweets refer to this stadium and discuss the matches and players.

The remaining eight most-prominent bins show a similar pattern. For the PanSp bins, the geocontext includes Irish bars, tourist attractions and wealthy neighborhoods in the northern part of the city which are attractive to tourists, while all of the ArgSp bins contain geocontext features relevant to locals of CABA such as soccer clubs, soccer stadiums such as La Bombonera (Figure 2, T4), dance schools, small commercial businesses and residential buildings in neighborhoods such as *Villa Soldati*, located in the South-West of the city. Similarly, all of the PanSp bins have associated tweets with location mentions and photo postings as top-ranked topics whereas none of the ArgSp bins do. Mentioning the name of the city and posting pictures are typical activities of tourists or of users addressing tourists (e.g., in advertisements of touristic attractions) (Kim et al. 2014). The analysis therefore suggests that tourism plays an important role in the use of PanSp dialect in CABA and that national sports clubs, local commerce and residential buildings tend to prioritize ArgSp.

4.3 Analysis 3: Dialects in Social Contexts

We have chosen several social contexts defined as bins containing buildings of a selected, well-defined social function. The building types chosen were: 1) tourist attractions, 2) Starbucks cafes, 3) soccer stadiums, and 4) hospitals. We then counted how many bins of each type demonstrated a relative prominence of ArgSp vs PanSp.

In Figure 3, maps for each category are presented showing bins with a relative prominence of ArgSp and PanSp marked by red and blue circles, respectively. Empty bins containing no tweets of either type are marked in grey. For the tourist attractions, 52% of the non-empty bins showed a relative prominence of PanSp, while for Starbucks Cafes, 59% of non-empty bins are PanSp oriented. While these numbers are far from conclusive, due to the sparse statistics, the pattern is consistent with the connection, observed in §4.2, between PanSp and tourism, if one accepts that tourists are likely to visit Starbucks cafés. For the soccer-stadium case, 100% of non-empty bins demonstrate a relative preponderance of ArgSp, which also reinforces the connection between ArgSp and soccer found in in §4.2. Finally, hospital bins showed no preference for either dialect.

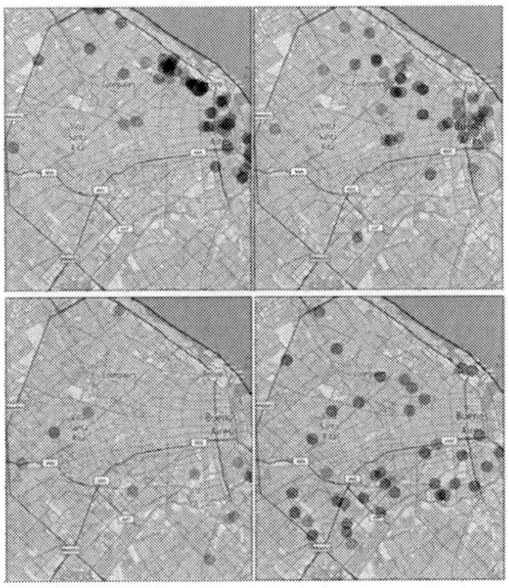

Figure 3: *Distribution of bins with a relative prominence of PanSp (blue) and ArgSp (red) tweets for specific social contexts.* Top left: touristic hotspots, Top right: Starbucks cafés, Bottom left: soccer stadiums, Bottom right: Hospitals. Black= no data

5 Discussion

The three analyses presented show ways in which different elements of the tweets can be combined to extract valuable information about the user's linguistic behavior and about relevant geographical and social contexts that can influence this behavior. The ability to connect multiple tweets to individual users via the user ID is a powerful tool enabling determination of user attributes such as bi-dialectalism which are unavailable via textual analysis alone. Similarly, the presence of precise GPS coordinates allows connections to be made between text and local geographical features that can be used to characterize the associated social contexts. In the work presented here, although evidence of a pattern is present, some analysis was done manually, leading to small data sets and low statistical significance. Development of algorithms to detect geocontext features and characterize tweet content would allow automation of bin analysis, greatly increasing the statistics and hence the strength of the approach.

Several other important issues must also be considered in going forward. First, despite the large size of our Twitter corpus (1.9M geolocated tweets), the quantity of data was a limiting factor for analyzing the small scales. Considering a binning of 100 x 100, one can expect only 190 tweets per bin, on average. Of course, due to spatial variations in population density, the number of tweets in the city center are far higher than those on the outskirts. Data scarcity is aggravated by the small fraction (~1%) of tweets for which the variants could be identified. Methods to improve variant identification are thus highly relevant. For instance, the number of tokens (and hence the number of collected tweets) could likely be increased by using a morphological tagger such as FreeLin[4]. However, since precise identification of the variants was our top priority, we opted for a manually-crafted set of tokens for which the lack of ambiguity could be verified.

Second, the social context within the bins may not be uniform. For instance, in Analysis 3, the Starbucks cafes represented only one of several buildings within the bins and therefore may not have been representative of the overall social context. By contrast, soccer stadiums, which are much larger, are more likely to fill an entire bin, thus providing a uniform social context. This increased context uniformity may partially account for the strong correlation observed between soccer stadiums and ArgSp dialect in Figure 3, bottom left.

Larger bins tend to encompass a greater diversity of social contexts lessening the degree of correlation between the chosen context and the prevalence of specific linguistic features. On the other hand, smaller bins tend to suffer from insufficient numbers of tweets, requiring optimization of the bin size. A similar problem arises, due to the lack of altitude information in most social-media GPS coordinates, when the bins contain multi-story buildings with different businesses on each floor.

The work presented here represents only a first step in the application of this methodology. Many opportunities exist for future work, including use of tweet-selection methods that do not rely on specific tokens (Nguyen et al. 2016) and expansion of the range of social contexts considered. These tools hold great promise to provide insights into the relation between language use and social dynamics, especially on small spatial scales.

References

Jacob Abitbol-Levy, Márton Karsai, Jean-Philippe Magué, Jean-Pierre Chevrot, and Eric Fleury. 2018. Socioeconomic dependencies of linguistic patterns in twitter: A multivariate analysis. In *WWW '18: Proceedings of the 2018 World Wide Web Conference*. Association for Computing Machinery Inc, pages 1125–34.

Steven Bird, Edward Loper, and Ewan Klein. 2009. *Natural Language Processing with Python*. O'Reilly, Sebastopol.

Justin Bland and Terrel A. Morgan. 2021. Geographic variation of *voseo* on Spanish Twitter. In Diego Pascual y Cabo and Idoia Elola (eds.), *Current Theoretical and Applied Perspectives on Hispanic and Lusophone Linguistics*, pages 7–38. John Benjamins, Amsterdam.

Jacob Eisenstein, Brendan O'Connor, Noah A. Smith, and Eric P. Xing. 2010. A latent variable model for geographic lexical variation. In *Proceedings of the 2010 Conference on Empirical Methods in Natural Language Processing*. Association for Computational Linguistics, pages 1277–87.

María Beatriz Fontanella de Weinberg. 1999. Sistemas pronominales de tratamiento usados en el mundo hispánico. In Violeta Demonte and Ignacio Bosque (eds.), *Gramática descriptiva de la lengua española,* vol 1., pages 1399–1426. Espasa Calpe, Madrid.

Bruno Gonçalves and David Sánchez. 2016. Learning about Spanish dialects through Twitter. *Revista Internacional Lingüística Iberoamericana,* 14(2):65–75.

Jack Grieve, Chris Montgomery, Andrea Nini, Akira Murakami, and Diansheng Guo. 2019. Mapping Lexical Dialect Variation in British English Using Twitter. *Frontiers in Artificial Intelligence,* 2(11). https://doi.org/10.3389/frai.2019.00011.

Dirk Hovy and Christoph Purschke. 2020. Capturing regional variation with distributed place representations and geographic retrofitting. In *Proceedings of the 2018 Conference on Empirical Methods in Natural Language Processing, EMNLP 2018*. Association for Computational Linguistics, pages 4383–94. https://doi.org/10.18653/v1/D18-1469.

Olga Kellert and Nicholas Matlis. 2022. Geolocation of multiple sociolinguistic markers in Buenos Aires,

[4] https://nlp.lsi.upc.edu/freeling/

PLoS One 17(9):e0274114. https://doi.org/10.1371/journal.pone.0274114.

Suin Kim, Alice Oh, Ingmar Weber, and Li Wei. 2014. Sociolinguistic Analysis of Twitter in Multilingual Societies. In *Proceedings of the 25th ACM conference on Hypertext and social media.*

William Labov. 2006. *The social stratification of English in New York city.* 2nd ed. Cambridge University Press, Cambridge, UK.

Guy Lansley and Paul A. Longley. 2016. The geography of Twitter topics in London. *Computers Environment Urban Systems*, 58:85–96. https://doi.org/10.1016/j.compenvurbsys.2016.04.002.

Delia Mocanu, Andrea Baronchelli, Nicola Perra, Bruno Gonçalves, Qian Zhang, and Alessandro Vespignani. 2013. The Twitter of Babel: Mapping World Languages through Microblogging Platforms, *PLoS ONE* 8(4):e61981. https://doi.org/10.1371/journal.pone.0061981.

Dong-Phuong Nguyen, A. Seza Doğruöz, Carolyn P. Rosé, and Franciska M.G. de Jong. 2016. Computational sociolinguistics. A survey, *Computational Linguistics,* 42(3):537–593.

Stephan Schlosser, Daniele Toninelli, and Michela Cameletti. 2021. Comparing methods to collect and geolocate tweets in Great Britain. *Journal of Open Innovation: Technology, Market, and Complexity*, 7(1):1–20.

dialectR: Doing Dialectometry in R

Ryan Soh-Eun Shim*
Institute for Natural Language Processing
University of Stuttgart
soh-eun.shim@ims.uni-stuttgart.de

John Nerbonne
Linguistics
Groningen, Freiburg & Tübingen
j.nerbonne@rug.nl

Abstract

We present dialectR, an open-source R package for performing quantitative analyses of dialects based on categorical measures of difference and on variants of edit distance. dialectR stands as one of the first programmable toolkits that may freely be combined and extended by users with further statistical procedures. We describe implementational details of the package, and provide two examples of its use: one performing analyses based on multidimensional scaling and hierarchical clustering on a dataset of Dutch dialects, and another showing how an approximation of the acoustic vowel space may be achieved by performing an MFCC (Mel-Frequency Cepstral Coefficients)-based acoustic distance on audio recordings of vowels.

1 Introduction

The quantitative analysis of dialect relatedness has yielded respectable results in the field of dialectometry, where sophisticated methods of measuring linguistic distance have been developed which correlate to a large degree with perceptual measurements of intelligibility (Gooskens and Heeringa, 2004; Beijering et al., 2008). The use of such methods offers an objective basis to the determination of dialect distributions, including boundaries at times, and which overcomes some of the subjective biases inherent in earlier approaches that utilized the notion of isogloss for dialect classification.

However, despite the success of these methods, access to their use has generally relied on GUI-based software such as Visual DialectoMetry (VDM) (Goebl, 2006), DiaTech (Aurrekoetxea et al., 2013), and Gabmap (Nerbonne et al., 2011; Leinonen et al., 2016), which are easy to use, but which accept the trade-off of impeding easy modification for those who wish to extend existing methods. Users who wish to perform statistical analyses outside of what is provided or make changes to the existing pipeline do not have easy access to the internals of such software, and consequently have to start from a higher technical threshold. In fact, these packages have not been modified by others. A notable exception is the L04 software,[1] which operates in the UNIX ecosystem and would allow for some degree of user modification, but few, if any users have taken advantage of this. In addition to providing for more flexibility that exists in current packages, the present effort also facilitates the work of those who like the provisions of the older packages, but who wish to try out contemporary approaches, something the existing packages likewise do not readily support.

In view of this situation, we present dialectR, an open-source software package that allows the construction of dialectometric pipelines in the statistical programming language R (R Core Team, 2020). It is largely inspired by Gabmap, but attempts to overcome some shortcomings of its monolithic presentation. Our vision is to facilitate more wide-ranging dialectological experimentation with the data analysis possibilities in R. For example, dialectologists should be able to experiment more directly with geostatistical analyses, which, with honorable exceptions (Grieve, 2018), have largely been ignored in dialectometry. For a second example, we note that, although dialectometry makes extensive use of multi-dimensional scaling (see below), other dimension-reducing techniques (for non-distance matrices), such as factor analysis or principal component analysis, have received less attention, again with some honorable exceptions (Pickl, 2013; Nerbonne, 2015). The present paper offers a foundation from which much more extensive experimentation may be launched. We offer

*The project began in a course taught by JN, where RS-ES suggested the idea of an R-package. The authors went back and forth on design decisions, but RS-ES implemented the software, and wrote most of the first version of the paper. JN wrote some subsections and collaborated on the others.

[1] http://www.let.rug.nl/kleiweg/L04/

Proceedings of the Ninth Workshop on NLP for Similar Languages, Varieties and Dialects, pages 20–27
October 16, 2022. ©2022 Association for Computational Linguistics

further examples below.

2 Software Design

The component of dialectR which most interests users is probably the edit distance computation of pronunciation differences based on transcriptions, which is written in C++11 and interfaced to R through the R package Rcpp (Eddelbuettel and François, 2011). Once a distance matrix between data-collection sites has been produced, dialectR additionally offers a number of ready-made functions for common analyses, such as an RGB-based multidimensionsal scaling for visualizing dialect continuua (Nerbonne et al., 1999), or a function for visualizing discrete dialect groupings based on hierarchical clustering (Nerbonne et al., 2008). Moreover, in the case where the input data is acoustic, we show how an additional acoustic distance proposed in Bartelds et al. (2020) can be leveraged, something missing in all alternative packages and web applications. We describe specifics of these components in the following subsections.

2.1 Distance Computation

Methods in dialectometry have revolved around aggregating linguistic differences between data collection sites since the inception of the field, in large part to overcome the noisy geographic distribution of sites and sample material (Goebl, 2018). A pioneering attempt in this direction can be seen in Séguy (1971), who worked with questionnaire data, where the number of possible answers are relatively limited (e.g. "what do you call a serving-size, unsweetened pastry?"). Séguy's method is essentially to count the number of different responses to the same survey questions at two dialect sites, and his paper marked the first important breakthrough in the establishment of the subfield.

To give a practical example of how such categorical could be used to quantify linguistic differences, suppose we have lexical data for two related dialect sites as shown in Table 1. To quantify how different these two sites are, a difference of 1 can be counted for every mismatch between vocabulary items, ignoring the pairs where data is unavailable. The total count is then normalized by taking the mean, resulting in a lexical distance of 0.25, meaning that there is a 75% lexical similarity between the two sites (Nerbonne and Kleiweg, 2003).

Such an approach provides a simple notion of lexical distance that can be used to aggregate over

Site	**Vocabulary Items**				
Brownsville	*dog*	*hat*	*horse*	*bathroom*	*pinkie*
White Plain	*dog*	*cap*	*horse*	*bathroom*	-

Table 1: Sample data as taken from LAMSAS for the illustration of lexical distance.

items, but a number of issues remain. For one, it would be desirable for morphologically related words to carry a smaller distance than words that are completely unrelated. Thus if in response to the question "if the sun comes out after a rain, you say the weather is doing what?", elicitations such as *fair off*, *fairs off*, and *faired off* come up, these variants of the same lexical item should count as less distant when compared with terms such as *clearing up* and *breaking away* (Nerbonne and Kleiweg, 2003). Similarly, it would also be insightful for there to be a metric that can quantify the degree of difference between phonetic transcriptions of related dialects. The solution to both issues may be found in edit distance, which forms the basis for methods developed in in the 1990s in Groningen.

Edit distance was first applied to dialect data in Kessler (1995), where it was applied on phonetic transcriptions of Irish Gaelic dialects and assigned to groups with hierarchical clustering, which proved to yield sensible results that correlate well with provincial boundaries. This in turn inspired further work at the University of Groningen that refines upon various aspects of the edit distance algorithm and the clustering algorithms (Nerbonne et al., 2008; Wieling et al., 2012), among other procedures. The original edit distance algorithm is a measure of distance between two strings, where the distance is derived from how many insertions, deletions, and substitutions it would take for one string to transform into the other. As an example, consider how in the table below, the string "koguma", the word for sweet potato in Korean, may be transformed into "kokoimo", a possible origin of the Korean term from the Tsushima dialect in Japan, with one insertion followed by three substitutions:

koguma	insert k	1
kokguma	replace g/o	1
kokouma	replace u/i	1
kokoima	replace a/o	1
kokoimo	Sum distance	4

However, in comparing two sequences with edit distance, longer sequences possess a much higher chance of containing more differences than shorter sequences. If used directly, this would bias the results by causing varieties with longer sequences to appear more different. Thus for a fair comparison of string distance across multiple samples, we follow Heeringa et al. (2006) by providing the option to normalize the distance by dividing the length of the alignment between the two strings. We furthermore also provide the option to use a variant of edit distance that forbids the alignment of vowels and consonants, which results in more plausible alignments, and thus also results in an improvement in the computed distance.

Moreover, due to the possibility of informants giving multiple responses in a single site, we provide the option to normalize for multiple responses with Bilbao distance (Aurrekoetxea et al., 2020), which is as follows:

$$D_B(A,B) = \frac{\sum_{i=1}^{|A|} \min_{b_j \in |B|} d(a_i b_j) + \sum_{j=1}^{|B|} \min_{a_j \in |A|} d(a_i b_j)}{|A| + |B|}$$

Where, in plain words, for every element in a given set A, we compute its minimal distance to all the elements of set B, using only that in the sum, and where we proceed the same way with respect to set B, seeking for each b in B, the closest element in A. The mean of the distances is then taken for normalization. We illustrate this with an example: suppose we have elicited responses to the question "what do you call the place where people are buried?" [2] from two sites, A and B. Site A has obtained the responses of {*graveyard*, *boneyard*}, and Site B has obtained the responses of {*cemetery*, *kirkyard*, *graveyard*}. Using a length-normalized edit distance as metric, the distance for every response in Site A as compared against the responses in Site B is shown in Table 2. We choose the combination for each response that minimizes the distance, add them up, and divide the sum by the total number of elements, which yields:

$$D_B(A,B) = \frac{0 + 0.44 + 0.75 + 0.5 + 0}{2 + 3} = 0.338$$

Finally, after the above computations have been applied to all pairs of words between sites, we discount the pairs where there is no data and take the average. This results in a distance matrix of normalized dialect distances, which is amenable to further statistical treatment.

[2]Question and responses sampled from Linguistic Atlas Project, item number 78.8.

A \ B	*cemetery*	*kirkyard*	*graveyard*
graveyard	0.78	0.56	0
boneyard	0.75	0.5	0.44

Table 2: Example data for illustration of Bilbao distance, where the cells indicate the length-normalized edit distance between responses.

2.2 Visualization

dialectR provides two visualization methods common in dialectometry: one based on multidimensional scaling, and another based on hierarchical clustering. We discuss their implementation in dialectR below.

2.2.1 Multidimensional Scaling

Multidimensional scaling refers to a family of dimensionality reduction techniques, where complex data is reduced to a smaller number of dimensions that can be more easily interpreted. Multidimensional scaling has been applied to distance tables extensively in dialectometry for the purpose of showing dialect continuum phenomena (Nerbonne et al., 1999; Embleton et al., 2013), and usually provides more robust results than those of clustering. The `mds_map` function in dialectR uses a refinement of Torgerson's multidimensional scaling (Torgerson, 1952), where provided a matrix of dissimilarities, the algorithm projects each data point into a lower dimensional space with the goal of preserving the distance between them as best possible.

The distance matrix of edit distance between varieties as described in section 2.1 can therefore in the aforementioned manner be given as input; reduced to three dimensions, where each dimension is rescaled to a range of [0, 1] with min-max scaling, and transformed proportionately to RGB values respectively. The three colors are then mixed, and at last projected onto the geographic locations of each variety. Figure 4 shows the results of applying this method on Dutch dialect data provided in the Goeman-Taeldeman-Van Reenen-project (Taeldeman and Goeman, 1996).

2.2.2 Hierarchical Clustering

Complementing the possibility of showing dialect continuua, in dialectology it is often also desirable to pursue a notion of distinct dialect groups.

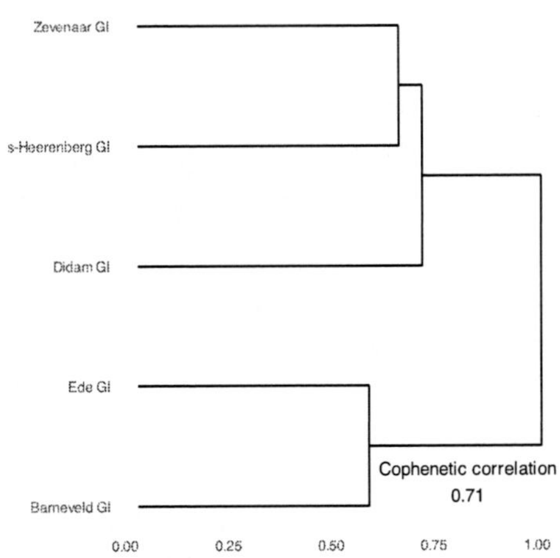

Figure 1: A partial dendrogram of the Goeman-Taeldeman-Van Reenen-project.

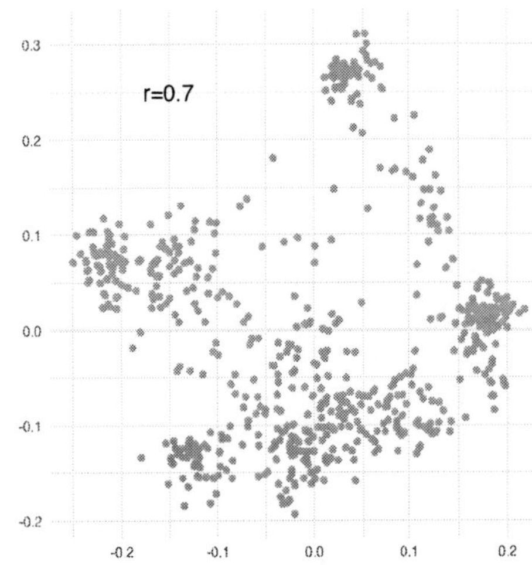

Figure 2: Dutch data from the Goeman-Taeldeman-Van Reenen-project reduced to two dimensions with multidimensional scaling, where the colors are groupings as obtained by hierarchical clustering.

This is achieved in dialectometry through hierarchical clustering, which dialectR implements by building upon the `hclust` function built natively in R. This allows for a number of agglomeration methods to be specified, including the weighted average method (alternatively known as the WPGMA method) and Ward's method, which differ in how proximity between clusters is defined, and can lead to somewhat different results. The result of applying hierarchical clustering on our distance matrix is a dendrogram, an example of which is shown in Figure 1, where the cophenetic distance between nodes can be seen. A cophenetic correlation coefficient between the original distance matrix and the results of clustering can also be calculated, which indicates how well the dendrogram has preserved the original distances in the data, and comes down to 0.71 for the Dutch dialect dataset using Ward's method.

However, due to the instability of hierarchical clustering, steps of validation and bootstrapping may be necessary to confirm the validity of the clusters. One possible method of validation is to plot the cluster groupings against the results of the a multidimensional scaling. This would result in Figure 2, where the difference in spread of the seven clusters would point to the possibility that certain edge cases remain ambiguous between clusters due to the continuous nature of the dialect data. The implementation of further bootstrapping and validation procedures such as described in Nerbonne et al. (2008) is also possible with the help of numerous related packages such as Suzuki and Shimodaira (2006) and Hennig (2020), the ready availability of which is a strength of dialectR over comparable closed systems.

2.3 Acoustic Distance

As an example of the benefit of the framework presented here, we turn to an open-source implementation of recent work that is not yet available in other comparable closed systems such as Gabmap and DiaTech. In order to demonstrate the advantage of an open system, we re-implemented the acoustic distance in Bartelds et al. (2020) in Python,[3] and include it here in R through the reticulate package (Ushey et al., 2020).

The method transforms audio samples into numerical feature representations based on 39-dimensional Mel-frequency cepstral coefficients (MFCCs), which include the first 12 cepstral coefficients and energy in each frame; the first and second derivatives from each of the cepstral coefficients and energy features; and one first and one second derivative related to the energy feature. These coefficients are computed with a window size of 25 ms and a stride of 10 ms. Cepstral means and variance normalization are used to reduce the effect of noise. After obtaining MFCCs for the two audio samples under consideration, dynamic time warping is then performed upon them to derive a measure of their distance. Bartelds et al. apply

[3]`https://github.com/b05102139/acoustic_distance`

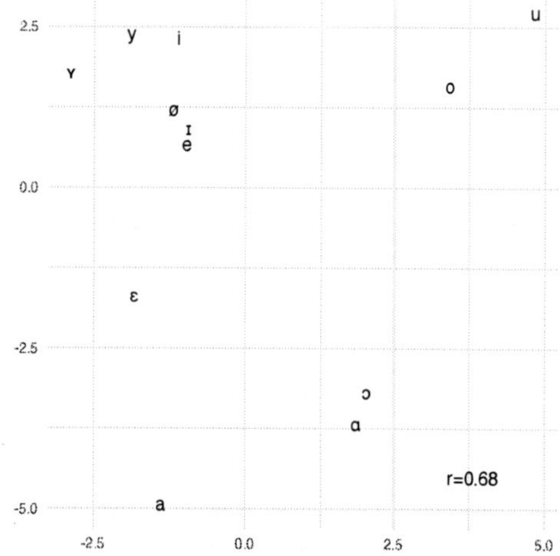

Figure 3: Acoustic vowel space as approximated with acoustic distance.

this method to audio samples in the Speech Accent Archive (Weinberger and Kunath, 2011), where a correlation of $r = -0.71 (p < 0.0001)$ was found between human judgments of native-likeness and the distance derived from their method. An approximate acoustic vowel space was also derived by applying their method to vowels, which we replicate in Figure 3 by using the recordings of vowels in the international phonetic alphabet as recorded by Peter Ladefoged[4] and plotting the two first dimensions of a multidimensional scaling.

This method enables the reduction of time and effort needed for transcription-based methods, where the human resources needed to transcribe the dialect audio into IPA may not be available. The implementation of this method relies heavily on speech processing packages in the Python ecosystem, and serves to illustrate the broader potential of doing dialectometry with open-source software, where the ability to utilize external resources in Python through the reticulate package constitutes a further advantage (Ushey et al., 2020).

3 Example Session

We show in this section an example session, by analyzing Dutch dialect data in the Goeman-Taeldeman-Van Reenen-project with dialectR. The IPA transcription dataset comes installed with the package, along with a sample Keyhole Markup Language (KML) file that is required in order to

Concepts / Sites	*aarde*	*adem*	*appels*
AalsmeerNH	ʔɒrde	ʔɒdəm	ʔapəls
AalstBeLb	ɛət	osəm	ɑpəls
AalstBeOv	eɛrdə	osəm	ɑpələn

Table 3: Excerpt of the transcriptions in the Goeman-Taeldeman-Van Reenen-project, where the cells are phonetic transcriptions of concepts collected at multiple sites.

provide geographic data of the collection sites. The Keyhole Markup Language is an XML-based markup language for geographic data, and is principally associated with Google Earth,[5] which users may utilize to create KML files for their own data. An excerpt of the phonetic transcriptions is shown in Table 3. An excerpt of the KML file is shown below:

```
<Placemark>
    <name>Zwolle Ov</name>
    <Point>
    <extrude>1</extrude>
    <coordinates>6.10418,52.5146,0</coordinates>
    </Point>
</Placemark>
```

The transcription data can be called with the `data` function built natively in R, and the geographic data can be loaded with `get_points` and `get_polygons`, which respectively extract the points and polygon data from the KML file into dataframes:

```
library(dialectR)
data(Dutch)
pathToKML <- system.file("extdata",
                         "DutchKML.kml",
                         package="dialectR")
dutchPoints <- get_points(pathToKML)
dutchPolygons <- get_polygons(pathToKML)
```

With the transcription data and geographic information ready, we can call `distance_matrix` and set the option of `alignment_normalization` to true, which computes the edit distance between the pronunciations of all corresponding words in all pairs and normalizes the score by length; we also set `funname` to `leven`, which uses the plain edit distance for its computation, as opposed to `vc_leven`, which implements the vowel-consonant constraint. The details of both of these options are discussed in Section 2.1.

[4] http://www.phonetics.ucla.edu/course/chapter1/vowels.html

[5] https://earth.google.com/web/

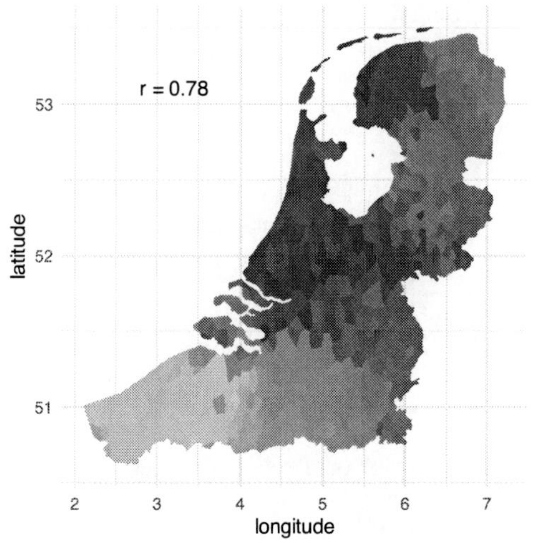

Figure 4: Three dimensions of the multidimensional scaling plotted respectively as RGB values, mixed together, and projected onto their respective locations.

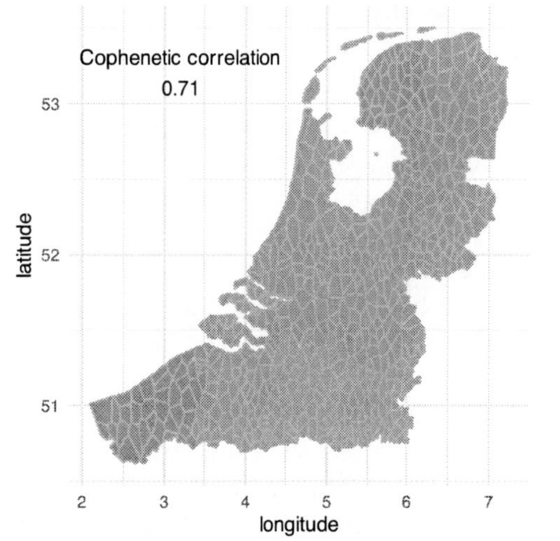

Figure 5: The groupings of hierarchical clustering as projected onto their respective locations.

We call `mds_map` upon the resulting distance matrix along with the required geographic information, which results in Figure 4:

```
distDutch <- distance_matrix(Dutch,
             funname="leven",
             alignment_normalization=TRUE)
mds_map(distDutch, dutchPoints, dutchPolygons)
```

We briefly remark that Friesland (the area in blue) clearly stands out as a variety most distinctly separate from its surroundings, which is consistent with its status as an independent language. The low Saxon area (the green area on the top right) and the west of Flanders (lower left) also show a notable similarity, which Wieling and Nerbonne (2011) also noted.

For purposes of illustration, we also show here how the edit distance and its variants as implemented in `distance_matrix` can be called independently of the function:

```
leven("graveyard/boneyard",
      "cemetery/kirkyard/graveyard",
             alignment_normalization = T,
             delim = "/")
```

Where the `alignment_normalization` parameter normalizes the distance by dividing the length of the alignment between two strings, and the `delim` parameter allows for comparing multiple responses in one or both of the sites with Bilbao distance.

To gain more specific insights into how one might classify significant similarities in a given area, we are now in a place to complement the multidimensional scaling analysis as performed above with hierarchical clustering. In dialectR this can be called via `cluster_map`, which results in Figure 5:

```
cluster_map(distDutch,
            kml_points = dutchPoints,
            kml_polygon = dutchPolygons,
            cluster_num = 7,
            method = "ward.D2")
```

We observe that the projection of our hierarchical clusters onto the geographic locations of the collection sites results in sensible aggregate isoglosses that largely correspond with the classification of dialectologists.

4 Conclusion and Future Work

We presented dialectR, an open-source package that attempts to facilitate community-based extensions to dialectometric methods by situating itself in the statistical environment of R. In doing so, we echo the sentiment in Nerbonne et al. (2011) regarding the future of Gabmap, a web application for dialectometry that served as the primary reference for the present package: "[t]here are also opportunities for further development. Probably the most important of these would involve making it easier for others to contribute modules, i.e. adopting an open-source development mode. Once it becomes easier for others to contribute, then scientific imagination is the limiting factor".

We suggested several lines of research above which dialectR might be used to support, including the use of geostatistical analysis or a wider range of dimension-reducing techniques. We further demonstrated how dialectR could be used to incorporate acoustics-based aggregate analyses in Sec. 2.3 above. So it is fitting that we close with yet another suggestion for work that dialectR might be used to support.

Edit distance measures for phonetic transcriptions have been shown to improve in sensitivity when used with sensitive segment weights (Wieling et al., 2012). Work in this direction has sought to take into account that frequent sound substitutions should be taken as more similar than infrequent ones (e.g., a substitution of [ɛ] should count as more similar to [e] than to [o]). Such a procedure has been used for the measurement of foreign accent strength (Wieling et al., 2014) and for the rectification of "field worker isoglosses", which refers to a systematic difference in transcription that occurs due to the field workers preferences, as opposed to any real linguistic differences between the dialect sites (Wieling and Nerbonne, 2011). These applications together point towards its usefulness as a future module, either to be incorporated into the current package, or, alternatively, to be made available alongside it.

As increasingly sophisticated statistical methods come to be used to examine dialect data (Wieling and Nerbonne, 2015; Wieling et al., 2018), the possibility of interfacing with dedicated packages in R facilitates the community-based effort to keep the latest methods within the reach of the general user.

Acknowledgements

We would like to thank the anonymous reviewers for providing valuable feedback in improving this work.

References

Gotzon Aurrekoetxea, Karmele Fernandez-Aguirre, Jesus Rubio, Borja Ruiz, and Jon Sanchez. 2013. 'DiaTech': A new tool for dialectology. *Literary and Linguistic Computing*, 28(1):23–30.

Gotzon Aurrekoetxea, John Nerbonne, and Jesus Rubio. 2020. Unifying analyses of multiple responses. *Dialectologia*, 25:59–86.

Martijn Bartelds, Caitlin Richter, Mark Liberman, and Martijn Wieling. 2020. A new acoustic-based pronunciation distance measure. *Frontiers in Artificial Intelligence*, 3.

Karin Beijering, Charlotte Gooskens, and Wilbert Heeringa. 2008. Predicting intelligibility and perceived linguistic distance by means of the Levenshtein algorithm. *Linguistics in the Netherlands*, 25:13–24.

Dirk Eddelbuettel and Romain François. 2011. Rcpp: Seamless R and C++ integration. *Journal of Statistical Software*, 40(8):1–18.

Sheila Embleton, Dorin Uritescu, and Eric S. Wheeler. 2013. Defining dialect regions with interpretations: Advancing the multidimensional scaling approach. *Literary and Linguistic Computing*, 28(1):13–22.

Hans Goebl. 2006. Recent advances in Salzburg dialectometry. *Literary and Linguistic Computing*, 21(4):411–435.

Hans Goebl. 2018. Dialectometry. In Charles Boberg, John Nerbonne, and Dominic Watt, editors, *The handbook of dialectology*, pages 123–142. John Wiley & Sons, Ltd.

Charlotte Gooskens and Wilbert Heeringa. 2004. Perceptive evaluation of Levenshtein dialect distance measurements using Norwegian dialect data. *Language Variation and Change*, 16(3):189–207.

Jack Grieve. 2018. Spatial statistics for dialectology. In Charles Boberg, John Nerbonne, and Dominic Watt, editors, *The handbook of dialectology*, pages 415–433. Wiley Online Library.

Wilbert Heeringa, Peter Kleiweg, Charlotte Gooskens, and John Nerbonne. 2006. Evaluation of string distance algorithms for dialectology. In *Proceedings of the workshop on linguistic distances*, pages 51–62, Sydney, Australia. Association for Computational Linguistics.

Christian Hennig. 2020. *fpc: Flexible procedures for clustering*. R package version 2.2-9.

Brett Kessler. 1995. Computational dialectology in Irish Gaelic. In *Seventh Conference of the European Chapter of the Association for Computational Linguistics*, Dublin, Ireland. Association for Computational Linguistics.

Therese Leinonen, Çağrı Çöltekin, and John Nerbonne. 2016. Using Gabmap. *Lingua*, 178:71–83.

John Nerbonne. 2015. Various variation aggregates in the LAMSAS South. In Michael D. Picone and Catherine Evans Davies, editors, *Language Variety in the South III*. University of Alabama Press, Tuscaloosa, Alabama.

John Nerbonne, Rinke Colen, Charlotte Gooskens, Therese Leinonen, and Peter Kleiweg. 2011. Gabmap – A web application for dialectology. *Dialectologia*, SI II:65–89.

John Nerbonne, Wilbert Heeringa, and Peter Kleiweg. 1999. Comparison and classification of dialects. In *Proceedings of the Ninth Conference on European Chapter of the Association for Computational Linguistics*, EACL '99, page 281–282, USA. Association for Computational Linguistics.

John Nerbonne and Peter Kleiweg. 2003. Lexical distance in LAMSAS. *Computers and the Humanities*, 37(3):339–357.

John Nerbonne, Peter Kleiweg, Wilbert Heeringa, and Franz Manni. 2008. Projecting dialect distances to geography: Bootstrap clustering vs. noisy clustering. In Christine Preisach, Hans Burkhardt, Lars Schmidt-Thieme, and Reinhold Decker, editors, *Data analysis, machine learning and applications*, pages 647–654. Springer Berlin Heidelberg, Berlin, Heidelberg.

Simon Pickl. 2013. *Probabilistische Geolinguistik*. Franz Steiner Verlag, Stuttgart.

R Core Team. 2020. *R: A language and environment for statistical computing*. R Foundation for Statistical Computing, Vienna, Austria.

Jean Séguy. 1971. La relation entre la distance spatiale et la distance lexicale. *Revue de Linguistique Romane*, 35:335–357.

Ryota Suzuki and Hidetoshi Shimodaira. 2006. Pvclust: An R package for assessing the uncertainty in hierarchical clustering. *Bioinformatics*, 22(12):1540–1542.

Johan Taeldeman and Ton Goeman. 1996. Fonologie en morfologie van de Nederlandse dialecten: een nieuwe materiaalverzameling en twee nieuwe atlasprojecten. *Taal en Tongval*, 48:38–59.

Warren S. Torgerson. 1952. Multidimensional scaling: I. Theory and method. *Psychometrika*, 17(4):401–419.

Kevin Ushey, JJ Allaire, and Yuan Tang. 2020. *reticulate: Interface to 'Python'*. R package version 1.18.

Steven H. Weinberger and Stephen A. Kunath. 2011. The speech accent archive: Towards a typology of English accents. In *Corpus-based studies in language use, language learning, and language documentation*, pages 265–281. Brill, Leiden, The Netherlands.

Martijn Wieling, Jelke Bloem, Kaitlin Mignella, Mona Timmermeister, and John Nerbonne. 2014. Measuring foreign accent strength in English: Validating Levenshtein distance as a measure. *Language Dynamics and Change*, 4(2):253–269.

Martijn Wieling, Eliza Margaretha, and John Nerbonne. 2012. Inducing a measure of phonetic similarity from pronunciation variation. *Journal of Phonetics*, 40(2):307–314.

Martijn Wieling and John Nerbonne. 2011. Measuring linguistic variation commensurably. *Dialectologia*, SI II:141–162.

Martijn Wieling and John Nerbonne. 2015. Advances in Dialectometry. *Annual Review of Linguistics*, 1(1):243–264.

Martijn Wieling, Esteve Valls, Rolf H. Baayen, and John Nerbonne. 2018. Border effects among Catalan dialects. In Dirk Speelman, Kris Heylen, and Dirk Geeraerts, editors, *Mixed-effects regression models in Linguistics*, pages 71–97. Springer International Publishing, Cham.

Low-Resource Neural Machine Translation: A Case Study of Cantonese

Evelyn Kai-Yan Liu
Uppsala University
kaiyan.liu.7557@student.uu.se

Abstract

The development of Natural Language Processing (NLP) applications for Cantonese, a language with over 85 million speakers, is lagging compared to other languages with a similar number of speakers. In this paper, we present, to our best knowledge, the first benchmark of multiple neural machine translation (NMT) systems from Mandarin Chinese to Cantonese. Additionally, we performed parallel sentence mining (PSM) as data augmentation for the extremely low resource language pair and increased the number of sentence pairs from 1,002 to 35,877. Results show that with PSM, the best performing model – bidirectional LSTM with Byte-Pair Encoding (BPE) – scored 11.98 BLEU better than the vanilla baseline and 9.93 BLEU higher than our strong baseline. Our unsupervised NMT (UNMT) results also refuted previous assumption (Rubino et al., 2020) that the poor performance was related to the lack of linguistic similarities between the target and source languages, particularly in the case of Cantonese and Mandarin. In the process of building the NMT system, we also created the first large-scale parallel training and evaluation datasets of the language pair. Codes and datasets are publicly available at https://github.com/evelynkyl/yue_nmt.

1 Introduction

There are over 85 million Cantonese speakers around the globe, and it is the de facto spoken language in Hong Kong, Macau, and the Canton region in China (Wong et al., 2017; Eberhard et al., 2021). The language is also deemed the most influential and well-known variety of Chinese languages after Mandarin (Matthews and Yip, 2013); nevertheless, Cantonese has rather limited linguistic resources. While there are varying sizes of Cantonese-English corpora, such as Hong Kong Hansards (Legislative Council of the Hong Kong Special Administrative Region, 2022) and Hong Kong Laws Parallel Text (Ma, 2000), the latter of which contains nearly 3 million parallel sentences between the two languages, the same cannot be said for the pair of Cantonese and Mandarin. English and Cantonese share very few linguistic features, and are considered distant languages. On the contrary, Cantonese and Mandarin are typologically similar in that they share more linguistic features such as grammatical structures and basic lexical items than Cantonese does with English (Wong and Lee, 2018). As such, our work aims to take advantage of the typological similarities between the two languages and investigate whether the similarities would enable decent translation quality despite having a limited amount of training data.

The existing Cantonese (Hong Kong variant) - Mandarin corpora are quite small and mostly in the domain of conversational transcripts and social media (Luke and Wong, 2015; Wong et al., 2017). This can be further demonstrated by the dependency treebank built by Wong et al. (2017), which consists of only 13,918 words/tokens, as compared to 285,000 in Mandarin in Universal Dependencies (UD; Nivre et al., 2020). Most state-of-the-art (SoTA) deep learning algorithms require a large amount of data to perform well. It holds true especially for more complex tasks, such as machine translation (MT), question answering, and neural text generation (Koehn and Knowles, 2017; Puri et al., 2020; Malandrakis et al., 2019). As a consequence, most of these complex tasks are not commonly applied to Cantonese.

Language, however, is the core of one's cultural identity (Coupland, 2007). In light of that, the main goal of this paper is to benchmark different Mandarin to Cantonese NMT approaches to pave the way for future research on Cantonese NMT systems. The contributions of the paper include providing the first baseline of Cantonese NMT and the first large training and evaluation parallel dataset of the language pair. Our hypothesis is that creating an MT system with a high-resource, typolog-

Proceedings of the Ninth Workshop on NLP for Similar Languages, Varieties and Dialects, pages 28–40
October 16, 2022.

ically close language might produce decent translation outputs. If that is the case, the limited resources of Cantonese can be improved by utilizing the MT system, hence enabling implementations of NLP systems with better performance for the low-resource language.

2 Linguistic Considerations of Cantonese and Mandarin

Most Chinese texts encountered in NLP is in Mandarin, largely due to its high availability in linguistic resources. Nearly all Cantonese speakers can read and write in written Mandarin, and it is conventionally preferred in academic and legal settings to write in written Mandarin to convey a sense of formality (Snow, 2004). As a consequence, there is very little Cantonese text data available, which, in turn, makes Cantonese seldom included in a majority of the NLP research and systems (Lee et al., 2022).

Nevertheless, Cantonese and Mandarin are typologically similar languages, where they have a similar grammatical system and share basic lexical items such as times, numbers, and personal pronouns that are identical in orthography (Zhang, 1998). Even though the two languages are closely related, there are, indeed, a plethora of linguistic differences. The most notable one is the phonological systems, in which their similarities are minimal in terms of sound inventory and intonation (Zhang, 1998; Tang and Van Heuven, 2009). On the aspects of syntactic structure, the main difference between the two languages is their word orders, where Cantonese allows a more flexible word ordering compared to Mandarin (Ding and Féry, 2014). Furthermore, there are distinctive grammatical features in Cantonese that do not exist in Mandarin (Zhang, 1998), including, but not limited to, post-verbal elements, structural particles, directional verbs, definiteness, and aspect markers. In terms of lexical dissimilarity, there are seven to eight thousand distinct words and expressions in Cantonese that are written in a different character from any Mandarin words, or that carry a different meaning from the Mandarin words of similar forms (Zhang, 1998). These distinct words attribute almost one third of the total vocabulary in Cantonese, and half of them are commonly used in daily conversation among Cantonese speakers.

Take a parallel sentence pair from the UD data as an example to illustrate the differences and similarities between the two languages. Sentence 1 denotes its expression in Cantonese, while Sentence 2 refers to the sentence in Mandarin.

(1) 嗰**時**啲 CD鋪 仲多過
That **time**'s CD shops even more than
而家啲 **七十一**。
now's **7-11**.

"There were more CD shops at that time than the 7-11 (convenience stores) we have now."

(2) 那**時**候 唱片店 比現在
At that **time** CD shops compared to now
七十一 還要多。
7-11 even more.

"There were more CD shops at that time than the 7-11 (convenience stores) we have now."

As can be observed, the lexical tokens between the two sentences are quite different, with only four words (in bold) in overlap and three of them being a numerical item and one being a timing word. On the contrary, the syntactic structures are roughly similar, with word order differences such as the placement of time, subject, and comparison expression.

The distinctive lexical, syntactic, and phonological differences result in the language pair being mutually unintelligible (Zhang, 1998). Consequently, transforming from Mandarin to Cantonese should be treated as a translation task.

3 Related Work

3.1 Cantonese Parallel Corpus

Wong et al. (2017) constructed a parallel corpus of Cantonese and Mandarin in Standard Traditional Chinese scripts. This corpus is the first, albeit small (1,002 sentence pairs), Cantonese-Mandarin parallel corpus. It is created by transcribing television programs in Hong Kong as Cantonese data and using the original subtitles of the programs in Mandarin (Wong et al., 2017).

3.2 Parallel Sentence Mining (PSM)

PSM, sometimes referred to as bitext mining, identifies sentence pairs that are, or are close to, translations of one another (Feng et al., 2020). It makes use of two comparable corpora, which contain non-translated bilingual documents that are aligned on topics but not at the sentence-level (Rapp et al., 2016). PSM has been commonly applied to MT for lower resource languages as a data augmentation to improve the performance of an MT system (Stefanescu et al., 2012; Uszkoreit et al., 2010; Munteanu and Marcu, 2005). It can also be applied to a larger-scale scenario that contains a multilingual machine translation system with thousands of language directions (Fan et al., 2021). Hence, PSM enables one to source high quality parallel sentences effectively and efficiently and is the most useful in multilingual research, especially in a low resource setting. Moreover, mining sentences from comparable corpora overcomes some of the limitations that exists in parallel datasets (Zweigenbaum et al., 2018). In particular, large parallel corpora typically cover only a subset of the variety of language pairs, and they are often in very specific domains and genres. Furthermore, most of the parallel sentences are constructed by using human translations; therefore, these translations are likely to contain translation biases such as calques and other phenomena (Zweigenbaum et al., 2018). Contrarily, comparable corpora often display more variety and are generally original texts instead of translations. As such, it holds more promises as a complement to parallel corpora to aid in terms of variety and quantity of the data.

The goal of PSM is to find semantically similar sentences by calculating multilingual sentence embeddings, followed by finding the K-nearest neighbor sentences for all sentences in both directions, and finally, calculating all possible sentence combinations (Feng et al., 2020). The higher score a sentence pair has, the better it could serve as a translation pair (Reimers and Gurevych, 2020). Generally, scores higher than 1 indicate that it is of quality. Reimers and Gurevych (2020) reported that using LaBSE (Feng et al., 2020) as the mining model returned the best results in their experiments.

3.3 Low-resource NMT

While NMT has demonstrated its performance in resource-rich language pairs, research has shown that the same performance does not apply in limited data situations (Koehn and Knowles, 2017; Sennrich and Zhang, 2019). As reported by Gu et al. (2018), NMT systems cannot achieve reasonable translation results if the corpus has less than 13K parallel sentences. As such, to improve the quality of low-resource NMT models, researchers have proposed a plethora of methods, which can be categorized into two groups:

1. **Monolingual data**. Exploiting data from the target language is low-cost and effective. Approaches range from back translation which takes advantage of the target-side monolingual corpus (Sennrich et al., 2016a), bilingual text mining (Feng et al., 2020), joint training in both translation directions (Zheng et al., 2019), as well as language models pre-training (Conneau and Lample, 2019; Lewis et al., 2019).
2. **Auxiliary languages' data**. Leveraging other language pairs' corpora for pre-training or joint representation learning has shown great success even with extremely low-resource language pairs (Zoph et al., 2016; Kocmi and Bojar, 2018). There are several methods of leveraging multilingual data for low-resource NMT, including transfer learning (Conneau et al., 2019; Chronopoulou et al., 2020), multilingual training (Gu et al., 2018; Zhang et al., 2020), as well as pivot translation (Wu and Wang, 2009; Wang et al., 2021).

3.3.1 Unsupervised NMT

There has been tremendous progress in using unsupervised NMT (UNMT) as opposed to supervised NMT in recent years (Artetxe et al., 2018). While a UNMT model performs well when trained on a large, high quality, and comparable dataset, it does not perform well for languages with lesser availability of data (Chronopoulou et al., 2020). To solve this issue, Chronopoulou et al. (2020) proposed pre-training a monolingual LM (MonoLM) on a high-resource language, then fine-tuning the LM on the language pair, followed by an initialization of a UNMT model. They also introduced a new vocabulary extension approach that enables fine-tuning a pre-trained LM to any unseen language. The results showed that their approaches outperformed XLM (Conneau and Lample, 2019), a SoTA cross-lingual language model pre-training framework, on several language pairs. Furthermore, they added residual adapters (Rebuffi et al., 2018) to the layer of each of the pre-trained MonoLM. Residual adapters are feed-forward networks that prevent catastrophic forgetting of the model (Bapna and Firat, 2019). Chronopoulou et al. (2020) reported that adapters enable fine-tuning parameters in a more time-saving and cost-efficient manner with little to no cost on the performance as compared to the originally proposed model.

4 Methodology and Experimental Setup

We implemented the following NMT systems on the direction of Mandarin to Cantonese in the experiment:

1. Word-based bidirectional LSTM model with general attention mechanism as the baseline ($BiLSTM$),
2. Word-based (1) + fine-tuning as a strong baseline ($BiLSTM_t$),
3. Word-based (2) + PSM ($BiLSTM_t$ + PSM),
4. BPE-based fine-tuned BiLSTM + PSM ($BiLSTM_{bpe+t}$ + PSM),
5. Word-based Transformer ($Trans_w$ + PSM),
6. BPE-based Transformer ($Trans_{bpe}$ + PSM),
7. Unsupervised NMT via language model pre-training and transfer learning with adapters ($RELM_{adap}$ + PSM)

4.1 Data, Bitext mining, and Prepossessing

Original Dataset This paper used the Cantonese-Mandarin parallel corpus by Wong et al. (2017) in Universal Dependencies (Nivre et al., 2020) as the foundation, which we refer to as UD in this paper. It consists of 1,002 sentence pairs (see Section 3.1).

Data Augmentation: Bitext Mining Considering the small size of the corpus, we used a data augmentation technique by mining sentence pairs. The Cantonese and Mandarin Wikipedia sites were extracted to perform the mining.[1] The bitext mining was performed via the SoTA LaBSE (Feng et al., 2020) to select pairs of semantically similar sentences following the scripts from Reimers and Gurevych (2019). Feng et al. (2020) suggested that sentences with a score of 1 are of quality, and 1.2 of high quality. However, we performed a qualitative review on a subset of the results and observed that sentences that scored 1.1286 are already of high quality and are semantically similar to each other. As such, we set the score threshold to 1.1286. After filtering out sentences below the threshold, we found 34,873 sentence pairs with equal to or over 1.1286 score. Having performed bitext mining, our total number of sentence pairs for training and evaluation has increased from 1,002 to 35,877. The increase in data size enables us to train a NMT system that is possible to perform well, since NMT systems are not able to achieve decent results when the training data has less than 13K pairs (Gu et al., 2018).

Final Datasets The newly complied data served as a synthetic parallel dataset to augment the UD dataset and alleviated the lack of sufficient training data. We refer to the combination of the two datasets as UD + Bitext, which was used to train all experimental models except the baselines. UD and UD + Bitext sets were both used for training and evaluation. Table 1 shows the distribution of the datasets used in the experiments.

No. of sentences	UD	UD + Bitext
Training	801	24,396
Validation	100	5,382
Test	101	6,099
Total	1,002	35,877

Table 1: Ratio of the datasets in the experiment (all randomly divided)

Preprocessing No word segmentation is done for the UD dataset as it is already tokenized. The mined parallel sentences were tokenized using Jieba.[2] We removed blank lines but did not normalize punctuation or non-Chinese characters. We used Byte Pair Encoding (BPE) preprocessing for $BiLSTM_{bpe+t}$ + PSM, $Trans_{bpe+t}$ + PSM, and $RELM_{adap}$ + PSM while word-based preprocessing was used for the baselines, $BiLSTM_t$ + PSM, and $Trans_w$ + PSM. We used fastBPE for $RELM_{adap}$ + PSM since the pre-trained model used this technique and subword NMT (Sennrich et al., 2016b) for the rest of the models with BPE representation. We trained the BPE tokenizers on our datasets with a maximum number of 8K BPE tokens in the vocabulary for models with these word representations.

4.2 Experiments

We trained (i) a BiLSTM model with attention and (ii) a Transformer model and compare them with (iii) an unsupervised NMT (UNMT) model using the RELM framework. Both (i) and (ii) were trained using Adam optimizer (Kingma and Ba, 2014) and cross-entropy loss function. We conducted the supervised NMT (SNMT) experiments

[1] https://dumps.wikimedia.org/backup-index.html

[2] https://github.com/fxsjy/jieba

using JoeyNMT (Kreutzer et al., 2019), while the UNMT is trained via PyTorch (Paszke et al., 2019). More details about the training parameters in the experiments can be found in Appendix A.

4.2.1 BiLSTM-based NMT

NMT Baselines We trained two word-based BiLSTM models with a learning rate of 3e-04 as our baselines. The vanilla baseline was implemented without exhaustive fine-tuning. Considering the sensitivity of under-resourced NMT to hyperparameters tuning (Sennrich and Zhang, 2019), it is crucial to optimize the model. Hence, a strong baseline was implemented following the parameter settings in Sennrich and Zhang (2019). We used 1 layer of encoder with 64 embedding dimension and 128 hidden units, and a batch size of 64. For regularization, we applied 0.2 drop-out and 0.3 hidden drop-out. A beam size of 5 was used for decoding.

BiLSTM with augmented data After parallel sentence mining, we extended our baselines to examine the effectiveness of data augmentation. We trained two models of different encoding schemes with the augmented data (approach 3 and 4) using the same model architecture (1 layer encoder of BiLSTM). The training parameters of these models were adjusted based on the strong baseline in consideration of the increased size in training data. Both approaches were trained on 3e-04 learning rate, an embedding dimension of 128, a hidden size of 256, 0.25 drop-out and 0.3 hidden drop-out, a batch size of 64, as well as a beam size of 10.

4.2.2 Transformer-based NMT

With the additional data from parallel sentence mining, it increases the chance of having a better performing Transformer NMT. Thus, we implemented two exhaustively tuned Transformer-based models on both word-level and BPE-level. The models were trained with identical parameters, including a learning rate of 2e-04, a batch size of 10, 2 layers of encoders with 4 attention heads, 0.1 drop-out rate, and a beam size of 5. The only differences are the embedding dimension and hidden size, where we used 64 each for the BPE-level model and 128 each for the word-level one.

4.2.3 UNMT via Transfer Learning

As mentioned in Section 3.3.1, researchers have reported success on transferring a pre-trained monolingual LM to a UNMT model even with some resource-poor language pairs (Chronopoulou et al., 2020). In light of that, we trained a UNMT system using the RELM framework (Chronopoulou et al., 2020) using the UD + Bitext dataset for monolingual model. For monolingual LM pre-training, we used 385,486 sentences (Mandarin) as the training data. Then, we fine-tuned part of the LM on the target language using only adapters with the same amount of parallel sentences. Finally, we trained a Transformer-based UNMT model by initializing the encoder and decoder with the fine-tuned model plus the adapters in both translation directions. We followed the default parameters of RELM for model training, with a learning rate of 1e-04, a batch size of 32, 512 embedding dimension and hidden size, 3 layers and 4 heads, a hidden and non-hidden drop-out rate of 0.1, A multilayer perceptron (MLP) attention, along with a beam size of 5.

4.3 Evaluation

4.3.1 Datasets

We used two datasets for evaluation, including (i) UD, and (ii) UD + Bitext. They were used as input to the translation systems for evaluating the quality of the NMT models aside from the automatic metric. It allows us to perform a qualitative investigation on the translation outputs of the proposed Mandarin-Cantonese NMT systems.

4.3.2 Methods

The automated evaluation metric used in this paper is detokenized SacreBLEU scores (Post, 2018). We report test set scores on the checkpoints with the highest BLEU score in the validation set. In addition, we performed manual evaluation on a subset of the evaluation data to get a better sense of the translation quality. The SacreBLEU results are reported and discussed below.

5 Results

Table 2 reports the primary results of our experiments. Having such a limited amount (~1K sentence pairs) of data, as expected, completely fails to train a vanilla BiLSTM translation model. Applying training tricks and exhaustive hyperparameter tuning, as suggested by Sennrich and Zhang (2019), has led to an improved result (+2.05 BLEU). However, the score and quality is too low for the translation outputs to be comprehensible.

Among all the models in the experiment, the data-augmented BiLSTM models are the best-performing, with the word-level model scoring

Architecture	Model	SacreBLEU
BiLSTM	Word level vanilla NMT, baseline 1	1.24
	Word level, $BiLSTM_t$, baseline 2	3.29
	Word level, $BiLSTM_t$ + PSM	12.37
	BPE level, $BiLSTM_{t+bpe}$ + PSM	**13.22**
Transformer	Word level + PSM ($Trans_{word}$)	3.56
	BPE level + PSM ($Trans_{bpe}$)	11.66
UNMT	$RELM_{adap}$ + PSM	1.85

Table 2: Experimental results on the Mandarin-Cantonese translation direction. PSM refers to the parallel sentence mining technique to increase data size. The highest score is in bold.

12.37 BLEU and the BPE-level one scoring 13.22 points. Word-level MT models are typically slower to converge, and thus, require more training to have on-par performance with their BPE-level counterparts (Sennrich et al., 2016b; Wu et al., 2016). Given that the two models were trained on an identical number of epochs, it is reasonable that the BPE-level one, which converges faster, performed better. The Transformer-based models are outperformed by the BiLSTM models. It is not surprising given the limited data in the experiments. The UNMT system with pre-trained LM scored 1.85 on SacreBLEU (+0.61 points compared to the vanilla baseline) and is the second-worst performing model in the experiment. The strong baseline (model 2, fine-tuned vanilla NMT) outperforms it by 1.44 BLEU even with only 1K sentence pairs.

6 Analysis

Effect of corpus size Bitext mining improved the model performance substantially (+9.08 BLEU, $BiLSTM_t$ + PSM compared to $BiLSTM_t$) with merely some minor changes in the training parameters in view of the increased data size. It shows that this technique is successful in assisting model learning and thus improving its performance by increasing the size of the training data.

6.1 Out-of-vocabulary (OOV)

Upon careful examination of the translations, we observed that OOV is a critical issue for both BiLSTM and Transformer models. OOV occurs when the translation output contains unknown tokens (UNK), which are unseen words or rare words whose occurrences are less frequent than other words in the vocabulary in the training data. The issue is a major challenge for any language in a low-resource scenario (Liu and Kirchhoff, 2018). In a low-resource setting, the dictionary created from the selected training data is not able to cover all the possible words and characters in the language. Consequently, when evaluated on an independent test set, it is highly likely that many terms that were not covered in the training data have then become unknown tokens. Given that our limited size of training data, OOV is a severe problem that negatively impacts model performance. Table 3 shows examples of translations generated by BiLSTM and Transformer models with word and Byte-Pair Encoding (BPE) representations.

Word-level systems For word-level BiLSTM and Transformer systems, we observed that the translation quality of the validation set is better than the test set, and they did not produce UNK tokens like the BPE-level models. They still, however, suffer from OOV. Due to the lack of UNK tokens, we are unable to measure the severity of this issue for word-level systems. The reason behind the absence of UNK tokens is word-based NMT models' inability to translate unseen words (Sennrich et al., 2016b); instead, they copy unknown words to the outputs, resulting in plenty of words copied directly from the training data of the source language. The quality of the translation from word-based models, as a result, is similar to the BPE-level one for the BiLSTM models. In contrast, the performance is significantly worse for the Transformer model. The result from the word-level Transformer model contains either single, irrelevant words or numerous duplicate words, making it uninterpretable. Referring to Table 3, the output sentence from this model is completely different from the reference sentence, either in terms of topic, sentence structure, or semantics. The output from word-level BiLSTM bears a closer resemblance to the reference text, albeit barely intelligible. It also copied many words from other sentences in the training data, as some words like **轉到** "turned" and **都係** "is also" are unrelated and thus should not be used in the sentence.

BPE-level systems BiLSTM with BPE representations has the highest number of UNK tokens compared to the rest of the experimental models

Model	Sentence from BPE-level model	Sentence from word-level model
Gold standard		
Original sentence	沙田區議員曾提出重建西林寺爲旅遊地	
Translation	District Councillors of Sai Tin had proposed to renovate Sai Lam Temple as a tourist attraction.	
BiLSTM		
Original output:	沙田<unk>曾經委任做旅遊<unk>	沙田都係之後轉到西林寺爲旅遊地
Translation	<unk> Sai Tin was assigned as a tourist <unk>.	Sai Tin then turned the Sai Lam Temple to a tourist attraction
Transformer		
Original output	而家都係沙田<unk>西林寺爲旅遊地	問題
Translation	Sai Lam Temple is still a tourist attraction in Sai Tin <unk>.	Problem

Table 3: Translation examples from the word-level and BPE-level models illustrating Out-of-Vocabulary (OOV) issue

(UNK to word ratio is 63.3% on the test set). In spite of that, the SacreBLEU of this model surpassed the rest, meaning that the accuracy of the non-UNK translated tokens is quite decent. For the BPE-level Transformer model, its occurrence frequency of UNK tokens is much lower than its BiLSTM counterpart (UNK to word ratio 38.5% as compared to 63.3%). Although $BiLSTM_{bpe+t}$ + PSM's BLEU score is higher than $Trans_{bpe}$ + PSM's, our analysis suggests the opposite in terms of translation quality. We found the translations by $Trans_{bpe}$ + PSM contains fewer UNK tokens and a closer semantic meaning to the reference sentences. These findings corroborate the UNK to word ratios reported above. Despite having a less severe OOV issue, the Transformer model still performs worse in terms of BLEU score, yet it intriguingly performs better on the aspects of translation quality. As shown in Table 3, the sentence output by the BPE-level Transformer model contains fewer UNK tokens, as well as a closer semantic meaning to the reference sentence. It is due to the fact that the Transformer model does not produce the exact words as the reference text, but a rephrased version; conversely, the BiLSTM model, as a sequence-to-sequence model, is more prone to direct-copying from the training text (Sutskever et al., 2014; Gu et al., 2016). Hence, its output would theoretically have more exact words. Since BLEU (Papineni et al., 2002) is concerned about the exact match in the translated text and the reference text, one of the plausible explanations of the above phenomenon is that the metric favors models that have a copying tendency.

Moreover, consistent with the findings of Artetxe et al. (2018), we observed that BPE is of scant help in terms of UNK tokens when the name entities or phrases are infrequent. Despite subword translations such as BPE being beneficial to OOV problems in general, such an advantage is hardly observed in this study. A likely explanation is that our source and target languages are both character-rich languages. While they can have over 50,000 characters in their languages, only a fraction of those are used regularly (Wang et al., 2020). Yet, many infrequently used characters can take up a considerable amount of vocabulary slots (Wang et al., 2020). As such, when two languages do not have many overlapping character sets, BPE might not be an optimal choice compared to other subword tokenization schemes such as Byte level BPE (BBPE; Wang et al., 2020) or unigram language modeling (Kudo, 2018). Future studies can explore the impacts of different subword tokenization techniques on this language pair to further increase the NMT performance.

UNMT The UNMT model performs considerably worse than the supervised MT models. The gap between the two approaches is very significant when we consider the identical data size. The BLEUs of the supervised approach are at least 9.81 higher than the UNMT model, whose score is only marginally better than the vanilla baseline. As such, for very low-resource language pairs, training an MT system with 36K synthetic parallel data is a better option. The majority of the translation output by the UNMT model are duplicates of some word, making the result unintelligible. Hence, we are not able to analyze it in-depth. Despite the success of Chronopoulou et al. (2020), our experimental results are in line with the previous work on UNMT for low-resource languages (Rubino et al., 2020). It is worth noting that even though our language pair (Cantonese and Mandarin) is highly similar typologically, the model performance is still similar to that of Rubino et al. (2020) in terms of BLEU. As such, in the case of Cantonese and Mandarin, we refuted their assumption that the poor performance was related to the lack of linguistic similarities between the target and source languages. We believe that the poor performance is largely tied to the amount of monolingual data in the LM pretraining step. It is also possible that although Cantonese and Mandarin are typologically close, the differences in word ordering or grammatical features made them linguistically less similar. However, compared to the language pairs in Rubino et al. (2020), our target and source languages share many more linguistic similarities. Hence, it is more likely that the poor performance is due to the limited data of our language pair. As a consequence, more training data is required to better aid the model to learn the language representations.

In addition, the language pair in this research differs greatly from the language pairs that performed well in the previous studies, such as English-French and German-English (Artetxe et al., 2018; Lample et al., 2018). Since both Cantonese and Mandarin are logographic languages, using a different subword representation method than the default BPE one might lead to a better-performing model.

7 Limitations

Translation systems are prone to making generalizations based on the frequency of gender-role, race, religion, and other stereotypes occurrences in the datasets. One typical example is "Man is to Programmer as Woman is to Homemaker" (Bolukbasi et al., 2016). The Cantonese-Mandarin UD parallel treebank used in this study was sourced from a television show, which might contain stereotypes in the dialogues. Besides, the bitext mined sentence pairs were sourced from the Wikipedia sites of Cantonese and Mandarin. Given that Wikipedia is an open-source community where everyone can contribute, its content could be vulnerable to social injustice and stereotypes as well. Their presence in the training data, if any, would reinforce the stereotypes in the translation system. One way to mitigate such potential issues is by treating it as a domain adaptation problem, as recommended by Saunders and Byrne (2020).

In terms of evaluation, the main automated metric in this study is SacreBLEU. Using only one metric, however, is not able to provide a full picture of the model performance and its translation quality. Although we used manual analysis along with SacreBLEU, having a non-matching based metric such as BERTScore (Zhang* et al., 2020) or SIMILE (Wieting et al., 2019) would be helpful in evaluating the contextual similarity between the input and the translation.

8 Conclusion and Future Work

In this paper, we presented the first benchmark of various NMT approaches for Cantonese. Due to the minimal amount of training data, the baseline models failed to produce intelligible results. We alleviated this issue by using parallel sentence mining as data augmentation and have increased the training data size from $\sim$1K to $\sim$36K. It resulted in a tremendous boost in performance (+9.08 BLEU) and produced higher-quality translations. Additionally, we provided a large parallel training and evaluation dataset of Cantonese and Mandarin for future research.

One of the interesting findings in this paper is that our Transformer MT systems performed worse than the BiLSTM systems in terms of SacreBLEU. This is reasonable given the large amount of data required by Transformer-based models and the limited amount of training data. What is more intriguing is that using varied word representations in an NMT system leads to very different results. We found that BPE-level models generally perform better. The BPE-level Transformer model produces more comprehensible translations despite having a lower BLEU score than the two BiLSTM models. We hypothesize that this is because of the evaluation metric's (BLEU) architecture favoring models with a copying tendency. Besides the supervised models, we also implemented an unsupervised NMT with LM pre-training. It is, however, among the worst-performing models, in spite of the large amount of training data in comparison with the rest of the models.

Future work can be dedicated to different approaches to improve the performance of Mandarin-Cantonese NMT systems. While this study has investigated the direction of Mandarin to Cantonese as a way to alleviate the lower resource in Cantonese, our next step would include both translation directions as well. In addition, one could explore various approaches to mitigate the severe OOV issue, such as applying Jyutping romanization of the characters (Du and Way, 2017; Aqlan et al., 2019) or using BBPE (Wang et al., 2020) or unigram language modeling (Kudo, 2018) rather than BPE as the subword tokenization technique.

Another research direction is to train a multilingual NMT system (MNMT). With various source languages, the model is able to learn universal language representations from all the languages, thus enabling the systems to be language agnostic (Lee et al., 2017; Johnson et al., 2017; Feng et al., 2020). In our case, it may enable Cantonese to take advantage of the universal language representations in terms of linguistics and knowledge, hence allowing the system to perform well regardless the amount of available data (Gu et al., 2018).

References

Fares Aqlan, Xiaoping Fan, Abdullah Alqwbani, and Akram Al-Mansoub. 2019. Arabic–Chinese neural machine translation: Romanized Arabic as subword unit for Arabic-sourced translation. *IEEE Access*, 7:133122–133135.

Mikel Artetxe, Gorka Labaka, Eneko Agirre, and Kyunghyun Cho. 2018. Unsupervised neural machine translation. In *International Conference on Learning Representations*.

Ankur Bapna and Orhan Firat. 2019. Simple, scalable adaptation for neural machine translation. In *Proceedings of the 2019 Conference on Empirical Methods in Natural Language Processing and the 9th International Joint Conference on Natural Language Processing (EMNLP-IJCNLP)*, pages 1538–1548, Hong Kong, China. Association for Computational Linguistics.

Tolga Bolukbasi, Kai-Wei Chang, James Y Zou, Venkatesh Saligrama, and Adam T Kalai. 2016. Man is to computer programmer as woman is to homemaker? debiasing word embeddings. In *Advances in Neural Information Processing Systems*, volume 29. Curran Associates, Inc.

Alexandra Chronopoulou, Dario Stojanovski, and Alexander Fraser. 2020. Reusing a Pretrained Language Model on Languages with Limited Corpora for Unsupervised NMT. In *Proceedings of the 2020 Conference on Empirical Methods in Natural Language Processing (EMNLP)*, pages 2703–2711, Online. Association for Computational Linguistics.

Alexis Conneau, Kartikay Khandelwal, Naman Goyal, Vishrav Chaudhary, Guillaume Wenzek, Francisco Guzmán, Edouard Grave, Myle Ott, Luke Zettlemoyer, and Veselin Stoyanov. 2019. Unsupervised cross-lingual representation learning at scale. *arXiv preprint arXiv:1911.02116*.

Alexis Conneau and Guillaume Lample. 2019. Cross-lingual language model pretraining. In *Advances in Neural Information Processing Systems*, volume 32. Curran Associates, Inc.

Nikolas Coupland. 2007. *Style: Language variation and identity*. Cambridge University Press.

Picus Sizhi Ding and Caroline Féry. 2014. Word order, information structure and intonation of discontinuous nominal constructions in Cantonese/ordre des mots, structure de l'information et intonation des phrases nominales discontinues en cantonais. *Cahiers de Linguistique Asie Orientale*, 43(2):110–143.

Jinhua Du and Andy Way. 2017. Pinyin as subword unit for Chinese-sourced neural machine translation.

Eberhard, David M, and Gary F Simons. 2021. Ethnologue: Languages of the world. twenty-fourth edition.

Angela Fan, Shruti Bhosale, Holger Schwenk, Zhiyi Ma, Ahmed El-Kishky, Siddharth Goyal, Mandeep Baines, Onur Celebi, Guillaume Wenzek, Vishrav Chaudhary, et al. 2021. Beyond english-centric multilingual machine translation. *J. Mach. Learn. Res.*, 22(107):1–48.

Fangxiaoyu Feng, Yinfei Yang, Daniel Cer, Naveen Arivazhagan, and Wei Wang. 2020. Language-agnostic bert sentence embedding. *arXiv preprint arXiv:2007.01852*.

Jiatao Gu, Hany Hassan, Jacob Devlin, and Victor O.K. Li. 2018. Universal neural machine translation for extremely low resource languages. In *Proceedings of the 2018 Conference of the North American Chapter of the Association for Computational Linguistics: Human Language Technologies, Volume 1 (Long Papers)*, pages 344–354, New Orleans, Louisiana. Association for Computational Linguistics.

Jiatao Gu, Zhengdong Lu, Hang Li, and Victor O.K. Li. 2016. Incorporating copying mechanism in sequence-to-sequence learning. In *Proceedings of the 54th Annual Meeting of the Association for Computational Linguistics (Volume 1: Long Papers)*, pages 1631–1640, Berlin, Germany. Association for Computational Linguistics.

Melvin Johnson, Mike Schuster, Quoc V. Le, Maxim Krikun, Yonghui Wu, Zhifeng Chen, Nikhil Thorat, Fernanda Viégas, Martin Wattenberg, Greg Corrado, Macduff Hughes, and Jeffrey Dean. 2017. Google's multilingual neural machine translation system: Enabling zero-shot translation.

Diederik P Kingma and Jimmy Ba. 2014. Adam: A method for stochastic optimization. *arXiv preprint arXiv:1412.6980*.

Tom Kocmi and Ondřej Bojar. 2018. Trivial transfer learning for low-resource neural machine translation. *arXiv preprint arXiv:1809.00357*.

Philipp Koehn and Rebecca Knowles. 2017. Six challenges for neural machine translation. In *Proceedings of the First Workshop on Neural Machine Translation*, pages 28–39, Vancouver. Association for Computational Linguistics.

Julia Kreutzer, Jasmijn Bastings, and Stefan Riezler. 2019. Joey NMT: A minimalist NMT toolkit for novices. In *Proceedings of the 2019 Conference on Empirical Methods in Natural Language Processing and the 9th International Joint Conference on Natural Language Processing (EMNLP-IJCNLP): System Demonstrations*, pages 109–114, Hong Kong, China. Association for Computational Linguistics.

Taku Kudo. 2018. Subword regularization: Improving neural network translation models with multiple subword candidates. In *Proceedings of the 56th Annual Meeting of the Association for Computational Linguistics (Volume 1: Long Papers)*, pages 66–75, Melbourne, Australia. Association for Computational Linguistics.

Guillaume Lample, Alexis Conneau, Ludovic Denoyer, and Marc'Aurelio Ranzato. 2018. Unsupervised machine translation using monolingual corpora only. In *International Conference on Learning Representations*.

Jackson L Lee, Litong Chen, Charles Lam, Chaak Ming Lau, and Tsz-Him Tsui. 2022. PyCantonese: Cantonese linguistics and NLP in python. In *Proceedings of the 13th Language Resources and Evaluation Conference*, pages 6607–6611. European Language Resources Association.

Jason Lee, Kyunghyun Cho, and Thomas Hofmann. 2017. Fully character-level neural machine translation without explicit segmentation. *Transactions of the Association for Computational Linguistics*, 5:365–378.

Legislative Council of the Hong Kong Special Administrative Region. 2022. Hong Kong Hansard Database.

Mike Lewis, Yinhan Liu, Naman Goyal, Marjan Ghazvininejad, Abdelrahman Mohamed, Omer Levy, Ves Stoyanov, and Luke Zettlemoyer. 2019. Bart: Denoising sequence-to-sequence pre-training for natural language generation, translation, and comprehension. *arXiv preprint arXiv:1910.13461*.

Angli Liu and Katrin Kirchhoff. 2018. Context models for oov word translation in low-resource languages. *arXiv preprint arXiv:1801.08660*.

Kang Kwong Luke and May LY Wong. 2015. The Hong Kong Cantonese corpus: design and uses. *Journal of Chinese Linguistics*, 25(2015):309–330.

Xiaoyi Ma. 2000. Hong Kong Laws Parallel Text.

Nikolaos Malandrakis, Minmin Shen, Anuj Goyal, Shuyang Gao, Abhishek Sethi, and Angeliki Metallinou. 2019. Controlled text generation for data augmentation in intelligent artificial agents. *arXiv preprint arXiv:1910.03487*.

Stephen Matthews and Virginia Yip. 2013. *Cantonese: A comprehensive grammar*. Routledge.

Dragos Stefan Munteanu and Daniel Marcu. 2005. Improving machine translation performance by exploiting non-parallel corpora. *Computational Linguistics*, 31(4):477–504.

Joakim Nivre, Marie-Catherine de Marneffe, Filip Ginter, Jan Hajič, Christopher D Manning, Sampo Pyysalo, Sebastian Schuster, Francis Tyers, and Daniel Zeman. 2020. Universal Dependencies v2: An evergrowing multilingual treebank collection. *arXiv preprint arXiv:2004.10643*.

Kishore Papineni, Salim Roukos, Todd Ward, and Wei-Jing Zhu. 2002. Bleu: a method for automatic evaluation of machine translation. In *Proceedings of the 40th Annual Meeting of the Association for Computational Linguistics*, pages 311–318, Philadelphia, Pennsylvania, USA. Association for Computational Linguistics.

Adam Paszke, Sam Gross, Francisco Massa, Adam Lerer, James Bradbury, Gregory Chanan, Trevor Killeen, Zeming Lin, Natalia Gimelshein, Luca Antiga, et al. 2019. Pytorch: An imperative style, high-performance deep learning library. *Advances in neural information processing systems*, 32.

Matt Post. 2018. A call for clarity in reporting BLEU scores. In *Proceedings of the Third Conference on Machine Translation: Research Papers*, pages 186–191, Brussels, Belgium. Association for Computational Linguistics.

Raul Puri, Ryan Spring, Mostofa Patwary, Mohammad Shoeybi, and Bryan Catanzaro. 2020. Training question answering models from synthetic data. *arXiv preprint arXiv:2002.09599*.

Reinhard Rapp, Serge Sharoff, and Pierre Zweigenbaum. 2016. Recent advances in machine translation using comparable corpora. *Natural Language Engineering*, 22(4):501–516.

Sylvestre-Alvise Rebuffi, Hakan Bilen, and Andrea Vedaldi. 2018. Efficient parametrization of multi-domain deep neural networks. In *Proceedings of the IEEE Conference on Computer Vision and Pattern Recognition*, pages 8119–8127.

Nils Reimers and Iryna Gurevych. 2019. Sentence-bert: Sentence embeddings using siamese bert-networks. In *Proceedings of the 2019 Conference on Empirical Methods in Natural Language Processing*. Association for Computational Linguistics.

Nils Reimers and Iryna Gurevych. 2020. Making monolingual sentence embeddings multilingual using knowledge distillation. In *Proceedings of the 2020 Conference on Empirical Methods in Natural Language Processing (EMNLP)*, pages 4512–4525, Online. Association for Computational Linguistics.

Raphael Rubino, Benjamin Marie, Raj Dabre, Atushi Fujita, Masao Utiyama, and Eiichiro Sumita. 2020. Extremely low-resource neural machine translation for Asian languages. *Machine Translation*, 34(4):347–382.

Danielle Saunders and Bill Byrne. 2020. Reducing gender bias in neural machine translation as a domain adaptation problem. In *Proceedings of the 58th Annual Meeting of the Association for Computational Linguistics*, pages 7724–7736, Online. Association for Computational Linguistics.

Rico Sennrich, Barry Haddow, and Alexandra Birch. 2016a. Improving neural machine translation models with monolingual data. In *Proceedings of the 54th Annual Meeting of the Association for Computational Linguistics (Volume 1: Long Papers)*, pages 86–96, Berlin, Germany. Association for Computational Linguistics.

Rico Sennrich, Barry Haddow, and Alexandra Birch. 2016b. Neural machine translation of rare words with subword units. In *Proceedings of the 54th Annual Meeting of the Association for Computational Linguistics (Volume 1: Long Papers)*, pages 1715–1725, Berlin, Germany. Association for Computational Linguistics.

Rico Sennrich and Biao Zhang. 2019. Revisiting low-resource neural machine translation: A case study. In *Proceedings of the 57th Annual Meeting of the Association for Computational Linguistics*, pages 211–221, Florence, Italy. Association for Computational Linguistics.

Don Snow. 2004. *Cantonese as written language: The growth of a written Chinese vernacular*, volume 1. Hong Kong University Press.

Dan Stefanescu, Radu Ion, and Sabine Hunsicker. 2012. Hybrid parallel sentence mining from comparable corpora. In *Proceedings of the 16th Annual conference of the European Association for Machine Translation*, pages 137–144.

Ilya Sutskever, Oriol Vinyals, and Quoc V Le. 2014. Sequence to sequence learning with neural networks. In *Advances in neural information processing systems*, pages 3104–3112.

Chaoju Tang and Vincent J Van Heuven. 2009. Mutual intelligibility of Chinese dialects experimentally tested. *Lingua*, 119(5):709–732.

Jakob Uszkoreit, Jay Ponte, Ashok Popat, and Moshe Dubiner. 2010. Large scale parallel document mining for machine translation.

Changhan Wang, Kyunghyun Cho, and Jiatao Gu. 2020. Neural machine translation with byte-level subwords. In *Proceedings of the AAAI Conference on Artificial Intelligence*, volume 34, pages 9154–9160.

Rui Wang, Xu Tan, Renqian Luo, Tao Qin, and Tie-Yan Liu. 2021. A survey on low-resource neural machine translation. *arXiv preprint arXiv:2107.04239*.

John Wieting, Taylor Berg-Kirkpatrick, Kevin Gimpel, and Graham Neubig. 2019. Beyond BLEU:training neural machine translation with semantic similarity. In *Proceedings of the 57th Annual Meeting of the Association for Computational Linguistics*, pages 4344–4355, Florence, Italy. Association for Computational Linguistics.

Tak-sum Wong, Kim Gerdes, Herman Leung, and John Lee. 2017. Quantitative comparative syntax on the Cantonese-Mandarin parallel dependency treebank. In *Proceedings of the Fourth International Conference on Dependency Linguistics (Depling 2017)*, pages 266–275, Pisa, Italy. Linköping University Electronic Press.

Tak-sum Wong and John Lee. 2018. Register-sensitive translation: a case study of mandarin and Cantonese (non-archival extended abstract). In *Proceedings of the 13th Conference of the Association for Machine Translation in the Americas (Volume 1: Research Track)*, pages 89–96, Boston, MA. Association for Machine Translation in the Americas.

Hua Wu and Haifeng Wang. 2009. Revisiting pivot language approach for machine translation. In *Proceedings of the Joint Conference of the 47th Annual Meeting of the ACL and the 4th International Joint Conference on Natural Language Processing of the AFNLP*, pages 154–162.

Yonghui Wu, Mike Schuster, Zhifeng Chen, Quoc V Le, Mohammad Norouzi, Wolfgang Macherey, Maxim Krikun, Yuan Cao, Qin Gao, Klaus Macherey, et al. 2016. Google's neural machine translation system: Bridging the gap between human and machine translation. *arXiv preprint arXiv:1609.08144*.

Biao Zhang, Philip Williams, Ivan Titov, and Rico Sennrich. 2020. Improving massively multilingual neural machine translation and zero-shot translation. In *Proceedings of the 58th Annual Meeting of the Association for Computational Linguistics*, pages 1628–1639, Online. Association for Computational Linguistics.

Tianyi Zhang*, Varsha Kishore*, Felix Wu*, Kilian Q. Weinberger, and Yoav Artzi. 2020. Bertscore: Evaluating text generation with bert. In *International Conference on Learning Representations*.

Xiaoheng Zhang. 1998. Dialect MT: A case study between Cantonese and Mandarin. In *COLING 1998 Volume 2: The 17th International Conference on Computational Linguistics*.

Zaixiang Zheng, Hao Zhou, Shujian Huang, Lei Li, Xin-Yu Dai, and Jiajun Chen. 2019. Mirror-generative neural machine translation. In *International Conference on Learning Representations*.

Barret Zoph, Deniz Yuret, Jonathan May, and Kevin Knight. 2016. Transfer learning for low-resource neural machine translation. In *Proceedings of the 2016 Conference on Empirical Methods in Natural Language Processing*, pages 1568–1575, Austin, Texas. Association for Computational Linguistics.

Pierre Zweigenbaum, Serge Sharoff, and Reinhard Rapp. 2018. A multilingual dataset for evaluating parallel sentence extraction from comparable corpora. In *Proceedings of the Eleventh International Conference on Language Resources and Evaluation (LREC 2018)*.

A Appendix

Table 4 lists the training hyperparameters used for the models in the experiments.

Experiments	Hyperparameters					
	Encoding	Learning rate	Batch size	Maximum epoch	Embedding dimension	Hidden size
$BiLSTM$	word	0.0003	256	600	128	128
$BiLSTM_t$	word	0.0003	64	800	64	128
$BiLSTM_t$ + PSM	word	0.0003	64	100	128	256
$BiLSTM_{bpe+t}$ + PSM	bpe	0.0003	64	100	128	256
$Trans_{word}$ + PSM	word	0.0002	10	300	128	128
$Trans_{bpe}$ + PSM	bpe	0.0002	10	300	64	64
$RELM_{adap}$ + PSM	bpe	0.0001	32	5000	512	512

Table 4: Hyperparameters of the experimental models in the study.

Experiments	Hyperparameters					
	Layer(s)	Head(s)	Drop-out	Hidden drop-out	Attention	Beam size
$BiLSTM$	2	0	0.2	0.2	MLP	10
$BiLSTM_t$	1	0	0.3	0.3	MLP	5
$BiLSTM_t$ + PSM	1	0	0.25	0.3	MLP	10
$BiLSTM_{bpe+t}$ + PSM	1	0	0.25	0.3	MLP	10
$Trans_{word}$ + PS	2	4	0.1	0	MLP	5
$Trans_{bpe}$ + PSM	2	4	0.1	0	MLP	5
$RELM_{adap}$ + PSM	3	4	0.1	0.1	MLP	5

Table 4: Hyperparameters of the experimental models in the study, continued.

Phonetic, Semantic, and Articulatory Features in Assamese-Bengali Cognate Detection

Abhijnan Nath[1], **Rahul Ghosh**[2], and **Nikhil Krishnaswamy**[1]

[1]Department of Computer Science, Colorado State University, Fort Collins, CO, USA
[2]Fossil Ridge High School, Fort Collins, CO, USA[†]
{abhijnan.nath,nkrishna}@colostate.edu

Abstract

In this paper, we propose a method to detect if words in two similar languages, Assamese and Bengali, are cognates. We mix phonetic, semantic, and articulatory features and use the cognate detection task to analyze the relative informational contribution of each type of feature to distinguish words in the two similar languages. In addition, since support for low-resourced languages like Assamese can be weak or nonexistent in some multilingual language models, we create a monolingual Assamese Transformer model and explore augmenting multilingual models with monolingual models using affine transformation techniques between vector spaces.

1 Introduction

Lexical cognates are words that are inherited by direct descent from a common etymological ancestor. Due to sound change and semantic shift, cognates may or may not be easy to detect without rigorous application of the comparative method. For example, English "two" is cognate with Armenian *erku*, as both are descended from Proto-Indo-European **dwóh*$_1$, with **dw->>tw-* and **dw->>erk-* being regular, if non-intuitive, parallel sound changes.

Unlike loanwords, cognates are inherited and not borrowed, and are therefore necessarily subject to diachronic sound change. Application of the comparative method to cognates can be used to discern the evolutionary paths of related languages, making them very useful for historical linguists, but first cognates must be distinguished from other classes of words like ordinary translations or words that simply sound similar.

In this paper we focus on cognate detection between two closely-related languages: Bengali (ISO code `bn`) and Assamese (ISO code `as`). Bengali (262 million speakers) and Assamese (15 million speakers) are two languages of eastern India and Bangladesh. They are both official languages of India (with most speakers located in the states of West Bengal and Assam, respectively), while Bengali is also the national language of Bangladesh. They share a common descent from Early Indo-Aryan via Magadhi Prakrit, and are both typically written using Bengali or Eastern Nagari script. The Bengali-Assamese languages (or Gauda-Kamarupa languages) is the subgrouping of Eastern Indo-Aryan that contains both these languages and related dialects. They share certain grammatical features like classifying affixes (e.g., Asm. -zɔn, Beng. -dʒɔn, referring to persons), as well as certain common phonetic innovations (such as the evolution of Sanskrit /ə/→/ɔ/).

Despite the similarities, the two languages have some important differences, particularly in their sound patterns. Table 1 shows Assamese and Bengali consonants that are pronounced differently despite being written with the same letter. For instance, Assamese lenited Sanskrit /s/ to /x/ whereas Bengali palatalized it to /ʃ/. However both sounds are now written with the same letters in their respective languages—স, শ, or ষ—usually transcribed as <s> or <sh>.

Assamese	Bengali
s,s,z,z	tɕ,tɕʰ,dʑ,dʑʱ
t,tʰ,d,dʱ	ʈ/t̪,ʈʰ/t̪ʰ,ɖ/d̪,ɖʱ/d̪ʱ
x,ɹ	ʃ,r

Table 1: Assamese-Bengali sound correspondences.

Therefore between these two languages, phonetic features, orthographic features, semantic features, or alignment of articulatory sequences may be more or less useful in determining cognate status, depending on the specific words in question. The word এক (/ek/), meaning "one" in both languages, is a clear case of common inheritance

[†]This work conducted during an internship with the Colorado State University Department of Computer Science.

Proceedings of the Ninth Workshop on NLP for Similar Languages, Varieties and Dialects, pages 41–53
October 16, 2022.

from Sanskrit with the same sound changes applied; one need only look at the orthographic and phonetic forms to see this. But for Assamese অকল (/ɔkɔl/), meaning "only," the Bengali cognate is actually একলা (/ekla/). In Bengali, অকল is actually an Arabic loan meaning "wisdom."

In this paper we explore the contributions of phonetic, semantic, orthographic, and articulatory alignment features to the task of cognate detection between Assamese and Bengali. We use heuristic edit distance metrics, embedding vectors from various large multilingual language models (MLMs), and neural networks to learn alignments between phonetic sequences. We also use an affine transformation technique to augment the embedding spaces of MLMs with Assamese-specific data. With combinations of features, we are able to achieve up to ~94% F1 on cognate detection. Our results also show that embeddings from a smaller monolingual BERT variant can be mapped using affine transformations into the embedding space of larger multilingual models, which can improve both precision (up to 30%) and recall (up to 20%) in detecting Assamese cognates in Bengali.

2 Related Work

Cognate detection has been approached from many angles in the NLP community. Kondrak (2001) identifies cognates in Algonquian using phonetic and semantic similarity. Mulloni and Pekar (2006) infer orthographic changes between cognates across languages. Jäger (2018) evaluates PMI and SVM-based methods in cognate detection over the Automated Similarity Judgment Project database (Brown et al., 2008). List (2014) finds relationships between data size and genetic relatedness in automated cognate detection between English, German, Dutch, and French. Bloodgood and Strauss (2017) explore using global constraints in this task. Dellert (2018) explores sequence alignment and sound correspondence features in cognate detection in Northern European languages; these are two of the feature types we also explore here. Rama et al. (2018) and Rama and List (2019) explore the application of automated cognate detection methods to phylogenetic reconstruction and inference, and Kanojia et al. (2021a) utilize WordNets to perform orthographic similarity-based cognate detection in various Indian languages, but notably not Assamese.

Bharadwaj et al. (2016) and Rijhwani et al. (2019) suggest that phonologically-aware articulatory representations from PanPhon (Mortensen et al., 2016) can either be used natively as embeddings or as features in attention-based neural models for downstream NLP tasks such as NER or entity linking for low-resource languages. Labat and Lefever (2019) and Lefever et al. (2020) suggest that adding semantic information to orthographic features works well for cognate detection in resource-rich languages like English and Dutch (90% F1). Similarly, Kanojia et al. (2021b) suggests that adding large multilingual model embeddings to cognitive features like gaze improves cognate detection in low-resource languages like Hindi and Marathi (86% F1). Work in translation lexicons (e.g., Schafer and Yarowsky (2002)) is also relevant here, for the hybrid approach to similarity metrics used. We combine multiple approaches which, to our knowledge, have never before been used all together. Works such as Ganesan et al. (2021) and Artetxe et al. (2018a,b) improve bilingual lexical induction using either linear or non-linear word embedding maps, but they use non-contextual embeddings like fastText or word2vec. We extend such research to cognate detection using contextualized embeddings from Transformer-based models to leverage additional monolingual representations in this task.

3 Datasets

Cognates in Bengali and Assamese must share a common descent from an ancestor language[1]; the best-documented of these is Sanskrit. However, many descendants of Sanskrit make scholarly reborrowings from Sanskrit (*tatsama*) that are fully reincorporated Sanskrit forms adapted to fit the modern phonology. These exist alongside *tadbhava* words inherited from Old Indo-Aryan with concomitant sound changes in the Middle Indo-Aryan phase.

For this data collection, we turned to Wiktionary. Namely, we scraped the categories of the form `[Descendant]_terms_derived_from_Sanskrit` for each of the two descendants.[2]. We took the union of these two sets and then took the subset of the union where both the Assamese and Bengali forms had the same documented Sanskrit ancestor. Checking against com-

[1]We do not adopt the definition of cognate that subsumes loanwords (e.g., Kondrak (2001)); we use the linguistic definition that treats loanwords and cognates as distinct.

[2]e.g., `https://en.wiktionary.org/wiki/Category:Assamese_terms_derived_from_Sanskrit`

mon ancestry filters out loanwords from the cognate datasets. Table 2 shows the number of cognates retrieved for each language. We should note that despite the union-intersection operations being symmetrical, this does not result in equally-sized datasets for the two languages; because Bengali has more overall entries in the English Wiktionary, there are more cases where multiple Bengali words have the same ancestor as a single documented Assamese word.

Descendant	Ancestor	# Cognates
Assamese	Sanskrit	205
Bengali	Sanskrit	335

Table 2: Cognate pair counts per language.

We then convert every word in every pair to its phonetic representation in the International Phonetic Alphabet (IPA). This is done using the Epitran package (Mortensen et al., 2018). The available Epitran distribution does not support certain low-resourced languages, among them Assamese, but the format is easily extensible, and so we wrote an Epitran graph-to-phoneme mapping for Assamese using resources like Omniglot[3] and Wikiwand/Assamese[4], as well as native speaker guidance for verification.

Having gathered positive examples of cognates, we complete the datasets with word pairs that are not examples of cognates. These may be: i) **hard negatives**: phonetically similar non-cognates; ii) **synonyms**: semantically similar words, like ordinary non-cognate translations; iii) **randoms**: pairs where the two words have no discernible phonetic or semantic relationship.

To collect **hard negative** examples, we use the PanPhon package (Mortensen et al., 2016) and calculate six different edit distances between the IPA transcription of every gathered cognate in one language, and the IPA transcription for every lemma in the other language (the list of lemmas was also scraped from Wiktionary). For each edit distance, we select the word that has the lowest edit distance to the cognate in question. This returns up to six hard negatives per cognate (less if more than one edit distance metric returns the same nearest neighbor). Example: Asm. কথা (/kɔtʰa/) "word", Beng. কটা (/kɔʈa/) "how many".

[3]https://omniglot.com/writing/assamese.htm

[4]https://www.wikiwand.com/en/Help:IPA/Assamese

To collect **synonyms**, we adapted our Wiktionary scraper to exploit the metadata organization of Wiktionary pages, and retrieved synonyms for each word in the collected cognates list where available. Example: Asm. কুটুম (/kutum/) "family", Beng. রিশতাদার (/riʃt̪ad̪ar/) "relatives."

Finally we generate the **randoms** pairings by pairing each cognate with a random word in the other language. As a final cleanup step, we remove any intersections between these three datasets and between these and the cognates dataset.

We then concatenated these subsets into three different datasets. 1) `Assamese-Bengali`, where the Assamese word is the baseline comparand to which the Bengali word is compared. 2) `Bengali-Assamese`, where the reverse is true. This is a small and subtle difference. The order of the words in word pairs between this dataset and the previous one are simply flipped, so the edit distances are symmetric, but because alignment score is calculated using a deep neural network estimator trained on randomized splits of the data, alignment scores between two reversed word pairs are similar but often not identical. 3) `All-languages`. This is a bidirectional dataset consisting of the concatenation of the previous two. In training and inference this allows the final classifier to learn from similarity metrics that flow in both directions.

The full dataset creation process for data of this size can be completed within an day, including native speaker verification. Table 11 in the Appendix gives the total train and test size of each category.

4 Methodology

Here we discuss the orthographic and phonetic features we extract from the data, our methods of assessing alignment between phonetic sequences, how we extract semantic similarity features from various language models, and how these different features combine in the cognate classification task.

4.1 Orthographic and Phonetic Similarity

Orthographic similarity is simply the Levenshtein edit distance (Levenshtein et al., 1966) between two strings. Since Assamese and Bengali use the same script with small modifications, we want to explore the importance of a simple string similarity metric as a feature in our classification task. Because of differences in the sound patterns of the two languages (see Sec. 1), phonetic distance is also important. We calculate phonetic similarity using 6 different edit distances from PanPhon over the IPA transcriptions of the word pairs in our dataset. These edit distances are: Fast Levenshtein Distance, Dolgo Prime Distance, Feature Edit Distance, Hamming Feature Distance, Weighted Feature Distance, Partial Hamming Feature Distance, all normalized by the maximum length of the two words in the pair. We hypothesize that these distance metrics collectively capture some important information about phonetic similarity between Assamese and Bengali cognate pairs.

4.2 Alignment-Scoring Network

To account for different phonotactics, epenthesis, elision, and metathesis between Assamese and Bengali, we build a model to align phonemes in the pair. This provides a more informative measure than simple edit distances.

We convert the IPA transcriptions to 21 subsegmental articulatory features using PanPhon[5]. These features include place and manner of articulation, voicing, etc., and the feature vectors were padded to the maximum length of a vector in the cognate pair. The features for word pairs in our datasets were then concatenated for input to the alignment-scoring network.

The alignment network is a two-layer deep feed-forward neural network with 512 neurons in each layer, all with ReLU activation and followed by 10% dropout. We trained for 5,000 epochs on the aforementioned concatenated features of the `All-languages` dataset (see Sec. 3), using a 80:20 train/validation split. The network was trained against the cognate/non-cognate binary label. This is not to predict cognate status directly, since we do not include any semantic information at this step, but the label acts as an rough indicator of "phonetically aligned" or not. A positive prediction means the model predicts that the two words in the pair are strongly phonetically-aligned according to the articulatory features. During inference, we get the pre-sigmoid logit value as a holistic alignment score between the two words.

4.3 Semantic Similarity

Even though cognates do not need to have similar meaning, many do preserve semantic similarity. Work such as Turton et al. (2021) suggest that contextual semantic information at the word level can be extracted from BERT and variants as embeddings. As such, we extract semantic information from both word-level and sentence-level embeddings from large multilingual Transformer-based models such as XLM-R (Conneau et al., 2020) and MBERT (Devlin et al., 2018), as well as from some smaller, Indian language-focused models: IndicBERT (Kakwani et al., 2020) and Muril (Khanuja et al., 2021).

XLM-R (100 languages) and MBERT (104 languages) are trained on multiple languages from across the globe. MBERT includes Bengali in its training data but not Assamese. XLM-R was trained with data from both languages but the Assamese training data size is a relatively small 5 million tokens, whereas the Bengali training data is over 100 times larger (and the training data of a well-resourced language like English is 100 times larger still). IndicBERT and MuRIL are focused on Indian languages and so have a larger relative training data size for languages like Assamese and Bengali. IndicBERT and MuRIL also outperform XLM and MBERT against several semantic downstream NLP task benchmarks like IndicGLUE (Kakwani et al., 2020), cross-lingual XTREME (Hu et al., 2020), etc.

4.3.1 Monolingual Assamese Model

In order to provide our cognate classifier with a potentially stronger representation of Assamese semantics, and to investigate how much information a much smaller monolingual Transformer model might be able to contribute, we trained a "light" ALBERT (`albert-base-v2`) model for 305,700 epochs with a vocabulary size of 32,000 on four publicly-available Assamese datasets: Assamese Wikidumps[6], OSCAR (Suárez et al., 2019)[7], PMIndia (Haddow and Kirefu, 2020)[8] and the Common Crawl (CC100) Assamese corpus (Conneau et al., 2020)[9] (in total, after preprocessing, around 14 million Assamese tokens) with the BERT Masked Language Model (Devlin et al., 2018) loss function. See Table 5 in the Appendix for model configuration.

4.3.2 Affine Transformations Between Embedding Spaces

Since embeddings are vectors that preserve similarity relations across dimensions, only embeddings retrieved from the same model architecture are guaranteed to be directly comparable. Absent this condition, differences in training data, training

[5]PanPhon does not contain suprasegmental or tonal information but both Bengali and Assamese are non-tonal languages.

[6]https://archive.org/details/aswiki-20220120

[7]https://oscar-corpus.com

[8]https://paperswithcode.com/dataset/pmindia

[9]https://paperswithcode.com/dataset/cc100

regime, and model architecture mean that embeddings retrieved from different models are likely to be orthogonal in most dimensions.

However, recent work in the vision community (McNeely-White et al., 2020, 2022) has demonstrated that by fitting affine matrices $M_{A \to B}$ and $M_{B \to A}$ between paired features denoting equivalent samples extracted from models A and B, features from one embedding space can be transformed to another embedding space with high fidelity. This entails solving for a mapping function $f(x; W)$ where $W \in \mathbb{R}^{d_A} \times \mathbb{R}^{d_B}$, between equivalent information samples (i.e., paired embedding vectors) from two models, using ridge regression. The aforementioned work has been applied to CNN architectures, and here we use this task to explore the application of similar principles to Transformer architectures.

The paired vectors we use to compute mappings between embedding spaces come in the form of word-level and sentence-level embeddings from the aforementioned large language models: IndicBERT, XLM-R, MBERT, MuRIL, and our Assamese ALBERT variant (Sec. 4.3.1).

Sentence-sensitive embeddings We took our list of extracted cognates and had a native speaker of each language manually create simple sentences for each word that were direct translations of each other. Sentences were of a form that was appropriate for the part of speech, left the sense of the word as unambiguous as possible, and were as simple as possible (e.g., see Table 3).

Language	Sentence	IPA
Bengali	এটি একটি <u>টাং</u>	eʈi ekʈi ʈaŋ
Assamese	এইটো এটা <u>ঠেং</u>	eitʊ eta t^hɛŋ
English	This is a <u>foot</u>/<u>leg</u>	

Table 3: Sample equivalent sentences with cognate words (and English translations) underlined.

Two additional special tokens (<m> and </m>) were added to the models' vocabularies. Before getting the sentence embeddings, the cognate words were surrounded by these tokens to account for subword tokenization potentially breaking up the cognate words. We then generate binary vectors for the cognates using the indices of the special tokens in the sentence. Our model attends to these binary maps by an element-wise tensor multiplication in the forward function and outputs a contextual representation of the word. For instance, when preprocessed, the Bengali sample sentence "this is a valley" is input to the model as এটি একটি **<m>**উপত্যকা**</m>**. Sentence-sensitive embeddings were generated only from MBERT and our ALBERT variant, as the other models all have at least some support for Assamese already.

Word-level embeddings For each of the five models, we input a "sentence" formatted as `[CLS]<word>[SEP]` and use the `[CLS]` token's `last_hidden_state` to get representations for each token in each sequence of the batch from the last layer of the model, which often encodes more semantic information. Jawahar et al. (2019) and Tenney et al. (2019) suggest that BERTs later layers encode comparatively more high-level semantic information than the middle layers. The `[CLS]` token here serves the same purpose as the `<m>` tokens in the sentence-sensitive embeddings: to account for potential subword tokenization effects.

Having extracted the different embeddings from each model, we use the native embeddings from each model to find cosine similarities between the words in every pair in the data. These cosine similarities are input features into the final evaluation.

Affine mapping procedure Native model embeddings are independently useful for downstream NLP tasks, but their utility may be degraded when the language model does not robustly support the language in question. E.g., in the case of MBERT, which was not trained on Assamese, many Assamese words may be treated as out of vocabulary items and broken up into subwords that do not capture the semantics of the original word. Therefore in this case, we explore if and how linearly mapping one set of embeddings from its native space to a target model space can still act as an effective feature in this cognate detection task.

To construct the mapping, we take the word or sentence embeddings from one model as inputs, and equivalent word or sentence embeddings from another model as outputs, and fit them to each other using scikit-learn's ridge regressor. The resulting $d_A \times d_B$ transformation matrix[10] computed from a set of paired vectors serves as a bridge transformation from one embedding space to another by minimizing the distance between paired points in $\mathbb{R}^{d_A} \times \mathbb{R}^{d_B}$ feature space that share equivalent semantics. Multiplying a source embedding by this precomputed bridge matrix should result

[10]All embeddings used here are 768 dimensions, except embeddings from XLM-R, which are 1280 dimensions.

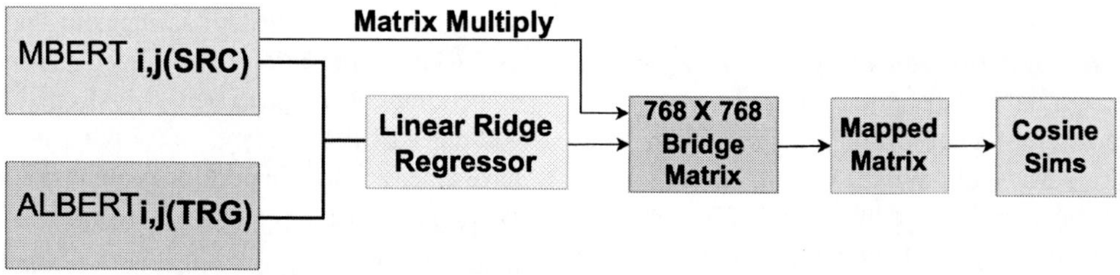

Figure 1: Cross-embedding space mapping pipeline resulting in directly comparable vector representations (MBERT→ALBERT used as example).

in approximately the same semantics in the target embedding space, meaning that a transformed embedding and one native to the target embedding space are now directly comparable using metrics like cosine similarity. Fig. 1 shows this procedure. We construct bridge matrices between the four MLMs mentioned previously, and our Assamese ALBERT variant. Like the word and sentence-sensitive embeddings, the cosine similarities between embeddings of word pairs after the mapping transformations are added to the dataset as input features to the final classification task, so we can examine all semantic similarity computations.

4.4 Evaluation

Having collected a variety of phonetic, semantic, and articulatory alignment metrics for all the paired words in our datasets, our task is now to train a classifier model to discriminate cognates from non-cognates in the data, using these features. We train two types of classification models: a logistic regressor (**LR**) and a neural network (**NN**). The NN consists of 3 layers of 512, 256, and 128 hidden units respectively, all with ReLU activation and followed by 10% dropout, and a final sigmoid activation, and is trained for 5,000 epochs with Adam optimization and BCE loss. The LR is more interpretable but the NN is better performing.

We train three versions of the model: one trained on the `All-languages` dataset, and evaluated on the test splits of that dataset and of the `Assamese-Bengali` and `Bengali-Assamese` datasets; and one each trained and evaluated only on the `Assamese-Bengali/Bengali-Assamese` datasets (pair-specific models, which are herein denoted in tables and charts with an asterisk (*) or additional label `train_ev`).

We trained all classifiers multiple times using different feature combinations to assess the contribution of different types of features. Table 4 shows the abbreviations we use in the following discussion for the different classes of features.

Abbr.	Features
`ped`	Phonetic Edit distances (PED)
`dl`	DNN logits (alignment score)
`ed`	PED with textual Levenstein dist.
`b`	All native MLMs (BERT variants)
`m`	All mappings w/o native MLMs
`ab-am`	All MLMs w/ word-level maps
`ab-sm`	All MLMs with sentence maps
`sm`	Sentence maps

Table 4: Abbreviations for feature combinations.

*`sm` - sentence maps from MBERT to ALBERT space.
*`b` - native MLM embeddings without cross-embedding space mappings (word or sentence).
*`ab-am` - includes native MLM embeddings along with word embedding maps without sentence maps

5 Results and Discussion

We achieve 94% F1, 93% recall, and 95% precision when using all features. The alignment score feature provides the greatest single boost, and we find that adding semantic information to phonetic features provides as much additional performance as adding orthographic features, though specific false positives and negatives diverge significantly.

Fig. 5 shows positive precision, recall, and F1 for the neural network classifier using all features.

	all	***bn-as***	***as-bn***	***bn-as****	***as-bn****
P(+)	95	97	94	90	90
R(+)	93	94	92	88	87
F1(+)	94	95	93	89	88

Table 5: NN classifier results (as %) for the `ed-dl-ab-am` feature combination (full feature set).

We can also see that the classifier performs very slightly better using Bengali as the baseline language than using Assamese. Similar results hold for other feature subsets: using the "bidirectional" `All-languages` model, feature sets `ed-dl-m`, `ped-dl-ab-am`, and `ed-dl-b` all show 94%

F1(+) for Bengali-Assamese but 93% F1(+) for Assamese-Bengali.

One possible reason for this is that Bengali forms are on average somewhat more conservative, tending to preserve consonant clusters more than Assamese, and in fact if we look at the false negatives for this result, we find many cases where one cognate has a consonant cluster and the other does not (see Table 6). Another possible reason may be the slightly higher number of Bengali baseline pairs in the dataset (see Sec. 3).

Bengali	**Assamese**
সাঁঝ (/ʃãdʑʱ/)	সন্ধিয়া (/xɔndʱija/)
শিক্ষা (/ʃikkʰa/)	শিকোৱা (/xikʊwa/)
মিষ্টি (/miʃʈi/)	মিঠা (/mitʰa/)

Table 6: Sample false negatives.

We also see that the model trained on the bidirectional data outperforms in each direction models trained on that direction alone.

The NN classifier outperforms the LR by ~4% in all metrics. This suggests that for detecting bilingual cognates using multiple feature types, the non-linear decision boundary of a multi-layer perceptron system is better-suited to this task than the linear decision boundary of the LR.

5.1 Influence of Features

By comparing the performance of different feature subsets we can expose what features are most important to the cognate detection task and when. We also add a layer of interpretability to the results by cross-checking against the weights assigned to the different features by the LR classifier.

5.1.1 Alignment Features

The alignment score (`dl`) is the singular feature that most increases performance (Table 7). Adding alignment scores to just edit distances (`ed`) causes performance to rise approximately 17%. The logistic regressor for the `ed-dl` feature set gives the alignment score feature a weight of ~3.2, making it strongly correlated with cognate status. It also performs best using the bidirectional data; with addition of alignment score, the pair-specific models perform about 4-6% lower.

5.1.2 Phonetic vs. Orthographic Features

When using only phonetic edit distances (`ped`), performance drops to 43% F1 in most evaluations (51% on the Assamese-Bengali pair-specific model). This is because many times Assamese-Bengali cognates are pronounced differently even if spelled similarly. Adding a textual Levenshtein distance metric (`ed`) can identify correspondence where phonetic edit distance struggles. The `ed` LR classifier gives textual Levenshtein distance a weight of ~-2.7, a strong inverse correlation.

Feat.	***all***	***bn-as***	***as-bn***	***bn-as****	***as-bn****
`ed`	76	76	76	76	76
`ed-dl`	**93**	**93**	**92**	**86**	**88**
`ped`	43	43	43	42	51

Table 7: F1(+) as % with and without alignment score (`dl`) and Levenshtein distance features.

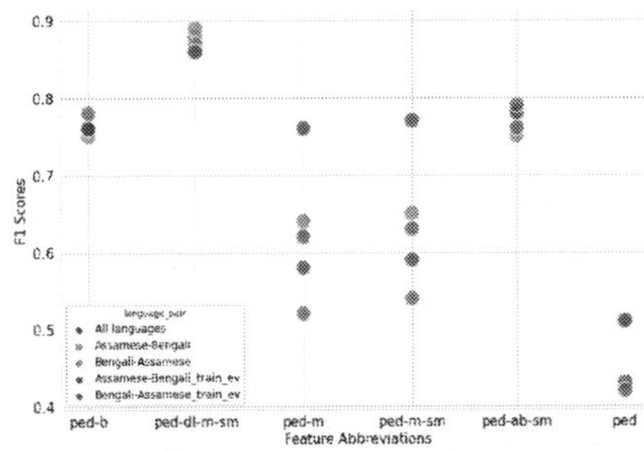

Figure 2: Influence of different semantic feature sets compared to phonetic edit distance baseline (`ped`).

5.1.3 Semantic Features

Addition of all the available semantic features to the `ed-dl` feature set results in a performance boost of only a few percentage points (cf. Tables 5 and 7). Nonetheless, by conducting further ablation tests, we can show where the semantic features actually provide important information.

Fig. 2 shows the effects of different subsets of semantic features—cosine similarities between native MLM embeddings, and between embeddings mapped from Assamese ALBERT to each MLM embedding space at the word and sentence level—compared to the lowest performing feature set, phonetic edit distances.

Adding any semantic information to phonetic features alone substantially improves performance of the neural network classifier on cognate detection. For instance, adding cosine similarities from the different pretrained MLMs (`ped-b`) brings performance back up to ~76%, or on par with the inclusion of textual Levenshtein distance. For this feature set, XLM cosine similarity has the highest weight: ~1.0, while MBERT cosine similarity is next: ~0.4 (MuRIL: ~0.3; IndicBERT: ~0.06).

In terms of overall performance, adding semantic similarly to phonetic edit distance is as good as adding textual edit distance, but the specific misclassified examples in each case are quite different. Table 8 shows the breakdown of false positives by negative example type using these two different feature sets. Feature set `ed` has a much higher false positive rate, and also that in most cases when semantic information is used instead of textual edit distance, the proportion of false positives that are synonyms goes down, suggesting that including semantic information from MLMs improves cognate detection by mitigating misclassification of synonyms. The exception to this is in the `ped-b` feature set for the Assamese-Bengali pair-specific model, where 60% of false positives are synonyms, pointing to the relative weakness of Assamese semantic representations in MLMs.

	all		*bn-as**		*as-bn**	
	ed	ped-b	ed	ped-b	ed	ped-b
HN	18	12	12	11	6	4
Syn.	18	5	8	1	5	6
Rnd.	4	1	2	0	1	0

Table 8: Number of false positives using `ed` vs. `ped-b` feature sets broken down by negative example type (hard negative, synonym, random). Bidirectional and pair-specific models shown.

Word-level mappings Adding cosine similarities taken after mapping Assamese ALBERT word-level embeddings into the embedding spaces of the MLMs (`ped-m`) also improves performance, but the effect is more nuanced than when using native cosine similarities. For most data splits, the performance boost is not as pronounced (e.g., an appreciable but modest increase from 43% to 54% F1 on the bidirectional model evaluated against Bengali-Assamese data), but a dramatic increase in performance is seen on the Assamese-Bengali pair-specific model, where positive F1 rises to 76%, equaling the performance of the same model using the native MLM similarities. We see that the LR weight assigned to cosine similarities between the mapped Assamese ALBERT embeddings and Bengali XLM embeddings is $\sim$1.0 while the equivalent weight for Assamese ALBERT-Bengali MBERT mappings is $\sim$0.4. These weights are nearly the same as those assigned to the native XLM and MBERT cosine similarities; this and the similar NN performance indicate that these mappings are contributing the same level of information. However, weights assigned to mappings into IndicBERT or MuRIL space are both close to 0. This may be due to the larger size of the MBERT and XLM training corpora. The resultant embedding vectors in MBERT/XLM space are more dispersed, and perhaps closer to isotropic (Ethayarajh, 2019), whereas IndicBERT and MuRIL vectors appear to be clustered in a tight high-dimensional cone. This means there is more "space" in MBERT and XLM to transfer in useful semantic information through techniques like affine mapping. This is particularly interesting in the case of MBERT, which did not train on Assamese data, yet the embedding space appears able to accommodate meaningful information from Assamese embeddings.

Sentence-level mappings Adding MBERT-Assamese ALBERT cosine similarities computed after mapping the MBERT embeddings into ALBERT space using the sentence-level transformation matrix (`ped-m-sm`) gives a further slight boost to the neural network model. The Assamese-Bengali pair-specific model reaches 77% F1. Adding sentence-level mappings alone to phonetic edit distances increases performance over `ped` by only $\sim$6%; the combination of word and sentence-level mappings is what provides this final small boost to the Assamese-Bengali pair-specific models. Adding sentence-level mapping information also further boosts the other data splits and models by a small amount.

Examining the effect of adding sentence mappings to `ped-b` (`ped-ab-sm`), we see that this time the two pair-specific models see an appreciable improvement from 76% to 78% (`Assamese-Bengali_train_ev`) and 79% (`Bengali-Assamese_train_ev`), suggesting that similarities computed after sentence-level mappings can help language-specific models more than language-agnostic or multilingual ones.

Table 9 shows the breakdown of false positives by type of negative example using these two feature sets. Table 10 shows the breakdown of false *negatives* for `ped`, `ped-m` and `ped-m-sm`.

	*bn-as**			*as-bn**		
	ped	pm	psm	ped	pm	psm
HN	31	48	45	47	10	15
Syn.	0	4	4	6	8	6
Rnd.	0	7	2	0	2	0

Table 9: Number of false positives in pair-specific model outputs using `ped`, `ped-m (pm)`, and `ped-m-sm (psm)` feature sets broken down by negative example type (hard negative, synonym, random).

When compared to the phonetic edit distance baseline, the Assamese-Bengali model sees a dra-

	*bn-as**			*as-bn**		
	`ped`	`pm`	`psm`	`ped`	`pm`	`psm`
FN	212	140	138	182	106	100

Table 10: Number of false negatives (undetected cognates) in pair-specific model outputs using `ped`, `ped-m (pm)` and `ped-m-sm (psm)` feature sets.

matic reduction in false positives, mostly due to reduction in misclassified hard negatives (phonetic neighbors). Since hard negatives are semantically distant from their phonetic-neighbor cognates, introducing Assamese semantic information helps semantically disambiguate cognates from hard negatives. Adding mapped sentence-sensitive embedding similarities slightly increases the number of hard negative false positives, while also slightly reducing synonym false positives, eliminating random false positives, and further reducing false negatives. The Bengali-Assamese model actually sees *more* false positives with mappings added. This model's overall performance boost is due to fewer false negatives, while with sentence mapping the Assamese-Bengali model reduces both false positives and negatives.

The trends in Tables 8–10 show that using semantic similarities from models with relatively strong support for Bengali helps Bengali-Assamese performance, while adding mapped embedding similarities help Assamese-Bengali performance by bringing in more Assamese-specific information through affine transformation.

6 Conclusion and Future Work

We have presented here a method for detecting cognates between Bengali and Assamese that uses a mixture of phonetic, orthographic, articulatory alignment, and semantic features. The choice of these languages was motivated by their relatedness and the relative dearth of NLP work particularly on Assamese, but we believe the methods presented herein are applicable to cognate detection and other types of heterogeneous similarity-based tasks on potentially any language pair.

We found that our articulatory alignment score was by far the most informative feature. We also introduced a technique to map representations between embedding spaces and used it to introduce semantic features from a monolingual Assamese model into four large multilingual models. Adding semantic features to phonetic features alone is interesting on multiple levels—particularly using mapped instead of native embeddings.

Our ablation tests on different types of semantic representations suggest that i) linearly transforming vectors from one model's embedding space to another's carries certain semantic information with high fidelity, and ii) a model trained on a low-resource setting can be mapped to a richer model's space. If these hypotheses hold, transformed embeddings from a low-resourced LM can not only reduce the computational cost involved in training large multilingual language models but also improve downstream NLP tasks.

NLP for minority languages may benefit from being able to detect cognates in better-resourced languages, both for computational historical linguistics, and for corpus building. For instance, other languages of Assam (e.g., Mishing, Bodo) are not Indo-Aryan, but have loanwords cognate to Indo-Aryan words, alongside vocabulary cognate to other families, like Sino-Tibetan. Our phonetic and alignment techniques may facilitate creating semantic models for these severely low-resourced languages unsupported by LLMs.

Collecting putative cognates is an essential step in most applications of computational historical linguistics, allowing finding regular sound correspondences (for which our alignment method could be adapted, e.g., by training individual attention weights over a sequence), identifying shared innovations, and reconstructing earlier word forms that could be used to reconstruct proto-languages a la Bouchard-Côté et al. (2013) and Jäger (2019).

The affine mapping technique we use warrants more exploration. Not every affine map is a linear map, and other techniques like shear and rotation mapping may expose how simple a transformation can be used. Other semantic techniques we wish to explore include pairwise scoring of cognate pair embeddings using a neural network. This has been shown to work well for coreference resolution and may be applicable for cognate detection. Lastly, we would like to improve our monolingual Assamese ALBERT model and evaluate it on other downstream tasks like question answering.

Acknowledgments

This research was supported in part by a subcontract on grant award FA8750-18-2-0016 from the U.S. Defense Advanced Research Projects Agency (DARPA). Views expressed herein do not reflect the policy or position of the Department of Defense or the U.S. Government. All errors are the responsibility of the authors.

References

Mikel Artetxe, Gorka Labaka, and Eneko Agirre. 2018a. Generalizing and improving bilingual word embedding mappings with a multi-step framework of linear transformations. In *Proceedings of the AAAI Conference on Artificial Intelligence*, volume 32.

Mikel Artetxe, Gorka Labaka, and Eneko Agirre. 2018b. A robust self-learning method for fully unsupervised cross-lingual mappings of word embeddings. In *Proceedings of the 56th Annual Meeting of the Association for Computational Linguistics (Volume 1: Long Papers)*, pages 789–798, Melbourne, Australia. Association for Computational Linguistics.

Akash Bharadwaj, David R Mortensen, Chris Dyer, and Jaime G Carbonell. 2016. Phonologically aware neural model for named entity recognition in low resource transfer settings. In *Proceedings of the 2016 Conference on Empirical Methods in Natural Language Processing*, pages 1462–1472.

Michael Bloodgood and Benjamin Strauss. 2017. Using Global Constraints and Reranking to Improve Cognates Detection. In *Proceedings of the 55th Annual Meeting of the Association for Computational Linguistics (Volume 1: Long Papers)*, pages 1983–1992.

Alexandre Bouchard-Côté, David Hall, Thomas L Griffiths, and Dan Klein. 2013. Automated reconstruction of ancient languages using probabilistic models of sound change. *Proceedings of the National Academy of Sciences*, 110(11):4224–4229.

Cecil H Brown, Eric W Holman, Søren Wichmann, and Viveka Velupillai. 2008. Automated classification of the world s languages: a description of the method and preliminary results. *Language Typology and Universals*, 61(4):285–308.

Alexis Conneau, Kartikay Khandelwal, Naman Goyal, Vishrav Chaudhary, Guillaume Wenzek, Francisco Guzmán, Édouard Grave, Myle Ott, Luke Zettlemoyer, and Veselin Stoyanov. 2020. Unsupervised Cross-lingual Representation Learning at Scale. In *Proceedings of the 58th Annual Meeting of the Association for Computational Linguistics*, pages 8440–8451.

Johannes Dellert. 2018. Combining information-weighted sequence alignment and sound correspondence models for improved cognate detection. In *Proceedings of the 27th international conference on computational linguistics*, pages 3123–3133.

Jacob Devlin, Ming-Wei Chang, Kenton Lee, and Kristina N Toutanova. 2018. BERT: Pre-training of Deep Bidirectional Transformers for Language Understanding.

Kawin Ethayarajh. 2019. How Contextual are Contextualized Word Representations? Comparing the Geometry of BERT, ELMo, and GPT-2 Embeddings. In *Proceedings of the 2019 Conference on Empirical Methods in Natural Language Processing and the 9th International Joint Conference on Natural Language Processing (EMNLP-IJCNLP)*, pages 55–65.

Ashwinkumar Ganesan, Francis Ferraro, and Tim Oates. 2021. Learning a Reversible Embedding Mapping using Bi-Directional Manifold Alignment. In *Findings of the Association for Computational Linguistics: ACL-IJCNLP 2021*, pages 3132–3139.

Barry Haddow and Faheem Kirefu. 2020. PMIndia–A Collection of Parallel Corpora of Languages of India. *arXiv preprint arXiv:2001.09907*.

Richard W Hamming. 1950. Error detecting and error correcting codes. *The Bell system technical journal*, 29(2):147–160.

Junjie Hu, Sebastian Ruder, Aditya Siddhant, Graham Neubig, Orhan Firat, and Melvin Johnson. 2020. Xtreme: A massively multilingual multi-task benchmark for evaluating cross-lingual generalisation. In *International Conference on Machine Learning*, pages 4411–4421. PMLR.

Gerhard Jäger. 2018. Global-scale phylogenetic linguistic inference from lexical resources. *Scientific Data*, 5(1):1–16.

Gerhard Jäger. 2019. Computational historical linguistics. *Theoretical Linguistics*, 45(3-4):151–182.

Ganesh Jawahar, Benoît Sagot, and Djamé Seddah. 2019. What does BERT learn about the structure of language? In *Proceedings of the 57th Annual Meeting of the Association for Computational Linguistics*, pages 3651–3657, Florence, Italy. Association for Computational Linguistics.

Divyanshu Kakwani, Anoop Kunchukuttan, Satish Golla, Gokul N.C., Avik Bhattacharyya, Mitesh M. Khapra, and Pratyush Kumar. 2020. IndicNLPSuite: Monolingual Corpora, Evaluation Benchmarks and Pre-trained Multilingual Language Models for Indian Languages. In *Findings of EMNLP*.

Diptesh Kanojia, Kevin Patel, Pushpak Bhattacharyya, Malhar Kulkarni, and Gholamreza Haffari. 2021a. Utilizing wordnets for cognate detection among indian languages. *arXiv preprint arXiv:2112.15124*.

Diptesh Kanojia, Prashant Sharma, Sayali Ghodekar, Pushpak Bhattacharyya, Gholamreza Haffari, and Malhar Kulkarni. 2021b. Cognition-aware Cognate Detection. In *Proceedings of the 16th Conference of the European Chapter of the Association for Computational Linguistics: Main Volume*, pages 3281–3292.

Simran Khanuja, Diksha Bansal, Sarvesh Mehtani, Savya Khosla, Atreyee Dey, Balaji Gopalan, Dilip Kumar Margam, Pooja Aggarwal, Rajiv Teja Nagipogu, Shachi Dave, et al. 2021. MuRIL: Multilingual representations for Indian languages. *arXiv preprint arXiv:2103.10730*.

Grzegorz Kondrak. 2001. Identifying cognates by phonetic and semantic similarity. In *Second Meeting of the North American Chapter of the Association for Computational Linguistics*.

Sofie Labat and Els Lefever. 2019. A Classification-Based Approach to Cognate Detection Combining Orthographic and Semantic Similarity Information. In *Proceedings of the International Conference on Recent Advances in Natural Language Processing (RANLP 2019)*, pages 602–610, Varna, Bulgaria. INCOMA Ltd.

Els Lefever, Sofie Labat, and Pranaydeep Singh. 2020. Identifying cognates in English-Dutch and French-Dutch by means of orthographic information and cross-lingual word embeddings. In *PROCEEDINGS OF THE 12TH INTERNATIONAL CONFERENCE ON LANGUAGE RESOURCES AND EVALUATION (LREC 2020)*, pages 4096–4101. European Language Resources Association (ELRA).

Vladimir I Levenshtein et al. 1966. Binary codes capable of correcting deletions, insertions, and reversals. In *Soviet physics doklady*, volume 10, pages 707–710. Soviet Union.

Johann-Mattis List. 2014. Investigating the impact of sample size on cognate detection. *Journal of Language Relationship*, 11(1):91–102.

David McNeely-White, Ben Sattelberg, Nathaniel Blanchard, and Ross Beveridge. 2022. Canonical Face Embeddings. *IEEE Transactions on Biometrics, Behavior, and Identity Science*.

David McNeely-White, Benjamin Sattelberg, Nathaniel Blanchard, and Ross Beveridge. 2020. Exploring the interchangeability of CNN embedding spaces. *arXiv preprint arXiv:2010.02323*.

David R Mortensen, Siddharth Dalmia, and Patrick Littell. 2018. Epitran: Precision G2P for many languages. In *Proceedings of the Eleventh International Conference on Language Resources and Evaluation (LREC 2018)*.

David R Mortensen, Patrick Littell, Akash Bharadwaj, Kartik Goyal, Chris Dyer, and Lori Levin. 2016. Panphon: A resource for mapping IPA segments to articulatory feature vectors. In *Proceedings of COLING 2016, the 26th International Conference on Computational Linguistics: Technical Papers*, pages 3475–3484.

Andrea Mulloni and Viktor Pekar. 2006. Automatic detection of orthographics cues for cognate recognition. In *Proceedings of the Fifth International Conference on Language Resources and Evaluation (LREC06)*.

Taraka Rama and Johann-Mattis List. 2019. An automated framework for fast cognate detection and bayesian phylogenetic inference in computational historical linguistics. Association for Computational Linguistics.

Taraka Rama, Johann-Mattis List, Johannes Wahle, and Gerhard Jäger. 2018. Are automatic methods for cognate detection good enough for phylogenetic reconstruction in historical linguistics? *arXiv preprint arXiv:1804.05416*.

Shruti Rijhwani, Jiateng Xie, Graham Neubig, and Jaime Carbonell. 2019. Zero-shot neural transfer for cross-lingual entity linking. In *Proceedings of the AAAI Conference on Artificial Intelligence*, volume 33, pages 6924–6931.

Mousmita Sarma and Kandarpa Sarma. 2014. *Sounds of Assamese Language*, pages 77–93.

Charles Schafer and David Yarowsky. 2002. Inducing translation lexicons via diverse similarity measures and bridge languages. In *COLING-02: The 6th Conference on Natural Language Learning 2002 (CoNLL-2002)*.

Pedro Javier Ortiz Suárez, Benoît Sagot, and Laurent Romary. 2019. Asynchronous pipeline for processing huge corpora on medium to low resource infrastructures. In *7th Workshop on the Challenges in the Management of Large Corpora (CMLC-7)*. Leibniz-Institut für Deutsche Sprache.

Ian Tenney, Dipanjan Das, and Ellie Pavlick. 2019. BERT rediscovers the classical NLP pipeline. In *Proceedings of the 57th Annual Meeting of the Association for Computational Linguistics*, pages 4593–4601, Florence, Italy. Association for Computational Linguistics.

Jacob Turton, Robert Elliott Smith, and David Vinson. 2021. Deriving Contextualised Semantic Features from BERT (and Other Transformer Model) Embeddings. In *Proceedings of the 6th Workshop on Representation Learning for NLP (RepL4NLP-2021)*, pages 248–262.

A Appendices

A.1 Sample Breakdown by Label

Table 11 gives breakdown of the Assamese-Bengali and Bengali-Assamese train/test splits based on their labels. Since we distinguish cognates from loanwords but otherwise do not single out loanwords in our datasets, loanwords may exist in the other categories. Given the phonetic similarity between loanwords and their sources, where loanwords do exist in our data, they are overwhelmingly likely to be in the hard negative category.

	as-bn		*bn-as*	
	`train`	`test`	`train`	`test`
Cog.	306	303	306	300
HN	776	769	721	716
Syn.	329	327	317	316
Rnd.	304	301	304	299
Total	1715	1700	1648	1631

Table 11: Number of Hard-Negatives (HN), Synonyms (Syn.), Cognates (Cog.), and Random pairs (Rnd.) in Assamese-Bengali and Bengali-Assamese train/test sets.

A.2 ALBERT (Monolingual Assamese Configuration)

Table 12 gives configuration details of the monolingual Assamese Transformer model that we trained for this research.

A.3 Further Details on Effects of Phonetic Features

Of the 6 phonetic edit distances we used, Hamming Feature Distance (divided by maximum length) and Partial Hamming Distance (divided by maximum length) appear to be the most correlated with cognate status according to the weights assigned to them by the logistic regressor. This suggests that Hamming distance's (Hamming, 1950) focus on using the minimum number of substitutions to transform one string into another works well for similar languages like Assamese and Bengali where most individual phonemes are largely preserved between cognate words.

Interestingly, the Dolgo Prime Distance variant gets a low (usually negative) weight in almost all feature combinations. This is interesting and suggests that Dolgo Prime Distance is not useful here due to it unduly conflating multiple phonemes into the same class. The Dolgopolsky-inspired stable phoneme classes used by PanPhon places /ʃ/ in the "coronal fricatives" class, while /x/ is in the "velar/postvelar obstruents" class. The unvoiced velar fricative /x/ is unique to Assamese and rare among Indian languages (Sarma and Sarma, 2014) and we know well that Bengali and Assamese have a regular /ʃ/-/x/ sound correspondence. So, as Dolgo Prime distance splits these up into different classes, when using this metric cognate words containing these corresponding sounds will have phonetic distance added to them when in fact they are regularly corresponding.

Parameters	Config
architecture	AlbertForMaskedLM
attention_probs_dropout_prob	0.1
bos_token_id	2
classifier_dropout_prob	0.1
embedding_size	128
eos_token_id	3
hidden_act	gelu
hidden_dropout_prob	0.1
hidden_size	768
initializer_range	0.02
inner_group_num	1
intermediate_size	3072
layer_norm_eps	1e-05
max_position_embeddings	514
num_attention_heads	12
num_hidden_groups	1
num_hidden_layers	6
position_embedding_type	"absolute"
transformers_version	"4.18.0"
vocab_size	32001

Table 12: ALBERT Model configuration trained on monolingual Assamese corpus.

Mapping Phonology to Semantics: A Computational Model of Cross-Lingual Spoken-Word Recognition

Iuliia Zaitova **Badr M. Abdullah** **Dietrich Klakow**
Department of Language Science and Technology (LST)
Saarland Informatics Campus, Saarland University, Germany
{ izaitova | babdullah | dietrich }@lsv.uni-saarland.de

Abstract

Closely related languages are often mutually intelligible to various degrees. Therefore, speakers of closely related languages are usually capable of (partially) comprehending each other's speech without explicitly learning the target, second language. The cross-linguistic intelligibility among closely related languages is mainly driven by linguistic factors such as lexical similarities. This paper presents a computational model of spoken-word recognition and investigates its ability to recognize word forms from different languages than its native, training language. Our model is based on a recurrent neural network that learns to map a word's phonological sequence onto a semantic representation of the word. Furthermore, we present a case study on the related Slavic languages and demonstrate that the cross-lingual performance of our model not only predicts mutual intelligibility to a large extent but also reflects the genetic classification of the languages in our study.

1 Introduction

Speakers of closely related languages are usually capable of understanding each other's speech to a great degree without having a prior exposure to the second language (L2) or switching a lingua franca for communication[1] (Jan and Zeevaert, 2007; Gooskens, 2019). The ability of the listener to comprehend spoken utterances in a different language (L2) using their native language (L1) competence is termed in the sociolinguistics literature as *intercomprehension*. Gooskens (2017) categorized the factors that facilitate intercomprehension into linguistic factors (e.g., inherent cross-linguistic similarity between L1/L2) as well as extra-linguistic factors (e.g., listener's attitude towards communicating in a different language than their own L1).

[1]A language used for communication between people who do not share a native language.

Several studies in the sociolinguistics literature have documented the levels of intercomprehension between related languages through empirical testing of mutual intelligibility with human subjects of different language backgrounds (Gooskens, 2007, 2017; Van Heuven, 2008, *inter alia*). It has been observed that objective measures of cross-language distance—such as lexical distance—are strong predictors of cross-linguistic intelligibility. Therefore, mutual intelligibility of related languages is largely driven by the presence of word cognates—words that encode the same concepts with similar phonological forms across languages.

From the psycholinguistic perspective, the listener's ability to recognize word forms in a different language is an example of the remarkable human ability to cope with the variability of speech (Pisoni and Levi, 2007). Thus, spoken-word recognition across different, but related languages can be considered as lexical access problem—processing the spoken-word form to activate and retrieve the lexical category that is intended by the speaker. In the cognitive modeling literature, the task of spoken-word recognition has been addressed as a mapping problem between an acoustic-phonetic representation of the word form onto its semantic representation in memory (see Weber and Scharenborg (2012) for a detailed overview). Recently, deep neural networks have been explored as models of spoken-word processing and recognition in several studies (Magnuson et al., 2020; Mayn et al., 2021; Matusevych et al., 2021). Our paper adds another contribution to this line of research by considering the cross-lingual aspects of spoken-word recognition and sheds light on its contribution to cross-linguistic intelligibility using a computational model. Our contribution is two-fold: (1) we present a neural model of spoken-word recognition and investigate the degree to which a monolingual model—i.e., has only been trained on a single language—is able to recognize the meaning of spo-

Proceedings of the Ninth Workshop on NLP for Similar Languages, Varieties and Dialects, pages 54–63
October 16, 2022. ©2022 Association for Computational Linguistics

ken words across related languages, and (2) we present a case study on the Slavic languages which are remarkably similar and mutually intelligible to various degrees. Concretely, we investigate the following research questions:

RQ1 Does the cross-lingual performance of model predict the mutual intelligibility of the languages in our study?

RQ2 Do the results of cross-lingual evaluation reflect the genetic relations among the studied Slavic languages?

RQ3 Which linguistic distance measures predict the cross-lingual performance of the monolingual models? and how do they compare to predictors of human performance?

2 Background and Related Work

2.1 Slavic Intercomprehension

Previous sociolinguistic research on intercomprehension and mutual intelligibility has focused on two related questions: (1) how to experimentally measure the level of mutual intelligibility across related languages using functional testing and human listeners? and (2) which measures of linguistic distance are strong predictors of cross-language intelligibility? (Golubović and Gooskens, 2015). One of the earliest sociolinguistic studies has investigated the intelligibility of Spanish and Brazilian Portuguese (Jensen, 1989). For languages within the Slavic language family, Golubović and Gooskens (2015) have tested mutual intelligibility across two modalities—i.e., text and speech—using three cross-language tasks: (1) word translation, (2) cloze test and (3) picture naming task. Golubović and Gooskens (2015) have observed that the degree of cross-language intelligibility is largely dependent on the genetic proximity of the languages under study. For example, language pairs within the same Slavic sub-family such as Czech and Polish (West Slavic group) are more mutually intelligible than language pairs that cross the group division (Czech and South Slavic languages such as Croatian or Bulgarian). Furthermore, the authors demonstrated that lexical and phonetic similarities across languages are strong predictors of their intelligibility.

Other studies on Slavic intercomprehension take an information-theoretic angle to analyze this phenomenon. For example, Jagrova et al. (2018) investigated the effect of in-context predictability (or lexical surprisal) on the written intelligibility of Czech text for Polish readers and vice versa. Moreover, the information-theoretic metric of word adaptation surprisal has been shown to predict asymmetric intelligibility of Slavic readers of Cyrillic script, namely Russian and Bulgarian (Mosbach et al., 2019). In the speech modality, Kudera et al. (2021) have analyzed the cognate facilitation effect on cross-language auditory lexical processing using a cross-lingual priming study. In summary, the studies we reviewed in this section have demonstrated a great degree of mutual intelligibility among speakers of Slavic languages, and this intelligibility can be predicted by linguistic measures of similarity to a great degree.

2.2 Computational Models of Spoken-word Processing

Using computational models based on deep neural networks (DNNs) to simulate spoken-word processing have been proposed in several prior studies. Magnuson et al. (2020) presented a minimal neural architecture based on an LSTM to map between acoustic word forms onto their respective sparse semantic representation. Mayn et al. (2021) analyzed the effect of speech variability on spoken-word recognition using a DNN model trained on German words from read speech corpora. As part of their experiments, the authors have shown that the model can fairly recognize word cognates from related Germanic languages (namely Dutch and English), and the cross-lingual performance of the model reflected language proximity. Matusevych et al. (2021) introduced a phonetic model of spoken-word processing and demonstrated that the model predicts perceptual difficulties of non-native speakers. It was also shown that neural models of spoken-word processing capture cross-linguistic, typological similarities in their representational geometry (Abdullah et al., 2021b). Macher et al. (2021) proposed a recurrent model that takes as input a phonological sequence and projects it onto a semantic space to investigate orthographic effects on word recognition. These computational studies have demonstrated the usefulness of neural networks to simulate human listeners who have been exposed to a single language, which enables researchers to test specific hypotheses or isolate the effect a particular linguistic level on language processing.

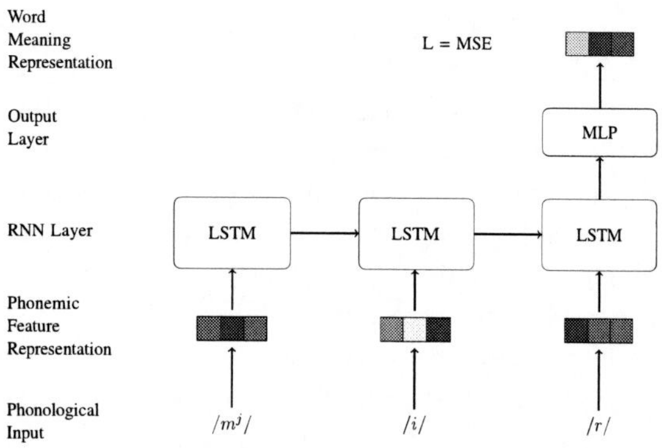

Figure 1: Schematic architecture of the model.

3 The Model

Similar to the work of Macher et al. (2021), our model takes a phonological sequence (spoken word form) as input, builds up a whole-word phonological representation of the sequence, and then projects it onto a semantic space (meaning representation) of the lexical item encoded by the word form. Formally, we model the spoken-word recognition task of as a mapping function $\mathcal{F}_{\boldsymbol{\theta}} : \Phi \rightarrow S$, where Φ is the (discrete) space of phonological word forms, S is the word semantic space, and $\boldsymbol{\theta}$ are the parameters of the mapping function. Since phonological word forms can have any length, we model the function $\mathcal{F}$ using a recurrent neural network (LSTM) followed by a multi-layer perceptron (MLP) (see Figure 1). Given the word form of the lexical category w as a phonological sequence $\Phi(w) = \boldsymbol{\varphi}_{1:\tau} = (\varphi_1, \varphi_2, \ldots, \varphi_\tau)$, a vector representation is computed as

$$\boldsymbol{v} = \mathcal{F}(\boldsymbol{\varphi}_{1:\tau}; \boldsymbol{\theta}) \in R^D \quad (1)$$

Here, D is the dimensionality of the semantic space. Since our goal is to map the phonological input onto a semantic representation, the learning objective is based on vector regression loss and it aims to minimize the term

$$\mathcal{L} = ||\boldsymbol{v} - \Lambda(w)||^2 \quad (2)$$

where $\Lambda(w) \in R^D$ is the ground-truth distributed representation, or semantic word embedding, of the lexical category w. We assume that continuous-space, distributed word representations are available to the model during training.

3.1 Phoneme Representation

Each phoneme in the input phonological sequence $\boldsymbol{\varphi}_{1:\tau} = (\varphi_1, \varphi_2, \ldots, \varphi_\tau)$ is represented as a feature vector based on the PHOIBLE feature set (Moran and McCloy, 2019). That is, we represent each of the 135 phonemes in our inventory as a discrete, multi-valued feature vector of 38 phonetic features similarly to the method introduced in Abdullah et al. (2021a). PHOIBLE includes distinctive feature data for every phoneme in every language. The feature system used is created by the PHOIBLE developers to be descriptively adequate cross-linguistically. In other words, using PHOIBLE feature set allows our model to capture phoneme similarities across languages even if the phonemes have distinct symbols. For each of the 38 available features, every phoneme receives a value, which is $+1$ if the feature is present, -1 if it is not, and 0 if the feature is not applicable.

To illustrate the structure of the phoneme feature representation, we visualize a two-dimensional projection of phoneme representations using the t-SNE algorithm (Van der Maaten and Hinton, 2008) in Figure 2.

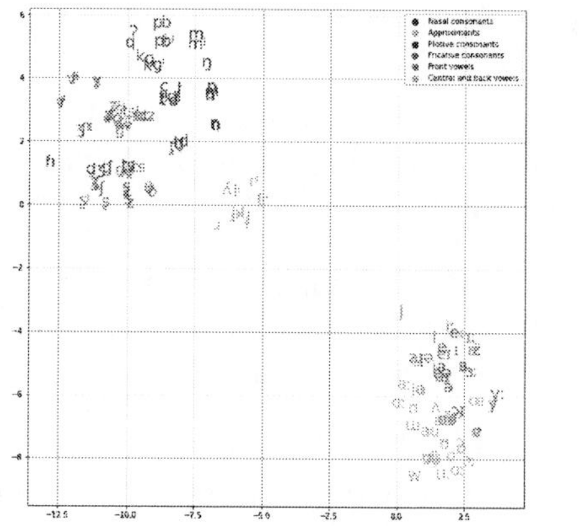

Figure 2: t-SNE visualization of phoneme embeddings vectorized with PHOIBLE feature set. One can notice two clear clusters of consonants (on the left) and vowels (on the right), as well as a visible difference in the positioning of front and back vowels, fricatives, plosives, etc.

3.2 Word Meaning Representation

To represent the word's meaning which our model has to build from the word phonological form, we use distributed word embeddings from fastText (Mikolov et al., 2018). FastText word vectors are pre-trained using the continuous bag-of-words (CBOW) algorithm with position-weights, in dimension 300, with character n-grams of length 5, a window of size 5 with contrastive negative sampling.

Figure 3: Major countries where Slavic languages are spoken. Red coloring – for West Slavic, yellow – for Eastern Slavic, and green – for South Slavic.

3.3 Model Hyperparameters and Training

We train six monolingual models for the following languages: Russian, Ukrainian, Polish , Czech, Bulgarian and Croatian. The final model for each language is trained using a batch size of 128 for 150 epochs. We employ the ADAM optimizer (Kingma and Ba, 2014) with the Mean Squared Error (MSE) loss as the vector regression objective function. To account for the different size of input phonemic sequences, we used zero padding to make the size of the input sequence equal to 16. We employ one layer of LSTM, followed by a one-layer MLP consisting of a linear followed by a *tanh* layer. Since every phoneme has 38 features (every phoneme embedding has the length of 38), and every input sequence has the length of 16, the dimensions of the input matrix are 38×16. We use the hidden dimension size of 512, which consequently maps the phonetic sequence to the 300-dimensional target of fastText embeddings. All the models are built using PyTorch (Paszke et al., 2019).

4 Experimental data

In our paper, we present a case study on the Slavic languages which have been shown to exhibit remarkable similarities and high degrees of mutually intelligibility at the conversational level (Sussex and Cubberley, 2006, Golubović and Gooskens, 2015). We use two languages of each of the three main branches of Slavic languages, that is, Russian and Ukrainian for East Slavic; Polish and Czech for West Slavic; and Bulgarian and Croatian for South Slavic[2]. One of the factors that drive our choice is the availability of high quality G2P tools available.

4.1 Phonetic Transcriptions

To obtain an IPA phonetic transcription for each orthographic form of each word embedding in our data, we employ eSpeak speech synthesizer[3]. For the Ukrainian data, we use Epitran transcription library (Mortensen et al., 2018), as this language is not currently supported by eSpeak. For the languages which we only used for evaluation (Belarusian, Slovak, Slovene, Latvian, Romanian, German, and Turkish), the original Northeuralex transcriptions were retrieved using Lexibank (List et al., 2021)[4].

4.2 Training Data

For the training data, we sample experimental word forms from fastText embeddings while excluding the word forms that appear in the test data. Apart from that, we exclude word forms that are classified as parts of speech not present in the test data to reduce noise during training. Parts of speech that are included are *noun, verb, adverb, adjective, pronoun*, and *numeral*.

For each lexical concept in the test data, we make sure that at least three word forms with the same lemma are within the training data. For example, if the word form (ноль, nol^j) is in the test data, it cannot be in the training data, but another word form (ноля, nol^ja) can. We hypothesize that the model will be able to capture the semantics of a word by learning to be invariant to inflections and derivations.

4.2.1 Evaluation Data

To evaluate the model performance, we employ parallel lists of word forms from lexicostatistical database NorthEuraLex (Dellert et al., 2019) which cover the 1,016 concepts in all languages. Having a concept for all testing data words in all languages

[2]Henceforth, we use ISO 639-1 codes for the languages: Russian – ru, Ukrainian – uk, Polish – pl, Czech – cs, Bulgarian – bg, Croatian – hr.

[3]http://espeak.sourceforge.net/index.html

[4]Since our input phoneme embeddings capture the features of each phoneme (described in §3.1), transcription difference between the tools should have minimal effect on the model's performance. We additionally tested several transcription tools for the same language, which did not result in a significant change of performance on our model's main task of retrieving meaning of a phonological sequence.

Table 1: Examples of Northeuralex concepts

Concept	Russian Orth	Russian IPA	Czech Orth	Czech IPA	Bulgarian Orth	Bulgarian IPA
EAR	ухо	/u x ɑ/	ucho	/u x o/	ухо	/u x ɔ/
NOSE	нос	/n o s/	nos	/n o s/	нос	/n ɔ s/
FOOD	еда	/je d a/	strava	/s t r a v a/	храна	/x r a n a/
BROTHER	брат	/b r a t/	bratr	/b r a t r/	брат	/b r a t/

allows us to systematically investigate the cross-linguistic performance of the models. Overall, we exclude 514 concepts and use 502 concepts for each of the 13 parallel test sets. Our reasons to exclude some concepts were: 1) the concept does not have a corresponding fastText embedding in any of the 6 training languages; 2) some concepts do not exist in some of the languages as a single word and use a descriptive term for some concepts (for example, the term *breast* corresponds to женская грудь /ʒɛnskəjə grut^{j}/) in Russian), which also makes it impossible to retrieve a fastText embedding; 4) a word in one of the 6 training languages maps to more than one concept, which could lead to confusion with its fastText embedding. An example of the NorthEuraLex data we use for testing is represented in Table 1.

5 Evaluation

During testing, the model computes the meaning representation of the phonemic sequence in the test language. To evaluate the model retrieval on the test set, the closest match between the model output and target vector for the model training language is retrieved using cosine similarity. Cosine similarity determines whether two vectors are pointing in roughly the same direction and is measured by the cosine of the angle between two vectors. Cosine similarity, on the abstract level, represents the proximity of the meaning retrieved by the listener to the actual meaning of the word. In other words, it would tell us how semantically similar two given vectors are. Cosine Similarity is computed between a model's output and all the 502 possible ground truth vector representations in the language of training. The vectors to be compared include all the word vectors used for monolingual testing. Given these competing word embeddings, we also calculate average Recall at 1 (R@1), Recall at 5 (R@5), Recall at 10 (R@10), as well as Mean Reciprocal Rank (MRR) for the test data. R@n as the proportion of times that the set of top n word embeddings which are closest to the model's output also includes the ground truth vector representation. If the ground truth is most similar to the output vector of a model, R@1 is 1, otherwise it is 0. Likewise, R@5 is 1, if the corresponding ground truth embedding is within the top 5 most similar words to the output vector, and R@10 is 1 if the embedding is within 10 most similar words. Hence, the average R@n is a number between 0 and 1. The Reciprocal Rank information retrieval measure calculates the reciprocal of the rank at which the first relevant document was retrieved. For evaluation of the test data, we compute an average of Reciprocal Rank for all the given word forms.

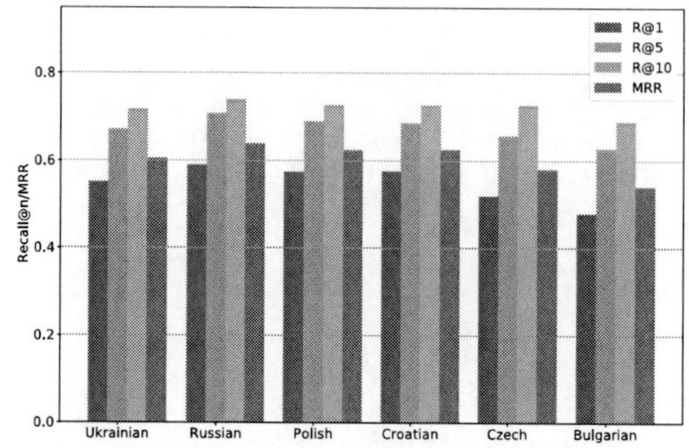

Figure 4: Monolingual performance of the models

5.1 Monolingual Evaluation

The procedures that are used for monolingual and cross-lingual evaluations are comparable, and differ only in the language of the test lexical concept. For both monolingual and cross-lingual evaluations, the retrieved fastTest meaning embeddings for both training and validation sets come from the same embedding space. For the monolingual evaluation, the output embedding for a particular phonemic sequence is compared to groundtruth embeddings of the concepts of test set. The monolingual performance of the models is shown in Figure 4. The monolingual scores for all models are very similar. Such consistency could of course be due to the generally good performance of the current model structure and parameters on any human language. However, it could also be related to structural similarity of the languages of Slavic group (such as, for example, all Slavic languages being synthetic and expressing syntactic relationships via inflection).

5.2 Cross-lingual Evaluation

To make the cross-lingual evaluation comparable across different languages, we compute the cosine similarity of the L2 target concept to all evaluation concepts in the embedding space of the model training language (L1). For instance, if the model has observed during training the Russian word люди /l^j u d i/ (eng.trans: people), during testing the model on Czech concepts we compute the meaning representation of *lidé* /l i d ə/ (eng.trans: people) and then estimate its similarity to test sequences in Russian with the target meaning representation being that of the Russian word люди /l^j u d i/. Such concept mapping during testing has two goals: (1) the pre-trained fastText embeddings for different languages live in different embedding spaces, so it is not possible to compare them as they are, and (2) we assume that a human listener also compares foreign words that they hear to words from their native language, and attempts to retrieve the meaning based on their L1 mental lexicon. For cross-lingual performance, we evaluated each model on all languages under analysis and added three more languages of the Slavic group (East Slavic – Belarusian, West Slavic – Slovak, South Slavic – Slovene) three other languages from the Indo-European language family, to which the Slavic language also belong (German, Romanian, and Latvian), and the Turkish language coming from the Turkic language family[5]. If the model produces human-like behaviour, we can expect it to be better at recognising spoken word forms from more related languages.

The recall at 10 (R@10) results for each model are shown in Figure 5. On the plots, scores for languages of the same language group as the model language, are located on the left side. We also use different color coding for different language group, i.e. reddish colors for East Slavic languages, blueish colors for West Slavic languages, and greenish for South Slavic. Languages outside the Slavic language family are colored in the shades of grey. First, we observe a clear distinction between the retrieval performance of the Slavic and non-Slavic test word forms. The retrieval performance on non-Slavic test word forms (Latvian, Romanian, German, and Turkish) is generally lower for all models except for Bulgarian, which recognizes Romanian evaluation set better than Ukrainian. However, given the geographic proximity between the speaker communities of Romanian and Bulgarian and the fact that both are within the Balkan Sprachbund, this could indicate an effect of lexical borrowing between the two languages. From these findings, we conclude that our hypothesis that the languages which are more genetically related are also more mutually intelligible within the proposed model is mostly supported, with notable exceptions that could related to geographic transfer.

Regarding the evaluation within the Slavic language family, the phonemic sequences in the language from the same subgroup of Slavic languages (such as, Ukrainian for Russian and Croatian for Bulgarian) are recognised significantly better than others by most models. However, there are a few exceptions to this trend. One notable exception in the cross-lingual evaluation is the performance of the Czech model, which seems to have an expected high retrieval performance on Slovak word forms, but unexpectedly does not seem to recognize Polish word forms with a comparable performance. Another surprising result is the fact that the Russian model seems to recognize Croatian and Bulgarian word forms better than Belarusian word forms.

To get further insights onto the cross-lingual performance of the model, we apply hierarchical clustering on the R@10 results between the six models we trained in this study using the Ward algorithm implemented in the SciPy Python library. The Ward's linkage function specifying the distance between two clusters is computed as the increase in the error sum of squares after merging two clusters into a single cluster. The dendrogram of the Ward clustering of R@10 results is shown in Figure 6. The dendrogram in Figure 6 shows we can correctly reconstruct the Slavic language tree from the cross-lingual retrieval performance of the six languages that we have trained models for.

5.3 Correlation with Linguistic Metrics

To investigate which data-driven, linguistic predictors make the model behave as it does, we use Pearson correlation between the cross-lingual model performance and two measures of phonetic-lexical distance. The first metric of phonetic-lexical distance is Levenshtein Distance (LD) where the difference between two strings is calculated as the minimum number of single-character edits (insertions, deletions or substitutions) required to change one word into the other. For the second metric, we use Phonologically Weighted Levenshtein Distance (PWLD), which is a measure of phonological similarity between different phonemic sequences or word forms (Fontan et al., 2016). The PWLD met-

[5]the ISO 639-1 codes for the languages: Belarusian – be, Slovak – sk, Slovene – sl, German – de, Romanian – ro, Latvian – lv, Turkish – tr.

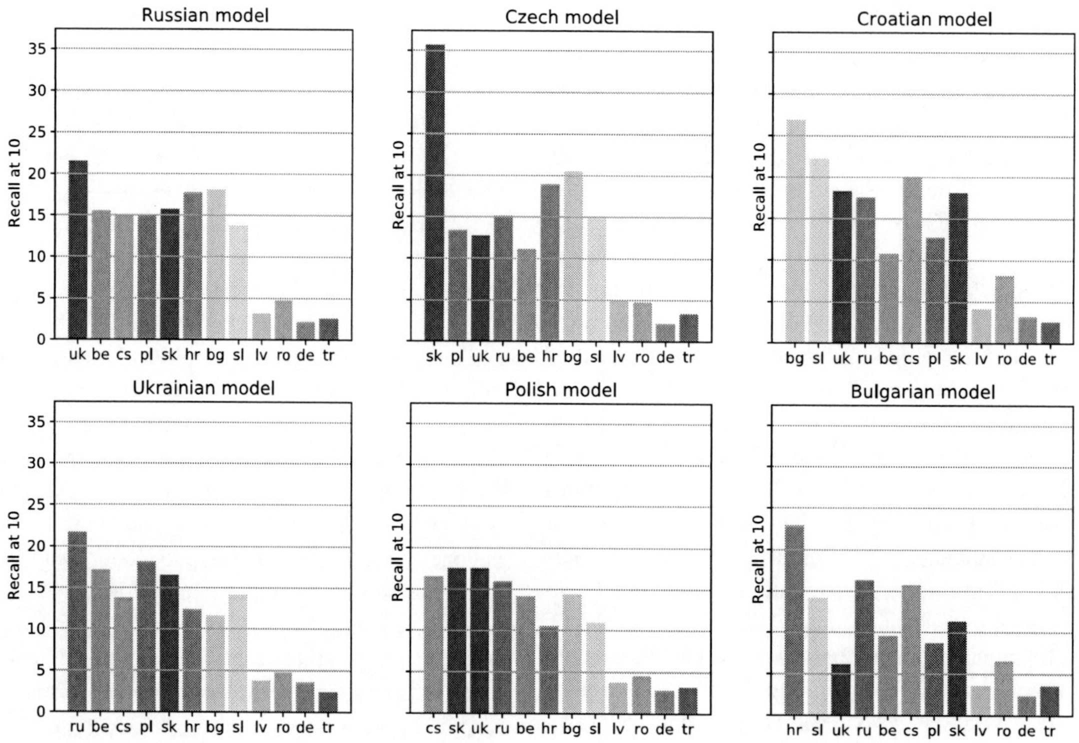

Figure 5: Recall at 10 results. Each plot corresponds to a model trained on one language, while y-axis shows evaluation languages. ISO 639-1 codes for the languages: Ukrainian – uk, Russian – ru, Belarusian – be, Czech – cs, Polish – pl, Slovak – sk, Croatian – hr, Bulgarian – bg, Slovene – sl, Latvian – lv, Romanian – ro, German – de, Turkish – tr.

Figure 6: Dendrogram of the Ward clustering of R@10 results.

ric is an extension of the string-based Levenshtein distance that also calculates the cost of each phone substitution based on phoneme features. We suppose that PWLD is more suitable for cross-lingual analysis than Levenshtein Distance, since it is more capable of catching less apparent phonological similarities, such as, for example in the pair of Czech and Bulgarian cognates *ucho /u x o/* and yxo */u x ɔ/*, where phonemes */o/* and */ɔ/* are very similar to each other. We use the same adaption of the original PWDL proposed in Abdullah et al. (2021a)

Table 2: Pearson correlation coefficient for metrics under analysis. Statistical significance is marked with * and *** for $p < 0.05$ and $p < 0.001$, respectively.

	R@10	MRR	cos sim	LD	PWLD
R10		0.98***	0.5***	-0.74***	-0.57***
MRR			0.5***	-0.75***	-0.56***
cos sim				-0.29*	-0.44***
LD					0.8***
PWLD					

to make it suitable for our analysis.

Table 2 shows the correlation scores of all the metrics under analysis. We observe that both metrics correlate with MRR and R@10, while the correlation with cosine Similarity scores are much lower. Surprisingly, PWLD has a lower correlation with the retrieval metrics than LD, even though it uses the same phoneme vectorization scheme as the model.

5.4 Qualitative Analysis

Figure 7 shows t-SNE visualization on the output on the Russian model. For t-SNE computation, we used output vectors for all the test data. On the visualization, only the concepts *FOG*, *WIND*, *FISH*, and *MOSQUITO* are shown. For concepts *WIND*, *FISH*, and *MOSQUITO* one can observe clear clusters of concepts, as they also appear to sound similarly in all the 6 languages. This is not the case with the concept *FOG*. As shown in Figure 7, t-SNE clustered the concept in different languages quite far from each other even for similarly sounding words. It is interesting that concepts *MOSQUITO* and *WIND* that do not sound similar, but probably have a contextual, distributional similarity, appear close to each other. This probably has to do with the nature of the target fastText embeddings, which are trained to predict the word's context. Additionally, we provide the top retrieved words for the model trained on Russian and tested on Ukrainian. Table 3 demonstrates other candidates in Ukrainian for some phonemic sequences in Russian. The English translation of the concept is given in the brackets.

From the lists of cross-lingual nearest neighbors reported in Table 3, one can notice that the model learns to push semantically similar words closer to each other, despite them having a very different phonetic shape (for instance, *soup-porridge-food* or *who-why-was*). This could again be related to be the nature of fastText embeddings (Mikolov et al., 2018) that we used as target embeddings for the model. As already mentioned, the vector for each word also contains information about this word's context. As a result, the output embeddings produced by the model for contextually close words appear to have a lot in common and are recognized as semantically similar.

Another observation from Table 3 is the clear advantage of shorter and non-content spoken word forms over longer ones. Most of the short words in the list are non-content words, that do not have any distinctive semantic context, and appear in any type of text. In this regard, these words can be seen as items that share fewer features compared to longer words and content words.

6 Discussion and Conclusion

In this paper, we presented a spoken-word recognition model based on a recurrent neural architecture that maps variable-length phonological sequences of word forms into their respective meaning representations. Our goal is to simulate auditory lexical processing in human listeners where we test the model on word forms from closely related

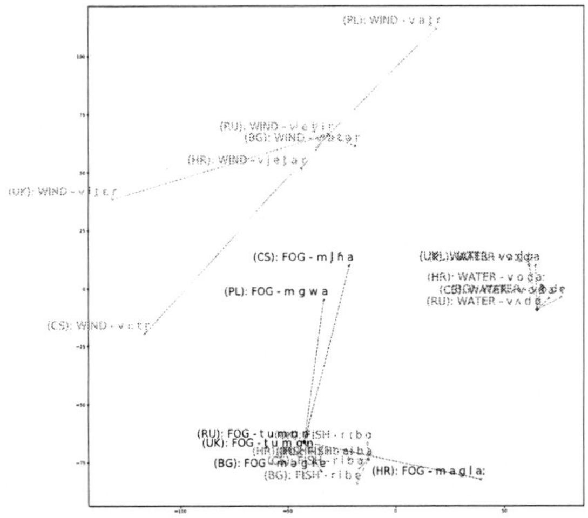

Figure 7: t-SNE on the concept retrieval of the Russian model.

languages and investigate the cross-lingual performance of the model. Furthermore, we presented a case study on the family of Slavic languages, which are known to be remarkable similar and exhibit (partial) mutual intelligibility to various degrees. We grounded our research on the findings from the sociolinguistics literature of Slavic mutual intelligibility and intercomprehension. Using our proposed model, we trained different instances of our model on six Slavic languages: Bulgarian, Croatian, Czech, Polish, Russian, and Ukrainian. Finally, we conducted a cross-lingual evaluation on our trained models to investigate their performance on retrieving and recognizing word forms from other L2 languages.

Returning to our research questions in §1, the cross-lingual analysis of our model performance has shown a trend where the model performance is better on languages that exhibit higher cross-linguistic intelligibility as documented in sociolinguistics studies (**RQ1**). However, this effect is more consistent within South and East Slavic languages, but less consistent in the case of West Slavic languages (Czech and Polish). The factors that drive this inconsistency remain unknown and would require further future work to identify and analyze. Despite this inconsistency, the clustering analysis on the cross-lingual concept retrieval performance resulted in a dendrogram that reflects the traditional genetic classification of the six studied Slavic languages onto West, East, and South languages (**RQ2**). Furthermore, we have shown that cross-linguistic phonetic-lexical similarities

Table 3: Top scored candidates in Ukrainian for the model trained on Russian

	/j a/ (‘I’)	**/r ɑ n a/ (‘wound’)**	**/k t o/ (‘who’)**	**/k ɑ ʃ a/ (‘porridge’)**	**/s u p/ (‘soup’)**
Nearest neighbors	/j A/ (‘I’)	/r ɑ n ɑ/ (‘wound’)	/x t / (‘who’)	k ɑ ʃ ɑ (‘porridge’)	s u p/ (‘soup’)
	/d ɛ'/ (‘yes’)	/j ɑ/ (‘I’)	/t u t/ (‘here’)	/r ɑ n ɑ/ (‘wound’)	/k ʃ / (‘porridge’)
	/s i m/ (‘if’)	/ ɑ p k ɑ/ (‘hat’)	/v r / (‘whisper’)	/v ɔ r ɔ / (‘whisper’)	/d ɛ' n/ (‘day)
	/x t ɔ/ (‘who’)	/j i ɑ/ (‘life’)	/t ɔ m u/ (‘why’)	/ʃ ɑ p k ɑ/ (‘hat’)	/x r t/ (‘food’)
	/j i ɑ/ (‘life’)	/d ɛ'/ (‘yes’)	/b i j/ (‘was’)	/k n ɑ/ (‘book’)	/k r^{j}*uk*/(‘*hook*’)

between the languages—operationalized as string and feature-based phonetic distance on a parallel word list—correlate with the cross-lingual concept retrieval performance of the model. This finding is consistent with the observation in the sociolinguistics literature regarding how lexical similarity between languages facilitates intercomprehension (e.g., the cognate facilitation effect). Therefore, the cross-lingual concept retrieval performance of our model can be predicted using measures of linguistic distance similar to those that predict cross-language comprehension performance (**RQ3**).

The work presented in this paper can be further extended in different directions. For instance, mutual intelligibility between related languages have been found in many cases to be asymmetric. For example, speakers of Portuguese seem to understand Spanish better than the other way around. Future work could analyze and investigate whether or not and to what extent such an asymmetric behavior is observed in our model.

7 Acknowledgements

The authors would like to thank the anonymous reviewers for their encouraging feedback and insightful comments on the paper. This research is funded by the Deutsche Forschungsgemeinschaft (DFG, German Research Foundation), Project-ID 232722074 – SFB 1102.

References

Badr M. Abdullah, Marius Mosbach, Iuliia Zaitova, Bernd Möbius, and Dietrich Klakow. 2021a. Do Acoustic Word Embeddings Capture Phonological Similarity? An Empirical Study. In *Proceedings of Interspeech 2021*, pages 4194–4198.

Badr M. Abdullah, Iuliia Zaitova, Tania Avgustinova, Bernd Möbius, and Dietrich Klakow. 2021b. How familiar does that sound? cross-lingual representational similarity analysis of acoustic word embeddings. In *Proceedings of the Fourth BlackboxNLP Workshop on Analyzing and Interpreting Neural Networks for NLP*, pages 407–419, Punta Cana, Dominican Republic. Association for Computational Linguistics.

Johannes Dellert, Thora Daneyko, and Alla et al. Münch. 2019. Northeuralex: a wide-coverage lexical database of northern eurasia.

Lionel Fontan, Isabelle Ferrané, Jérôme Farinas, Julien Pinquier, and Xavier Aumont. 2016. Using phonologically weighted levenshtein distances for the prediction of microscopic intelligibility. In *Annual conference Interspeech (INTERSPEECH 2016)*, page 650.

Jelena Golubović and Charlotte Gooskens. 2015. Mutual intelligibility between West and South Slavic languages. *Russian Linguistics*, 39:351–373.

Charlotte Gooskens. 2007. The contribution of linguistic factors to the intelligibility of closely related languages. *Journal of Multilingual and multicultural development*, 28(6):445–467.

Charlotte Gooskens. 2017. Dialect intelligibility. *The handbook of dialectology*, pages 204–218.

Charlotte Gooskens. 2019. Receptive multilingualism. *Multidisciplinary perspectives on multilingualism*, pages 149–174.

Klara Jagrova, Tania Avgustinova, Irina Stenger, and Andrea Fischer. 2018. Language models, surprisal and fantasy in Slavic intercomprehension. *Computer Speech Language*, 53.

D Jan and Ludger Zeevaert. 2007. *Receptive multilingualism: Linguistic analyses, language policies and didactic concepts*, volume 6. John Benjamins Publishing.

John B. Jensen. 1989. On the mutual intelligibility of Spanish and Portuguese. *Hispania*, 72(4):848–852.

Diederik Kingma and Jimmy Ba. 2014. Adam: A Method for Stochastic Optimization. *International Conference on Learning Representations*.

Jacek Kudera, Philip Georgis, Bernd Möbius, Tania Avgustinova, and Dietrich Klakow. 2021. Phonetic distance and surprisal in multilingual priming: Evidence from Slavic. In *Interspeech*, pages 3944–3948.

Johann-Mattis List, Robert Forkel, Simon J Greenhill, Christoph Rzymski, Johannes Englisch, and Russell D Gray. 2021. Lexibank: A public repository of standardized wordlists with computed phonological and lexical features.

Nicole Macher, Badr M. Abdullah, Harm Brouwer, and Dietrich Klakow. 2021. Do we read what we hear? modeling orthographic influences on spoken word recognition. In *Proceedings of the 16th Conference of the European Chapter of the Association for Computational Linguistics: Student Research Workshop*, pages 16–22, Online. Association for Computational Linguistics.

James S Magnuson, Heejo You, Sahil Luthra, Monica Li, Hosung Nam, Monty Escabi, Kevin Brown, Paul D Allopenna, Rachel M Theodore, Nicholas Monto, et al. 2020. Earshot: A minimal neural network model of incremental human speech recognition. *Cognitive science*, 44(4):e12823.

Yevgen Matusevych, Herman Kamper, Thomas Schatz, Naomi H Feldman, and Sharon Goldwater. 2021. A phonetic model of non-native spoken word processing. In *Proceedings of the 16th Conference of the European Chapter of the Association for Computational Linguistics*.

Alexandra Mayn, Badr M. Abdullah, and Dietrich Klakow. 2021. Familiar words but strange voices: Modelling the influence of speech variability on word recognition. In *Proceedings of the 16th Conference of the European Chapter of the Association for Computational Linguistics: Student Research Workshop*, pages 96–102, Online. Association for Computational Linguistics.

Tomas Mikolov, Edouard Grave, Piotr Bojanowski, Christian Puhrsch, and Armand Joulin. 2018. Advances in pre-training distributed word representations. In *Proceedings of the International Conference on Language Resources and Evaluation (LREC 2018)*.

Steven Moran and Daniel McCloy, editors. 2019. *PHOIBLE 2.0*. Max Planck Institute for the Science of Human History, Jena.

David R. Mortensen, Siddharth Dalmia, and Patrick Littell. 2018. Epitran: Precision G2P for many languages. In *Proceedings of the Eleventh International Conference on Language Resources and Evaluation (LREC 2018)*, Paris, France. European Language Resources Association (ELRA).

Marius Mosbach, Irina Stenger, Tania Avgustinova, and Dietrich Klakow. 2019. incom.py - a toolbox for calculating linguistic distances and asymmetries between related languages. In *Proceedings of the International Conference on Recent Advances in Natural Language Processing (RANLP 2019)*, pages 810–818, Varna, Bulgaria. INCOMA Ltd.

Adam Paszke, Sam Gross, Francisco Massa, Adam Lerer, James Bradbury, Gregory Chanan, Trevor Killeen, Zeming Lin, Natalia Gimelshein, Luca Antiga, Alban Desmaison, Andreas Kopf, Edward Yang, Zachary DeVito, Martin Raison, Alykhan Tejani, Sasank Chilamkurthy, Benoit Steiner, Lu Fang, Junjie Bai, and Soumith Chintala. 2019. Pytorch: An Imperative Style, High-Performance Deep Learning Library. In *Advances in Neural Information Processing Systems 32*, pages 8024–8035. Curran Associates, Inc.

David B Pisoni and Susannah V Levi. 2007. Some observations on representations and representational specificity in speech perception and spoken word recognition. *The Oxford handbook of psycholinguistics*, pages 3–18.

Roland Sussex and Paul Cubberley. 2006. *The Slavic Languages*. Cambridge University Press.

Laurens Van der Maaten and Geoffrey Hinton. 2008. Visualizing data using t-SNE. *Journal of machine learning research*, 9(11).

Vincent J Van Heuven. 2008. Making sense of strange sounds:(mutual) intelligibility of related language varieties. a review. *International journal of humanities and arts computing*, 2(1-2):39–62.

Andrea Weber and Odette Scharenborg. 2012. Models of spoken-word recognition. *Wiley Interdisciplinary Reviews: Cognitive Science*, 3(3):387–401.

Annotating Norwegian Language Varieties on Twitter for Part-of-Speech

Petter Mæhlum[1], Andre Kåsen[2], Samia Touileb[3] and Jeremy Barnes[4]

[1]University of Oslo
[2]National Library of Norway
[3]University of Bergen
[4]University of the Basque Country

pettemae@ifi.uio.no, andre.kasen@nb.no,
samia.touileb@uib.no, jeremy.barnes@ehu.eus

Abstract

Norwegian Twitter data poses an interesting challenge for Natural Language Processing (NLP) tasks. These texts are difficult for models trained on standardized text in one of the two Norwegian written forms (Bokmål and Nynorsk), as they contain both the typical variation of social media text, as well as a large amount of dialectal variety. In this paper we present a novel Norwegian Twitter dataset annotated with POS-tags. We show that models trained on Universal Dependency (UD) data perform worse when evaluated against this dataset, and that models trained on Bokmål generally perform better than those trained on Nynorsk. We also see that performance on dialectal tweets is comparable to the written standards for some models. Finally we perform a detailed analysis of the errors that models commonly make on this data.

1 Introduction

Norwegian Twitter data poses an interesting challenge for Natural Language Processing (NLP) tasks. Not only do these data represent a set of noisy, user-generated texts with the kinds of orthographic variation common on social media, but also because there is a considerable number of tweets written in dialectal Norwegian. These dialectal variants are quite common and add another level of difficulty for NLP models trained on clean data in one of the two Norwegian written forms (Bokmål or Nynorsk).

Barnes et al. (2021) compiled a dataset of tweets classified according to whether they are written in primarily Bokmål, Nynorsk, or a dialect of Norwegian. We build upon this work by annotating a subset for Part-of-Speech (POS). We investigate to what extent available Norwegian POS tagging models, that were trained on Bokmål and Nynorsk Universal Dependency data (Nivre et al., 2020), perform on this Twitter dataset.

To this end, we use five POS models: three off-the-shelf models, and two developed for the purpose of this work. Each of these models was trained on either a dataset of Bokmål or Nynorsk texts. We explore the performance of each model in terms of accuracy, and investigate which standardized written form can be used as training data and yield good results for non-standardized dialectal texts.

The main contributions of this work are:

- we annotate a moderately sized Twitter dataset with POS labels and include metadata related to which language variety it belongs (Bokmål, Nynorsk, Dialect, or Mixed),
- we perform a detailed error analysis of common model errors specific to our Twitter data,
- we include our insights into the annotation process for POS tagging of non-standardized written forms,
- we release two spaCy models built on top of a Norwegian BERT model.

2 Background

Johannessen (1990) outlined a system for automatic morphosyntactic analysis of Norwegian nouns in the framework of Koskenniemi (1983). This was among the first systems, if not even the very first, that automatically assigned Norwegian texts any morphological information. The first widely used tagger, however, was developed within the *Taggerprosjektet*[1] and came to be known as the Oslo-Bergen Tagger[2] (OBT). Rather than continuing and expanding the system of Johannessen (1990), OBT was implemented in the framework of Karlsson (1990). OBT was initially a rule-based Constraint Grammar tagger for Norwegian Bokmål.

[1]The project ran from April 1996 to December 1998.

[2]https://github.com/noklesta/The-Oslo-Bergen-Tagger

Proceedings of the Ninth Workshop on NLP for Similar Languages, Varieties and Dialects, pages 64–69
October 16, 2022. ©2022 Association for Computational Linguistics

Later, both support for Norwegian Nynorsk and a statistical disambiguation component were added (Johannessen et al., 2012). But one drawback of OBT is that it is made for written, edited text, and therefore might not scale well to sources that are not standardised.

Extending tagger coverage to spoken Norwegian dialect transcription, on the other hand, was the objective of both Nøklestad and Søfteland (2007) and Kåsen et al. (2019). Both sampled data either from the Norwegian part of the Nordic Dialect Corpus (NDC, Johannessen et al. (2009)) or the Language Infrastructure made Accessible (LIA) Corpus.[3] Annotations are found in the respective treebanks of the corpora and are accounted for in Øvrelid et al. (2018) and Kåsen et al. (2022).

Besides Norwegian, there is a large amount of work on the difficulty of processing noisy data from social media (Xu et al., 2015), including the difficulty of POS tagging on social media (Albogamy and Ramasy, 2015), with dialectal variation (Jørgensen et al., 2015), or whether lexical normalization is helpful (van der Goot et al., 2017). However, Norwegian currently lacks any of these studies.

3 Data

Resources for evaluating NLP pipeline tasks for Norwegian are scarce. The only dataset available for standard NLP tasks such as POS tagging, lemmatization, and parsing is the Norwegian Dependency Treebank (NDT, Solberg (2013), Solberg et al. (2014)) that has been converted to the Universal Dependencies standard (Øvrelid and Hohle, 2016). There is, however, a notable exception when it comes to transcribed spoken dialectal data, where the LIA and NDC treebanks as mentioned above are available with annotations for POS tags, morphological features, lemmas, and dependency-style syntax. Despite this, the transcribed texts in the LIA and NDC corpora do not share the same characteristics as the Twitter data. Twitter contains spelling errors and emoji,[4] along with mentions and hashtags. We observe that although our Twitter data contains some characteristics of spoken Norwegian, such as subjectless sentences as in 1, which is otherwise within the spelling norms, the spelling conventions differ from those of LIA and NDC, making it difficult to directly compare the data.

(1) *Kommer nok hjem snart .*
Comes probably home soon .
'(Unspecified) probably comes home soon .'

In LIA and NDC, all transcriptions are done according to a Norwegian-based semi-phonetic standard (Hagen et al., 2015), with strict marking of vowel quantity, palatalization, retroflexion, and more. We see that writers on Twitter do not conform to any specific spelling norm when writing in their own or another dialect. This means that although not all dialectal traits from a dialect are faithfully preserved, this still leads to much dialectal variation in the Twitter data, as things that could have had a common spelling is spelled according to the author's own preference. Especially phonetic differences are often not indicated on Twitter. Because of this, we needed a separate dataset that could be used to evaluate how various systems for Norwegian POS-tagging work on dialectal text as it is found on real data from social media platforms.

We sampled a balanced subset of the dataset introduced by Barnes et al. (2021), who developed to develop a dialect classifier for Norwegian tweets, with the aim to be able to further investigate issues related to dealing with dialectal data on Twitter. This subset includes a selection of 38 tweets in Bokmål, 31 tweets in Nynorsk, and 35 in dialects, which comprises their full test set. We acknowledge that the size of the dataset is small. The POS-tagged dataset is subject to restrictions due to it containing personal information, but is available upon request.

3.1 Norwegian Dialects

Norwegian is considered to have four main dialect groups based on four different traits. This has been a controversial matter and the four-way divide essentially follows Christiansen (1954). There are also recent proponents of a two-way divide (Skjekkeland, 1997). The four-way distinctions have a Northern, Middle, Western, and Eastern group, whereas the two-way divide only operates with a Western and Eastern group. But these distinctions are made with traits from the spoken language. And, as Mæhlum and Røyneland (2012, p. 29) point out, there is a discrepancy between how dialectologists and lay people classify dialects. What sort of dialectal traits Twitter users choose to

[3] https://tekstlab.uio.no/LIA/korpus.html

[4] Emoji has recently gained some interest in the linguistic literature (see https://ling.auf.net/lingbuzz/005981)

	Bokmål		*Nynorsk*		*Dialectal*		*Mixed*		*All*	
PUNCT	211	15.72%	151	13.92%	123	11.27%	35	13.46%	520	13.76%
NOUN	168	12.52%	150	13.82%	116	10.63%	37	14.23%	471	12.47%
VERB	157	11.7%	130	11.98%	129	11.82%	24	9.23%	440	11.65%
PRON	134	9.99%	97	8.94%	140	12.83%	29	11.15%	400	10.59%
ADP	120	8.94%	89	8.2%	85	7.79%	21	8.08%	315	8.34%
AUX	78	5.81%	84	7.74%	93	8.52%	19	7.31%	274	7.25%
ADJ	103	7.68%	67	6.18%	88	8.07%	13	5.0%	271	7.17%
PROPN	92	6.86%	74	6.82%	50	4.58%	18	6.92%	234	6.19%
ADV	77	5.74%	68	6.27%	74	6.78%	11	4.23%	230	6.09%
SCONJ	46	3.43%	42	3.87%	43	3.94%	5	1.92%	136	3.6%
DET	49	3.65%	38	3.5%	33	3.02%	14	5.38%	134	3.55%
CCONJ	34	2.53%	38	3.5%	44	4.03%	11	4.23%	127	3.36%
PART	36	2.68%	22	2.03%	29	2.66%	9	3.46%	96	2.54%
X	16	1.19%	15	1.38%	9	0.82%	10	3.85%	50	1.32%
NUM	11	0.82%	8	0.74%	14	1.28%	2	0.77%	35	0.93%
INTJ	7	0.52%	6	0.55%	14	1.28%	1	0.38%	28	0.74%
SYM	3	0.22%	6	0.55%	7	0.64%	1	0.38%	17	0.45%

Table 1: Distribution of each POS-tag in the Twitter test set, along with the total number of occurrences for each tag and their corresponding percent-wise distribution.

include may therefore lead to a different kind of divide than one can find in the dialectology literature. That being said, Venås (1990) shows that there has been a long tradition of writing in dialect, where the oldest text in Venås (1990) dates back to 1525.

3.2 POS Annotations

The texts from the test set were annotated using the Universal Dependencies POS tagset.[5] The tweets were tokenized with NLTK's tokenizer (Bird et al., 2009) and split into sentences manually. The NLTK tokenizer was chosen over other tokenizers as our preliminary testing on our Twitter dataset shows that it performs better on noisy Norwegian data. The tokenized data was then pre-annotated with Stanza's Bokmål tokenizer to alleviate the annotation task. The remaining task was to correct each POS-tag for these pre-annotated sentences. One annotator annotated the whole test set, while two other annotators annotated two separate subsets of the dataset to give an indication of how robust the annotations were. All three annotators were trained in linguistics and language technology, and are native Norwegian speakers. An overview of the distribution of each POS-tag for each written form is reported in table 1. We see that the percent-wise distribution of POS-tags is similar in Bokmål, Nynorsk and All, but that the PRON tag is somewhat more frequent than the VERB tag in the Dialect tweets. This could be due to the fact that some dialectal tweets only appear as dialectal due to specific dialectal pronouns.

3.3 Inter-Annotator Agreement

The inter-annotator score for the full doubly-annotated test set, using Cohen's κ, was 0.87, indicating quite high agreement. Looking at the specific categories, we see that the agreement was 0.92 for Bokmål, 0.83 for Nynorsk, and 0.88 for dialectal tweets. No specific error patterns are observed that would account for the difference in scores, but all annotators have more familiarity with the Bokmål variant. One common point of disagreement across all is the copula verb *å være* 'to be', which according to the UD guidelines should be tagged as AUX. This was commonly tagged as VERB by one of the annotators. There is also some disagreement when it comes to words such as *opp* 'up', and *ned* 'down', which can be tagged both as adverbs (ADV), adpositions (ADP), and verbal particles. Since there is no tag for verbal particles in UD, the annotators had to chose between the other two. Cases of disagreement were solved by discussing tags where one or more annotators disagreed.

[5] https://universaldependencies.org/u/pos/

4 Experiments

We test several models trained on available Norwegian UD datasets on our Twitter data. Specifically, we compare OBT, Stanza, UDPipe 2.0, a simple BiLSTM model, as well as training our own spaCy models.

Both Stanza (Qi et al., 2020) and UDPipe 2.0 (Straka, 2018) use a BiLSTM which takes features from 1) pre-trained word embeddings, 2) a trainable frequent word embedding that is randomly initialized before training, and 3) character-level LSTM features. While UDPipe only uses a softmax layer for classification, Stanza instead uses a biaffine classifier to ensure consistency between the UPOS and XPOS predictions.

The BiLSTM model we use is a simplified version of the models used in UDPipe and Stanza. The model does not take any pre-trained word embeddings as features, but rather uses the vocabulary of the dataset it is trained on to create the embeddings. The model uses a linear layer for classification.

The spaCy models are newly trained during the present work, and will be released publicly in the near future. Since spaCy is a fully configurable and trainable pipeline, we used the Norwegian BERT model described in (Kummervold et al., 2021) with a shared embedding layer for a tagger, morphologizer, and trainable lemmatizer in an effort to optimize the tagger task.

5 Results and Discussion

Table 2 gives an overview of the accuracy on the Twitter test set using our five models trained on either Bokmål or Nynorsk data. Note that due to their small number, we do not include the mixed category by itself, but these tweets are included in the ALL column. On our twitter Bokmål test set, the best model is the UDPipe Bokmål model, which achieves 89.6 accuracy. Generally, the models trained on the UD Bokmål data are consistently better than the Nynorsk versions on this data (an average of 26.5 percentage points (pp)). Interestingly, the same is not true for the Twitter Nynorsk data. One may assume that models trained on the Nynorsk UD data would always perform better, but in fact, the best performing model is the spaCy model trained on Bokmål (85.7 acc) and on average, the models trained on UD Bokmål perform 4.9 pp worse.

Finally, on the dialectal Twitter data, the spaCy Bokmål model once again performs best (83.3). Again training on the Bokmål data generally performs 12.8 pp better than training on Nynorsk data. This may be due to the subset of dialectal tweets, as a manual inspection showed a large number of tweets from Central and Northern dialects, which share more features with Bokmål. A larger number of tweets from Western and Southern dialects could potentially change this. At the same time, however, it seems clear that the spaCy Bokmål model performs quite well on all the Twitter test data (85.8 acc), so it may simply be a stronger model.

5.1 Error Analysis

We note that the models struggle with features that are typical of the noisy Twitter data containing several misspellings. One concrete example is *å*, which in normative writing most likely refers to the identically spelled infinitive marker *å* 'to'. However, as dialectal writing is much more relaxed, alternative spellings create new homographs that need to be dealt with. We see that some cases of 'å' refer to the conjunction *og* 'and', which in many dialects is homophonous with *å*. We also note that many of the errors come from erroneously tagging pronouns as other word classes, such as INTJ, PART, or NOUN. One reason why there are many errors of this type might simply be because these are frequent indicators of dialect. Barnes et al. (2021) show that certain pronouns such as *æ* and *mæ* (both 'I') are highly correlated with dialectal tweets. They are in some cases the only dialectal indicator in a tweet. Finally, we observe that there are problems with annotating enclitic elements and words that should have been written separately, or conversely, with compound words that have been split. The two latter problems are not exclusive to dialects, but are common in informal writing. Enclitic elements, such as the enclitic negation ('kke, 'kje, 'che, etc.) and enclitic pronouns such as *'n* 'he, him' and *'a* 'she, her' are sometimes added after words, and sometimes without any punctuation, and there are no tokenizers that the authors are aware of that can correctly separate out these enclitic elements. For example, a spelling like *ekkje*, 'is not', which is the copula *e* with the enclitic negation adverb *kkje* 'not' written as one word, has this issue. The same happens with other words that according to the norm should be written as two words, such as *i dag* 'today', being written as *idag*. This leads to tokens with multiple possible POS-tags. In these cases the annotators would consider what

	Bokmål	Nynorsk	Dialect	All
OBT Bokmål	77.8	-	62.3	-
OBT Nynorsk	-	73.1	57.3	-
BiLSTM_UD Bokmål	80.5	63.8	63.4	70.2
BiLSTM_UD Nynorsk	62.3	76.2	56.7	64.6
BiLSTM_UD Nynorsk_LIA	47.6	56.2	43.9	48.9
Stanza Bokmål	86.6	67.5	69.5	75.4
Stanza Nynorsk	45.8	82.8	52.0	58.1
UDPipe Bokmål	**89.6**	76.1	72.9	80.4
UDPipe Nynorsk	74.4	82.9	63.2	73.2
spaCy Bokmål	87.9	**85.7**	**83.3**	**85.8**
spacy Nynorsk	62.5	83.2	65.0	69.6

Table 2: Accuracy on our Twitter test set using five different models trained on either Bokmål or Nynorsk datasets.

would be the best functional fit. For example, the resulting adverbial phrase *idag* can be annotated as an adverb, and verbs negated by enclitics are tagged as verbs. However, these are the annotators' judgements, and their proper treatment is not clear from the UD guidelines.

6 Conclusion

In this paper, we have introduced the first dataset of Norwegian tweets annotated for Part-of-Speech, that also include the metadata for the language variety of each tweet (Bokmål, Nynorsk, Dialect, or Mixed). We tested several POS taggers trained on UD data and show that, for our Twitter data, it is generally better to train on the UD Bokmål data, even if testing on Nynorsk or Dialect. Our detailed error analysis showed that the models generally have problems with dialectal pronouns and unfamiliar compounds. Finally, we release the newly trained spaCy models, and make our annotated data available on request, in order to enable the reproduction of our results.

Acknowledgements

We thank Alexandra Wittemann and Annika Willoch Olstad for their valuable contributions as annotators.

Parts of this work were supported by industry partners and the Research Council of Norway with funding to *MediaFutures: Research Centre for Responsible Media Technology and Innovation*, through the centers for Research-based Innovation scheme, project number 309339.

References

Fahad Albogamy and Allan Ramasy. 2015. Towards POS tagging for Arabic tweets. In *Proceedings of the Workshop on Noisy User-generated Text*, pages 167–171, Beijing, China. Association for Computational Linguistics.

Jeremy Barnes, Petter Mæhlum, and Samia Touileb. 2021. NorDial: A preliminary corpus of written Norwegian dialect use. In *Proceedings of the 23rd Nordic Conference on Computational Linguistics (NoDaLiDa)*, pages 445–451, Reykjavik, Iceland (Online). Linköping University Electronic Press, Sweden.

Steven Bird, Ewan Klein, and Edward Loper. 2009. *Natural language processing with Python: analyzing text with the natural language toolkit*. "O'Reilly Media, Inc.".

Hallfrid Christiansen. 1954. *Hovedinndelingen av norske dialekter*, volume 1954. Bymålslaget Oslo.

Kristin Hagen, Live Håberg, Eirik Olsen, and Ashild Søfteland. 2015. Transkripsjonsrettleiing for LIA. Technical report, Technical report.

Janne B. Johannessen. 1990. *Automatisk morfologisk analyse og syntese*. Novus forlag, Oslo.

Janne B. Johannessen, Kristin Hagen, André Lynum, and Anders Nøklestad. 2012. Exploring Newspaper Language: Using the web to create and investigate a large corpus of modern Norwegian. *Studies in Corpus Linguistics*, 49:51.

Janne B. Johannessen, Joel Priestley, Kristin Hagen, Tor Anders Åfarli, and Øystein Alexander Vangsnes. 2009. The Nordic Dialect Corpus–an advanced research tool. In *Proceedings of the 17th nordic conference of computational linguistics (nodalida 2009)*, pages 73–80.

Anna Jørgensen, Dirk Hovy, and Anders Søgaard. 2015. Challenges of studying and processing dialects in social media. In *Proceedings of the Workshop on Noisy*

User-generated Text, pages 9–18, Beijing, China. Association for Computational Linguistics.

Fred Karlsson. 1990. Constraint grammar as a framework for parsing running text. In *COLING 1990 Volume 3: Papers presented to the 13th International Conference on Computational Linguistics*.

Andre Kåsen, Kristin Hagen, Anders Nøklestad, and Joel Priestley. 2019. Tagging a Norwegian dialect corpus. In *Linköping Electronic Conference Proceedings*, pages 350–355. Linköping University Electronic Press.

Andre Kåsen, Kristin Hagen, Anders Nøklestad, Joel Priestly, Per Erik Solberg, and Dag Trygve Truslew Haug. 2022. The Norwegian Dialect Corpus Treebank. In *Proceedings of the Language Resources and Evaluation Conference*, pages 4827–4832, Marseille, France. European Language Resources Association.

Kimmo Koskenniemi. 1983. *Two-level morphology: A general computational model for word-form recognition and production*, volume 11. University of Helsinki, Department of General Linguistics Helsinki, Finland.

Per E Kummervold, Javier De la Rosa, Freddy Wetjen, and Svein Arne Brygfjeld. 2021. Operationalizing a National Digital Library: The Case for a Norwegian Transformer Model. In *Proceedings of the 23rd Nordic Conference on Computational Linguistics (NoDaLiDa)*, pages 20–29.

Brit Mæhlum and Unn Røyneland. 2012. *Det norske dialektlandskapet: innføring i studiet av dialekter*. Cappelen Damm akademisk.

Joakim Nivre, Marie-Catherine de Marneffe, Filip Ginter, Jan Hajič, Christopher D. Manning, Sampo Pyysalo, Sebastian Schuster, Francis Tyers, and Daniel Zeman. 2020. Universal Dependencies v2: An evergrowing multilingual treebank collection. In *Proceedings of the 12th Language Resources and Evaluation Conference*, pages 4034–4043, Marseille, France. European Language Resources Association.

Anders Nøklestad and Åshild Søfteland. 2007. Tagging a Norwegian speech corpus. In *Proceedings of the 16th Nordic Conference of Computational Linguistics (NODALIDA 2007)*, pages 245–248.

Lilja Øvrelid and Petter Hohle. 2016. Universal dependencies for Norwegian. In *Proceedings of the Tenth International Conference on Language Resources and Evaluation (LREC'16)*, pages 1579–1585.

Lilja Øvrelid, Andre Kåsen, Kristin Hagen, Anders Nøklestad, Per Erik Solberg, and Janne B. Johannessen. 2018. The LIA treebank of spoken Norwegian dialects. In *Proceedings of the Eleventh International Conference on Language Resources and Evaluation (LREC 2018)*.

Peng Qi, Yuhao Zhang, Yuhui Zhang, Jason Bolton, and Christopher D. Manning. 2020. Stanza: A python natural language processing toolkit for many human languages. In *Proceedings of the 58th Annual Meeting of the Association for Computational Linguistics: System Demonstrations*, pages 101–108, Online. Association for Computational Linguistics.

Martin Skjekkeland. 1997. *Dei norske dialektane: tradisjonelle særdrag i jamføring med skriftmåla*. Høyskoleforl.

Per Erik Solberg. 2013. Building gold-standard treebanks for Norwegian. In *Proceedings of the 19th Nordic Conference of Computational Linguistics (NODALIDA 2013)*, pages 459–464.

Per Erik Solberg, Arne Skjærholt, Lilja Øvrelid, Kristin Hagen, and Janne Bondi Johannessen. 2014. The Norwegian dependency treebank. In *Proceedings of the Ninth International Conference on Language Resources and Evaluation (LREC'14)*, pages 789–795, Reykjavik, Iceland. European Language Resources Association (ELRA).

Milan Straka. 2018. UDPipe 2.0 prototype at CoNLL 2018 UD shared task. In *Proceedings of the CoNLL 2018 Shared Task: Multilingual Parsing from Raw Text to Universal Dependencies*, pages 197–207, Brussels, Belgium. Association for Computational Linguistics.

Rob van der Goot, Barbara Plank, and Malvina Nissim. 2017. To normalize, or not to normalize: The impact of normalization on part-of-speech tagging. In *Proceedings of the 3rd Workshop on Noisy User-generated Text*, pages 31–39, Copenhagen, Denmark. Association for Computational Linguistics.

Kjell Venås. 1990. *Den fyrste morgonblånen: tekster på norsk frå dansketida*. Novus forlag.

Wei Xu, Bo Han, and Alan Ritter, editors. 2015. *Proceedings of the Workshop on Noisy User-generated Text*. Association for Computational Linguistics, Beijing, China.

OcWikiDisc: a Corpus of Wikipedia Talk Pages in Occitan

Aleksandra Miletić
Department of Digital Humanities
University of Helsinki
aleksandra.miletic@helsinki.fi

Yves Scherrer
Department of Digital Humanities
University of Helsinki
yves.scherrer@helsinki.fi

Abstract

This paper presents OcWikiDisc, a new freely available corpus in Occitan, as well as language identification experiments done as part of the corpus building process. Occitan is a regional language spoken mainly in the south of France and in parts of Spain and Italy. It exhibits rich diatopic variation, it is not standardized, and it is still low-resourced, especially when it comes to large downloadable corpora. In an effort to remedy this lack, we created OcWikiDisc, a corpus extracted from the talk pages associated with the Occitan Wikipedia. The version of the corpus with the most restrictive language filtering contains 8K user messages for a total of 618K tokens. The language filtering is performed based on language identification experiments with four off-the-shelf tools, including HeLI (Jauhiainen et al., 2022) and a new fasttext-based language identification model from Meta AI's No Language Left Behind initiative (Costa-jussà et al., 2022).

1 Introduction

This paper provides two main contributions: we present OcWikiDisc, a new, freely available corpus in Occitan, and report results of language identification experiments executed as part of the corpus-building process. Occitan is a Romance language, mainly spoken in the south of France and in parts of Spain and Italy. It is considered a regional language in France but doesn't have the status of an official language. Despite recent efforts to endow it with various NLP tools, it still remains low-resourced, especially when it comes to large, freely available corpora. Our OcWikiDisc corpus aims to remedy this lack by relying on user-generated content available on the Web: we extract the corpus from the talk pages associated with the Occitan Wikipedia. Thus, OcWikDisc contains messages posted by users, typically in direct user-to-user interactions. As such, it offers interesting possibilities for research not only in NLP, but also in corpus-based dialectology and wider linguistic studies. To the best of our knowledge, it is the first such corpus for Occitan. It can be downloaded through Zenodo[1].

Since the extracted content contains a significant proportion of messages written in languages other than Occitan, we perform language identification (LID) experiments. We test four off-the-shelf tools: langid (Lui and Baldwin, 2012) and its Python 3 implementation, py3langid [2], developed by A. Barbaresi; HeLI (Jauhiainen et al., 2016, 2022); and the fasttext language identification models, both the original (Joulin et al., 2017) and the most recent (Costa-jussà et al., 2022), published as part of Meta AI's No Language Left Behind Initiative.[3] We identify optimal LID strategies based on the desired outcome (optimizing for precision vs recall) and use them to filter the extracted corpus. These results also offer useful pointers for LID of Occitan in general.

The remainder of the paper is organized as follows. In Section 2, we give a brief description of the main linguistic properties of Occitan. Section 3 offers more details on available NLP tools and resources for Occitan. In Section 4, we describe our corpus extraction process and present the initial corpus. Section 5 is dedicated to language identification experiments, leading to several filtered versions of the corpus, which are presented in Section 6. Finally, in Section 7, we give our conclusions and directions for future work.

2 Occitan: Linguistic Properties and Dialectological Situation

Occitan is a Romance language spoken in the south of France, in parts of Piedmont in Italy and in Val d'Aran in Spain. It does not have the status of an

[1] https://doi.org/10.5281/zenodo.7079580

[2] https://github.com/adbar/py3langid

[3] https://ai.facebook.com/research/no-language-left-behind/

Proceedings of the Ninth Workshop on NLP for Similar Languages, Varieties and Dialects, pages 70–79
October 16, 2022. ©2022 Association for Computational Linguistics

Figure 1: Occitan dialects

(1)

T'	aviái	laissat	un	messatge	totara
you.DAT	have.1SG.IMPF	leave.PST.PTCP	a.SG.M	message	just

'I had just left you a message'

official language in France, and as many such linguistic varieties, it is not standardized. Currently, two main spelling norms are in use: one close to medieval troubadours' spelling (often referred to as *classical*) and another one closer to the French language spelling conventions (often referred to as *mistralian*) (Sibille, 2002). Furthermore, Occitan has a rich system of dialects organized in six main groups: Auvernhat, Gascon, Lemosin, Lengadocian, Provençau and Vivaroaupenc (see Figure 1) (Bec, 1995). Diatopic variation can be seen on the lexical, phonological, morphological or syntactic level. For an illustration of each of these types of variation, see Miletic et al. (2020b).

Some of the main linguistic properties are shared by most dialects. For example, Occitan is a null subject language with tense, person and number inflection marks on finite verbs for each person. Many dialects exhibit number and gender inflection on all components of the noun phrase. Unlike contemporary French, Occitan maintains the use of the preterite (*passat simple*), which contrasts with the perfect tense (*passat compausat*), and the use of the imperfect subjunctive, even in informal language. Example 1, extracted from the OcWikiDisc corpus, illustrates some of these properties.

3 Occitan and NLP

Until recently, Occitan belonged to the group of under-resourced languages. This situation was due to a combination of factors. First, the linguistic situation described above, compounding strong diatopic variation, absence of standardization, and use of multiple spelling norms, contributed to data sparsity. This was coupled with insufficient recognition on the institutional level, leading to a lack of human and financial resources available for NLP of Occitan. This situation is currently evolving for the better: in France, regional languages have been recognized as part of the country's cultural heritage by the constitutional amendment Article 75-1 published in 2008. Since then, they have benefited from national and European initiatives to revitalize regional languages and help them enter the digital era. This has led to the creation of initial resources and tools for Occitan.

An electronic lexicon in Lengadocian (Bras et al., 2020; Vergez-Couret, 2016) (850K entries), an online corpus of 3,4M words called BaTelÒc (Bras and Vergez-Couret, 2016) and a PoS- tagged corpus of 12K tokens (Bernhard et al., 2018) were created as part of the RESTAURE project[4] (2016-2018). During the LINGUATEC project,[5] a 20K-token treebank following Universal Dependencies annotation guidelines was created (Miletic et al., 2020a). The existence of annotated training corpora led to initial experiments in PoS-tagging and parsing Occitan (Vergez-Couret and Urieli, 2014; Miletic et al., 2019). A first neural text-to-speech model has also

[4] https://restaure.unistra.fr/en/presentation/

[5] https://linguatec-poctefa.eu/fr/projet/

been created (Corral et al., 2020).

All of these resources represent important steps forward for Occitan. Nonetheless, the language still remains low-resourced, especially when it comes to large, freely available corpora. The annotated corpora cited above are downloadable for research purposes, but they are fairly small, whereas BaTelÒc, the largest currently available corpus in Occitan, is not downloadable due to copyright limitations. A popular solution in this type of situation is to turn to the linguistic content available on the internet. This typically consists in crawling the top-level domain of the given language and transforming it into a corpus (see, *e.g.* Ljubešić and Klubička, 2014). However, as pointed out by Barbaresi (2013), such an approach can be ill-suited for low-resourced languages and linguistic varieties. Many of them (including Occitan) do not have a dedicated top-level domain, which makes the identification of URL targets for crawling more challenging, and reliable LID systems more crucial in the process. Moreover, low-resourced languages can also have a limited presence on the Internet compared to more widely used languages. To illustrate, the latest version of the OSCAR corpus (Ortiz Suárez et al., 2019)[6], based on the CommonCrawl from November/December 2021, only contains 31K tokens in Occitan, compared to, *e.g.* 41G tokens in French. We therefore turn to a more targeted solution: extracting content from Wikipedia.

4 Extracting a Corpus from Wikipedia Talk Pages

Wikipedia content in Occitan has been extracted and used as a corpus in previous research. For example, it is mentioned as part of the training material for the transformer-based multilingual language model mBERT (Devlin et al., 2019), but also for the LID tools fasttext (Joulin et al., 2017), langid (Lui and Baldwin, 2012) and HeLI (Jauhiainen et al., 2016). To the best of our knowledge, these training corpora have not been distributed.

Wikipedia content in Occitan is also present in parallel corpora extracted from Wikipedia such as WikiMatrix (Schwenk et al., 2021). It would be possible to derive a monolingual Occitan corpus from it, but the resulting corpus would contain individual sentences that would appear without their linguistic context, and would be accompanied by limited metadata.

Our goal, as stated in Section 1, is to create a corpus suitable for a wider range of research: NLP applications, computational and corpus-based dialectology, as well as corpus-based linguistics. We therefore aim to preserve the linguistic integrity of the content in the corpus and to provide as much metadata as possible. Also, we choose to focus on the talk pages rather than the encyclopedia pages themselves. Wikipedia talk pages are dedicated to discussions between users, typically about article content and editing policies. These are direct user-to-user interactions on a variety of topics, but in general they share the same goal: improving the quality of the Wikipedia content. They often combine elements of dialogue with elements of argumentative writing (Ho-Dac et al., 2016). Given the nature of their content, the talk pages are a novel source of linguistic material for Occitan.

4.1 Data Extraction Process

As the starting point of the extraction, we use a Wikimedia data dump containing the current version of Wikipedia pages and the associated metacontent.[7] The basic data structure of the archive is encoded in XML, but the content of each page is rendered in wikitext, a text-based encoding convention that can mark some further structure (thread headings, comments), indicate hyperlinks (username mentions, internal or external page addresses) or allow for some formatting (headings, bulleting, emphasis).

Our global workflow is organized into two main steps: extraction and filtering. The extraction starts by selecting XML elements in an XML namespace dedicated to discussions. For each such discussion, the text content is extracted and individual posts are identified. We also extract some metadata encoded in the XML: contributor, timestamp, namespace and discussion title. However, these pieces of metadata are available at the discussion level, and the corresponding discussion can contain multiple messages, or even multiple threads of messages. Therefore, we also extract the header of the thread in which a given message was posted, along with the username and the timestamp present in the post's signature. All of these pieces of information are preserved as metadata associated with the message in the output.

In the second step, the text of each identified

[6] `https://oscar-corpus.com/post/oscar-v22-01/`

[7] Dump date: 01 May 2022.

message is cleaned for formatting commands written in wikitext and various types of non-linguistic content, such as snippets of JavaScript or HTML code.

4.2 Initial Extraction Result

The extracted corpus is formatted as a simple CSV file, in which each line represents a message extracted from the corpus. The line contains the message itself and all the extracted metadata associated with it.

Some basic quantitative information about the resulting corpus is given in Table 1. In order to provide token counts, we perform tokenization on whitespace and punctuation marks (including apostrophes). This rudimentary solution was chosen to accommodate the fact that the corpus content is multilingual (see below).

Messages	11,025
Tokens	1,186,239
Tokens/Message	107.60
Users	522
Messages/User	17.07

Table 1: OcWikiDisc: initial extraction

The building process for Web-based corpora typically includes a deduplication step, in which identical (or near-identical) texts are eliminated from the corpus. Currently, this operation is not done on the OcWikiDisc corpus. Given the structure of the data, it should not be possible for the same message with the same metadata to appear multiple times in the archive (each discussion being represented exactly once in the XML file). Some near-identical system messages were present in the initial extraction result, but these are systematically in English and can therefore be eliminated through LID (described below). There are also messages in Occitan that could be classified as near-duplicates, which typically contain demands for article validation, birthday and New Year's wishes. However, these were not produced by bots, but by the contributors, and as such, they represent genuine linguistic material. Furthermore, they are often part of message threads, and excluding them automatically could compromise the integrity of the content.

The Occitan content in the corpus is fairly uniform when it comes to the spelling norm: the community strongly recommends the use of the classical norm in the articles in order to facilitate searches, and this seems to be respected almost systematically in the discussions too. When it comes to the use of dialects, there is an incentive to preserve the identity of each individual dialect and especially to avoid writing in "pan-Occitan", an improvised standard. An initial exploration of the data shows Lengadocien as the most widely used dialect in OcWikiDisc, followed by Gascon and Provençau (see also Section 5.3.1).

However, an important part of the messages contain linguistic material in languages other than Occitan. We therefore perform language identification experiments in order to identify the optimal approach to filter the corpus content. In this first set of experiments on OcWikiDisc, we focus on identifying messages containing Occitan and leave the identification of individual dialects for future work.

5 Language Identification Experiments

Language identification is an NLP task which consists in automatically identifying the language of a given text (Jauhiainen et al., 2019). In order to perform this task on the extracted corpus, we first evaluate four off-the-shelf tools that integrate models for Occitan. Each of them is briefly presented below.

5.1 Language Identification Tools

langid (Lui and Baldwin, 2012) uses a multinomial naïve Bayes model with feature selection based on an information gain measure. The features are not complete words, but character n-grams (1 to 4 characters). It is specifically designed to control for genre differences and bias towards better resourced varieties. In addition to the original tool, we also test its Python 3 implementation, **py3langid**, developed by A. Barbaresi [8]. Both tools were trained on the same set of 97 languages.

HeLI (Jauhiainen et al., 2016, 2022) uses language models consisting of single words and character n-grams of length 1 to 6. During training, the models are created by attributing each word or n-gram a score based on its relative frequency in the given language. During language identification, for each word of the text to be classified, the tool first calls upon the word-level models. If the word is found in none of them, the tool backs off to n-gram models, going from longest to shortest, until at least one match for the word is found. The scores of all languages identified in a given instance are

[8] https://github.com/adbar/py3langid

averaged to obtain the final score for each of them. HeLI integrates models for 200 languages.

fasttext (Joulin et al., 2017) was designed as a general text classification model, but its LID models have been widely used. It implements a language representation based on bag of words and bag of n-grams. It uses a linear classifier combined with a rank constraint, supposed to improve the generalisation for classes with small numbers of instances. We test both the LID model distributed with the original version of the tool as well as a more recent one, released in July 2022 as part of Meta AI's No Language Left Behind initiative (Costa-jussà et al., 2022). This initiative being specifically aimed at low-resourced languages, we wish to evaluate the tool's performances on Occitan. The original model was trained on 176 languages, while the most recent one integrates 204.

5.2 Baseline Evaluation on Existing Occitan Data

We perform an initial LID evaluation on a test set containing only Occitan. The sample is derived from the four-dialect treebank presented in Miletic et al. (2020b) by transforming each treebank sentence into a test instance. The sample contains 1,520 instances, 73% of which are in Lengadocian, 17% in Gascon, and 5% in Provençau and Lemosin each. However, for the purposes of this experiment, all dialects were merged.

We report accuracy scores for each tool in Table 2. The more recent fasttext LID model (fasttext2) achieves the best result at 93.22%, with an improvement of almost 30 percentage points over the previous version of the model (*fasttext1*). The only other tool scoring above 90% is HeLI, with langid at and py3langid at 66.64% and 70.00% respectively.

Given these results, we keep fasttext2 and HeLI for some further experiments: we test using the top-2 predictions from each tool (heli_top2 and fasttext2_top2), and then using the union of the top prediction from each of them (fasttext2_heli). We scored the prediction as true if the list of labels contained Occitan. As shown in the section *Strategies* of Table 2, relying on two labels from HeLI achieves the same score as using the top prediction from fasttext2. Using the top 2 labels from fasttext2 improves accuracy for almost 2%, but using HeLI's top prediction instead brings a small additional improvement, equivalent to another 3 correct predictions on this dataset. This is the best overall result in this part of our evaluation.

Individual tools	
Tool	**Accuracy (%)**
fasttext1	62.30
langid	66.64
py3langid	70.00
heli	90.70
fasttext2	93.22
Strategies	
Strategy	**Accuracy (%)**
heli_top2	93.22
fasttext2_top2	95.00
fasttext2_heli	95.20

Table 2: LID results on all-Occitan dataset

As mentioned above, a concern when attempting LID on low-resourced languages is that they will be confused with better resourced closely related linguistic varieties. We can therefore expect the tools to encounter difficulties in distinguishing Occitan from other Romance languages. The confusion matrices based on the classification produced by fasttext2 and HeLI seem to confirm this. Table 3 shows the ten most frequent erroneous labels produced by the two tools.

For both tools, 7 out of 10 most frequently confused languages are from the Romance family. In the case of HeLI, Interlingua[9] and Haitian can also claim closeness to the Romance languages. On the other hand, the remaining languages for fasttext2 are somewhat surprising: there seems to be no straightforward linguistic argument for confusing Occitan with Vietnamese or Standard Malay.

This evaluation allowed us to quickly identify potentially useful strategies for LID on our corpus. However, since the initial test set only contains Occitan, it is not possible to evaluate the tools' precision in a satisfactory manner. We therefore proceeded to an evaluation on a sample extracted from OcWikiDisc in order to further test the tools in a context closer to their intended use. For these experiments, we select fasttext2 and HeLI as the most reliable systems.

[9]Interlingua is a constructed language whose vocabulary and grammar are largely based on Romance languages. See, e.g., (Gode and Blair, 1951; Gode et al., 1952)

fasttext2		heli	
Catalan	23	Catalan	38
French	11	Spanish	11
Vietnamese	10	Interlingua	7
Portuguese	8	Lombard	6
Spanish	6	French	6
English	5	Extremaduran	5
Asturian	5	Piemontese	4
Galician	5	Portuguese	4
Standard Malay	4	Haitian	3
Italian	4	Pfälzisch	3

Table 3: Top-10 erroneous labels for fasttext2 and HeLI

5.3 Evaluation on OcWikiDisc

As stated above, the content of OcWikiDisc is not written exclusively in Occitan. The content in other languages can appear as a monolingual post, or as a part of a multilingual message. These multilingual examples can also include Occitan. This has important implications both for LID itself and for our evaluation setup.

LID in multilingual and, in particular, code-switching data is a challenge for LID systems (Jauhiainen et al., 2019). One of the central issues is the need to determine how many labels need to be attributed to each classification instance. This often implies determining a threshold for the classification score and accepting all predictions that score above it to contribute to the prediction.

When it comes to the evaluation, this type of material raises questions about the manual annotation guidelines. For instance, if a message contains only a toponym (cf. *He lives in Teste de Buche*), a metalinguistic use of a word (cf. *the word 'caval' means 'horse'*), or a salutation (cf. *Bonjorn, I would like to participate in writing this article*) in a different language, should it be labelled as multilingual? We address these questions below.

5.3.1 Building a Multilingual Evaluation Sample

For the purposes of this evaluation, we create a test set of 100 messages extracted from the corpus. Roughly a third of the instances contain no Occitan (but can contain several other languages), a third contains only Occitan, and a third contains Occitan and at least one other language. The sample was manually annotated by a single annotator. For each post, the annotator indicated all languages appearing in it, even if one of them was only instantiated in a single word. Out of the 100 test instances, 58 are monolingual, with the average number of labels per instance at 1.49. The maximum number of labels per instance is 4.

The sample was also annotated with dialect and spelling norm information. The Occitan content in this sample systematically follows the classical spelling norm. As for the dialects, out of 68 messages containing Occitan, 36 were in Lengadocian, 6 in Gascon and 5 in Provençau, whereas for the remaining 21 it was impossible to specify the dialect. However, this information was not used in the experiments described in the following section, which focus solely on language identification.

Some factors should be borne in mind while considering the evaluation results presented below. In the current annotation all labels are presented equally: there is no means of knowing how the content of the post is distributed between different languages. It is also worth mentioning that this was not a trivial task for the human annotator: she reported uncertainty about a part of the languages in the test set and had to rely on help from other linguists to identify some of them.

5.3.2 Evaluation on a Multilingual Sample

We frame our evaluation as a task in identifying Occitan content in the corpus. We therefore focus our attention on the tools' performance relative to this language, at the expense of their global results.

In order to determine the number of labels from each tool to be evaluated, we first considered using a threshold on the classification scores. However, this proved problematic with fasttext2. The tool's second-best predictions are associated with an important drop in probability, with 75% of them scoring at <0.021. A meaningful threshold would therefore favour outputting only one label from fasttext2. Yet our initial evaluation suggests that additional labels would be useful for the task at hand. We therefore opted for a different approach: we base our evaluation on top-2 and top-5 labels from each tool. This, of course, affects the global precision scores, since it automatically produces incorrect labels for monolingual posts. However, as noted above, our aim is to optimize the detection of Occitan, and not the global LID scores.

The evaluation results are presented in Table 4. We evaluate tools individually on their top-2 and top-5 labels, but also on two ensemble strategies, combining the top prediction and the top-2 pre-

	Occitan			Global		
	Precision	Recall	F1-score	Precision	Recall	F1-score
fasttext2_top2	84.75	73.53	78.74	**56.50**	75.84	**64.76**
heli_top2	**93.33**	61.76	74.34	51.00	68.46	58.45
fasttext2_top5	79.49	**91.18**	84.93	26.00	**87.25**	40.06
heli_top5	88.06	86.76	**87.41**	25.41	83.22	38.93
fasttext2_heli_top1	**100.00**	57.35	72.90	**89.09**	65.77	**75.68**
fasttext2_heli_top2	85.00	**75.00**	**79.69**	42.80	**77.85**	55.24

Table 4: Evaluation results on OcWikiDisc sample

	Messages	Tokens	Tokens/Message	Users	Messages/User
ocwikidisc_precision	8149	618,153	75.86	206	33.69
ocwikidisc_balanced	9032	756,922	83.80	323	23.19
ocwikidisc_recall	9394	804,959	85.69	347	22.39
ocwikidisc_unfiltered	11025	1,186,239	107.60	522	17.07

Table 5: OcWikiDisc: filtered corpora

	Total languages	Top 11
ocwikidisc_precision	54	Occitan, Catalan, French, English, German, Spanish, Portuguese, Lombard, Romanian, Piemontese, Galician
ocwikidisc_balanced	124	Occitan, Catalan, Extremaduran, Lombard, Spanish, Interlingua, French, Galician, Piemontese, Portuguese, Lingala
ocwikidisc_recall	114	Occitan, Catalan, French, Spanish, Galician, Portuguese, Lombard, Italian, Asturian, Korean, Romanian
ocwikidisc_unfiltered	155	Occitan, Catalan, French, Spanish, Portuguese, Galician, Italian, Korean, Lombard, English, Asturian

Table 6: Overview of languages detected in different versions of the corpus

dictions from each tool. We report the results on Occitan, and include global evaluation scores for the sake of completeness.

In strategies combining output from fasttext2 and HeLI, we use the union of the labels produced by each tool. This yields an average of 1.1 labels per instance when using the top prediction from each, and 2.7 labels per instance on average when using the top 2 predictions.

In all scenarios, we evaluate the tools in terms of precision, recall and F1-score. For the global evaluation results, the scores are micro-averaged.[10]

First, let us comment briefly the global evaluation results. As expected, the scenarios with a higher number of labels achieved the best recall, but had significantly lower precision scores, leading to lower F1 scores. The best precision was obtained with the combination of the top prediction from fasttext2 and HeLI, which also shows the best F1 score. This could therefore be considered as a sound option for optimizing the LID results on all languages.

When it comes to the identification of Occitan, the results are more surprising. Unlike what we saw in the initial evaluation, combining the two tools does not seem to improve over the best individual results. The highest F1-scores were achieved by HeLI using the top-5 predictions (87.41) and fasttext2 (84.93) in the same setup. HeLI also displays balanced precision and recall scores in this setup, which recommends it as a reliable global solution for our task. Using the combination of the top predictions from fasttext2 and HeLI achieves perfect

[10]For the evaluation on Occitan only, we evaluate recall based on all manually annotated messages that are labelled as containing Occitan, whereas the precision takes into account all predictions that contain the label for Occitan.

	Users with >1 message	Messages from top 10	Tokens from top 10
ocwikidisc_precision	120 (58%)	5,173 (63%)	399,530 (65%)
ocwikidisc_balanced	166 (51%)	5,346 (59%)	435,345 (58%)
ocwikidisc_recall	188 (54%)	5,392 (57%)	456,839 (57%)
ocwikidisc_unfiltered	257 (49%)	5,757 (52%)	552,669 (47%)

Table 7: Distribution of content across users

precision on our sample, but it is coupled with a significant drop in recall (57.35). Unsurprisingly, the best recall was achieved when using the highest number of labels (fasttext_top5 and heli_top5).

Based on these results, we choose the following strategy for our corpus-building process. We annotate the corpus both with fasttext2 and with HeLI, outputting the top-5 labels from each. We create three filtered versions, favouring precision (using fasttext2_heli_top1), recall (using fasttext2_top5) and F1-score (using heli_top5), respectively. Each of the filtered versions is presented below. Through this approach, we hope to produce resources adapted to different types of applications and research. An unfiltered version of the corpus is also made available.

6 Filtered Corpus

In this section, we present the complete LID-annotated corpus and its three filtered versions. The basic information about them is available in Table 5, whereas the detected languages in each version of the corpus are presented in Table 6. To facilitate comparison, we repeat the same information for the unfiltered version of the corpus, initially given in Section 4.2.

As expected, the version of the corpus favouring precision (ocwikidisc_precision) is the most restricted, with 8K messages and 618K tokens. This represents roughly half of the unfiltered corpus (in tokens). The difference between the corpus favouring recall (ocwikidisc_recall) and the one favouring F1-score (ocwikidisc_balanced) is relatively small for all reported measures. It remains to be seen if there is a qualitative difference in their content.

It is important to note that the distribution of content across users is heavily skewed in all four versions of the corpus, both in terms of the number of messages and in terms of the number of tokens. The full distribution of messages across users is shown in Figure 2. As illustrated in Table 7, more than half of the content in each filtered version comes from the 10 most active users, and only 50-60% of users have produced more than one message. While this affects the representativeness of the corpus, it offers an interesting possibility for dialect identification: if the dialect of each of the most active users can be reliably identified manually, this information can be propagated onto all of their messages, thus annotating an important part of the corpus for dialect information. This direction will be explored in our future work.

The information on detected languages in Table 6 is based on the predictions of the strategy used to filter a given corpus. Note that the 10 most frequent languages after Occitan in each corpus predominantly belong to the Romance family. This could simply be the result of shared interests or collaboration efforts on Wikipedia, but it could also be an indicator of difficulties with the identification of closely related languages. We will be looking into this issue in the future.

7 Conclusions and Future Work

In this paper, we presented OcWikiDisc, a new corpus in Occitan extracted from Wikipedia Talk pages. The version of the corpus with the most restrictive language-based filtering contains 618K tokens. Along with its extracted content, it also contains metadata about users, time of posting and discussion subjects, as well as language annotation produced using LID tools. To the best of our knowledge, it is the largest downloadable corpus for Occitan. It can be downloaded from Zenodo.

We also presented LID experiments aimed at identifying Occitan content in the initial extracted corpus, which is multilingual. We tested four off-the-shelf LID tools. In an initial experiment on an all-Occitan sample, the best results were achieved by the new LID model from the fasttext tool and by HeLI. On a test sample extracted from OcWikiDisc, fasttext's new model had the highest recall score, whereas HeLI achieved the most balanced precision and recall. Combining the two tools optimized the

Figure 2: Number of messages per user across the four versions of the corpus

precision.

In the future, we will investigate making the LID on the corpus more fine-grained. Currently, we perform LID at message level. Given the amount of multilingual messages observed in our data, it could be beneficial to do it rather at sentence level, or even at word level. We will also examine the annotation of the Romance languages found in the corpus, since a certain amount of confusion arising from the closely related languages in the corpus can be expected.

Acknowledgements

The authors would like to thank Jean Sibille (University of Toulouse), Myriam Bras (University of Toulouse) and Marianne Vergez-Couret (University of Poitiers) for their help with the manual annotation of the test sample.

This work has been supported by the Academy of Finland through project No. 342859 "CorCoDial – Corpus-based computational dialectology".

References

Adrien Barbaresi. 2013. Challenges in web corpus construction for low-resource languages in a post-bootcat world. In *6th Language & Technology Conference, Less Resourced Languages special track*, pages 69–73.

Pierre Bec. 1995. *La langue occitane*, 6th edition. PUF.

Delphine Bernhard, Anne-Laure Ligozat, Fanny Martin, Myriam Bras, Pierre Magistry, Marianne Vergez-Couret, Lucie Steiblé, Pascale Erhart, Nabil Hathout, Dominique Huck, Christophe Rey, Philippe Reynés, Sophie Rosset, Jean Sibille, and Thomas Lavergne. 2018. Corpora with part-of-speech annotations for three regional languages of France: Alsatian, Occitan and Picard. In *Proceedings of the Eleventh International Conference on Language Resources and Evaluation (LREC 2018)*, pages 3917–3924, Miyazaki, Japan. European Language Resources Association (ELRA).

Myriam Bras and Marianne Vergez-Couret. 2016. BaTelÒc : a text base for the Occitan language. In *Language Documentation and Conservation in Europe*, pages 133–149. Honolulu: University of Hawaï Press .

Myriam Bras, Marianne Vergez-Couret, Nabil Hathout, Jean Sibille, Aure Séguier, and Benazet Dazéas. 2020. Loflòc : Lexic obèrt flechit occitan. In *Fidélités et dissidences (Actes du* XII*e congrès de l'Association Internationale d'Études Occitanes)*, pages 141–156, Albi. Centre d'Etude de la Littérature Occitane.

Ander Corral, Igor Leturia, Aure Séguier, Michael Barret, Benaset Dazéas, Philippe Boula de Mareüil, and Nicolas Quint. 2020. Neural text-to-speech synthesis for an under-resourced language in a diglossic environment: the case of Gascon Occitan. In *Proceedings of the 1st Joint SLTU (Spoken Language Technologies for Under-resourced languages) and CCURL (Collaboration and Computing for Under-Resourced Languages) Workshop «Language Resources and Evaluation Conference–Marseille–11–16 May 2020»*, pages 53–60. European Language Resources Association (ELRA).

Marta R. Costa-jussà, James Cross, Onur Çelebi, Maha Elbayad, Kenneth Heafield, Kevin Heffernan, Elahe Kalbassi, Janice Lam, Daniel Licht, Jean Maillard, Anna Sun, Skyler Wang, Guillaume

Wenzek, Al Youngblood, Bapi Akula, Loic Barrault, Gabriel Mejia Gonzalez, Prangthip Hansanti, John Hoffman, Semarley Jarrett, Kaushik Ram Sadagopan, Dirk Rowe, Shannon Spruit, Chau Tran, Pierre Andrews, Necip Fazil Ayan, Shruti Bhosale, Sergey Edunov, Angela Fan, Cynthia Gao, Vedanuj Goswami, Francisco Guzmán, Philipp Koehn, Alexandre Mourachko, Christophe Ropers, Safiyyah Saleem, Holger Schwenk, and Jeff Wang. 2022. No language left behind: Scaling human-centered machine translation. arXiv preprint: https://arxiv.org/abs/2207.04672.

Jacob Devlin, Ming-Wei Chang, Kenton Lee, and Kristina Toutanova. 2019. BERT: Pre-training of deep bidirectional transformers for language understanding. In *Proceedings of the 2019 Conference of the North American Chapter of the Association for Computational Linguistics: Human Language Technologies, Volume 1 (Long and Short Papers)*, pages 4171–4186, Minneapolis, Minnesota. Association for Computational Linguistics.

Alexander Gode and Hugh E Blair. 1951. *Interlingua: a grammar of the international language.* Storm Publishers.

Alexander Gode, Hugh E Blair, and Forrest F Cleveland. 1952. Interlingua-english, a dictionary of the international language and interlingua, a grammar of the international language. *American Journal of Physics*, 20(6):382–382.

Lydia-Mai Ho-Dac, Veronika Laippala, Céline Poudat, and Ludovic Tanguy. 2016. French Wikipedia talk pages: Profiling and conflict detection. In *4th Conference on CMC and Social Media Corpora for the Humanities*.

Tommi Jauhiainen, Heidi Jauhiainen, and Krister Lindén. 2022. HeLI-OTS, off-the-shelf language identifier for text. In *Proceedings of the 13th Conference on Language Resources and Evaluation (LREC 2022)*, pages 3912–3922.

Tommi Jauhiainen, Krister Lindén, and Heidi Jauhiainen. 2016. HeLI, a word-based backoff method for language identification. In *Proceedings of the Third Workshop on NLP for Similar Languages, Varieties and Dialects (VarDial3)*, pages 153–162, Osaka, Japan. The COLING 2016 Organizing Committee.

Tommi Jauhiainen, Marco Lui, Marcos Zampieri, Timothy Baldwin, and Krister Lindén. 2019. Automatic language identification in texts: A survey. *Journal of Artificial Intelligence Research*, 65:675–782.

Armand Joulin, Édouard Grave, Piotr Bojanowski, and Tomáš Mikolov. 2017. Bag of tricks for efficient text classification. In *Proceedings of the 15th Conference of the European Chapter of the Association for Computational Linguistics: Volume 2, Short Papers*, pages 427–431.

Nikola Ljubešić and Filip Klubička. 2014. {bs,hr,sr}WaC - web corpora of Bosnian, Croatian and Serbian. In *Proceedings of the 9th Web as Corpus Workshop (WaC-9)*, pages 29–35, Gothenburg, Sweden. Association for Computational Linguistics.

Marco Lui and Timothy Baldwin. 2012. langid. py: An off-the-shelf language identification tool. In *Proceedings of the ACL 2012 system demonstrations*, pages 25–30.

Aleksandra Miletic, Myriam Bras, Louise Esher, Jean Sibille, and Marianne Vergez-Couret. 2019. Building a treebank for Occitan: what use for Romance UD corpora? In *Proceedings of the Third Workshop on Universal Dependencies (UDW, SyntaxFest 2019)*, pages 2–11, Paris, France. Association for Computational Linguistics.

Aleksandra Miletic, Myriam Bras, Marianne Vergez-Couret, Louise Esher, Clamença Poujade, and Jean Sibille. 2020a. Building a Universal Dependencies Treebank for Occitan. In *Proceedings of The 12th Language Resources and Evaluation Conference*, pages 2932–2939, Marseille, France. European Language Resources Association.

Aleksandra Miletic, Myriam Bras, Marianne Vergez-Couret, Louise Esher, Clamença Poujade, and Jean Sibille. 2020b. A four-dialect treebank for Occitan: Building process and parsing experiments. In *Proceedings of the 7th Workshop on NLP for Similar Languages, Varieties and Dialects*, pages 140–149, Barcelona, Spain (Online). International Committee on Computational Linguistics (ICCL).

Pedro Javier Ortiz Suárez, Benoît Sagot, and Laurent Romary. 2019. Asynchronous pipelines for processing huge corpora on medium to low resource infrastructures. In *Proceedings of the Workshop on Challenges in the Management of Large Corpora (CMLC-7) 2019. Cardiff, 22nd July 2019*, pages 9 – 16, Mannheim. Leibniz-Institut für Deutsche Sprache.

Holger Schwenk, Vishrav Chaudhary, Shuo Sun, Hongyu Gong, and Francisco Guzmán. 2021. Wikimatrix: Mining 135M parallel sentences in 1620 language pairs from Wikipedia. In *Proceedings of the 16th Conference of the European Chapter of the Association for Computational Linguistics: Main Volume*, pages 1351–1361.

Jean Sibille. 2002. Ecrire l'occitan : essai de présentation et de synthèse. In *Les langues de France et leur codification. Ecrits divers – Ecrits ouverts*, Paris, France. Inalco / Association Universitaire des Langues de France, L'Harmattan.

Marianne Vergez-Couret. 2016. Description du lexique Loflòc. Research report, CLLE-ERSS.

Marianne Vergez-Couret and Assaf Urieli. 2014. Pos-tagging different varieties of Occitan with single-dialect resources. In *Proceedings of the First Workshop on Applying NLP Tools to Similar Languages, Varieties and Dialects*, pages 21–29.

Is Encoder-Decoder Transformer the Shiny Hammer?

Nat Gillin
Gillin Inc.
36 Natchez Street, Seahaven, USA
`gillin.nat@gmail.com`

Abstract

We present an approach to multi-class classification using an encoder-decoder transformer model. We trained a network to identify French varieties using the same scripts we use to train an encoder-decoder machine translation model. With some slight modification to the data preparation and inference parameters, we showed that the same tools used for machine translation can be easily re-used to achieve competitive performance for classification. On the French Dialectal Identification (FDI) task, we scored 32.4 on weighted F1, but this is far from a simple naive Bayes classifier that outperforms a neural encoder-decoder model at 41.27 weighted F1.

1 Introduction

Sometimes one might find more appealing to re-use the same code, scripts and infrastructure that already serve an NLP product for another purpose.

In this case, an eco-system of tools is already available to train machine translation models and serve the model with a RESTful API, then we need some language identification tools. Then, one might think,

> *Technically, an auto-regressive encoder-decoder model that produces a single token at inference is sort of like a classifier.*

Recent works had validated the thought (Li et al., 2018; Thant and Nwet, 2020; Hadar and Shmueli, 2021), most notably the "Don't Classify, Translate!" (DCT) idea simply re-used an encoder-decoder machine translation models as a hierarchical classifier to categorize e-commerce products.

To test the DCT model for language identification, we evaluated the approach on the French Cross-Domain Dialect Identification (FDI) dataset (Gaman et al., 2022) while participating in a Vardial shared task .[1]

[1] `https://sites.google.com/view/vardial-2022/shared-tasks`

An example of the input and output of the FDI data looks as follows:

> **`[IN]`:** *Le NE compte une importante communauté ukrainienne qui s'élève à environ 1,3 million de personnes.*
>
> **`[OUT]`:** BE

where the input text sometimes contains named-entities and they are masked with the `$NE$` token and the output is a two-char locale code to roughly represent the dialect.

2 Motivation

Our initial thought was to use the least effort in script changes to train a machine translation model to a multi-class classification one. Being frugal, the secondary objective is to ensure that we do not spend more than a day's worth of GPU hours.

Intuitively, we need the decoder to produce only one token that marks the class label, so we shouldn't be needing heavy machinery (i.e. deep layers) in the decoder. Previous works (Domhan et al., 2020; Susanto et al., 2019) have also shown that offsetting decoder layers with more encoder layers could improve inference latency. Also, when training encoder-decoder models on small datasets, deep decoder layers might be an overkill.

Therefore, we decided to re-use a "*mini*" transformer (Vaswani et al., 2017) with 6 encoder, 2 decoder layers trained with the Marian NMT toolkit (Junczys-Dowmunt et al., 2018).[2]

3 TL;DR (Experimental Setup)

We trained an encoder-decoder machine translation model using the Marian NMT framework with the following hyperparameters:

[2] Using this script from `https://github.com/alvations/myth/blob/master/train-sarah.sh`

Proceedings of the Ninth Workshop on NLP for Similar Languages, Varieties and Dialects, pages 80–85
October 16, 2022.

- **Transformer with 6 encoder, 2 decoder,**
  - 8 attention heads
  - vocabulary size of 8,000
  - embedding dimension of 1024
  - transformer feed-forward dim. of 4096
- **Adam optimizer parameters**
  - learning rate sets warm-up at 8,000
  - max learning rate set to 0.0001
  - inverse square root learning rate decay
- **Sentencepiece options**
  - character coverage was set to 100%
  - class labels were set as user-defined symbols, viz. `BE`, `CA`, `CH`, `FR` to represent *Belgian*, *Canadian*, *Swiss* and *France* French varieties.
  - the same sentencepiece vocabulary is used for the source input and target output
- **Data limit options**
  - *during training*, the maximum length of the text input were cropped to 1,000 sentencepieces
  - *during validation*, the maximum length of the text input was set to 5,000 sentencepieces
  - *at inference*, when applying it to the test set, the max length was set to 500 sentencepieces[3]
- **Other notable hyperparameters**
  - global dropout regularization was set at 0.1
  - beam size was set to 3 during inference
  - label backoff when decoder produces output that is not any of the label

The modified script with the above hyperparameter used to train the model is available on `https://github.com/alvations/myth/blob/master/train-esther.sh`. We refer to this model as `DCT mini` for the rest of the paper.

[3]~~Cos~~ Because we wanted to keep the inference time tractable in production, i.e. <300ms

3.1 How Low Can We Go?

To push the limits of the '*Don't Translate, Classify*' approach, we want to see how the smallest possible model performs on the FDI dataset. We trained a model with transformer with ***1 encoder, 1 decoder and 1 attention head***. The rest of the hyperparameters are same as the ones described Section 3 above. We refer to this model as `DCT micro` for the rest of the paper.

3.2 Non-neural Baseline

Additionally, to compare our models with a non-neural baseline, we trained a naive Bayes model similar to the ones reported in Tan et al. (2014).[4]. Sweeping through 1 to 12 character n-grams features, the best model based validated on the development is based on 6 to 10 character n-grams. We refer to this model as `Naive Bayes` for the rest of the paper.

4 Results

Systems	Micro	Macro	Weighted
`Naive Bayes`	45.82	31.19	41.27
`DCT Mini`	39.14	26.27	32.35
`DCT Micro`	34.21	19.05	24.16
NRC	**49.34**	**34.37**	**45.81**
SUKI	39.18	26.61	34.22

Table 1: F1-scores of the Systems on the FDI Test Set

Table 1 reports the F1-scores of the systems we mentioned earlier and the best systems' results of the other teams (NRC and SUKI) that participated in the shared task (Aepli et al., 2022).

The `Naive Bayes` baseline result is unsurprisingly strong and the DCT approaches were competitive but much weaker at around 10 points F1-score lower. While we expected a drop in quality, the drastic F1 score drop from `DCT Mini` to `DCT Micro` is startling. A naive probabilistic model outperforming neural models on classification task is not a novel finding (Bernier-Colborne et al., 2019) and sometimes neural models when trained inappropriately with bad hyperparameter sets do not outperform the old-school statistical/probabilistic approaches (Nat, 2016; Zhang and Duh, 2020).

[4]Using script from `https://github.com/alvations/bayesline-DSL/blob/master/dsl-2019.py`

4.1 A Naive Bayesline

We note a performance difference of the naive Bayes models between the validation and test data. In retrospect, evaluating the naive Bayes models on the test data labels, the best feature is 4 to 6 character n-grams, and it achieves the 44.98 weighted F1 score, 34.33 and 47.15 on macro and micro F1 scores. But note that picking the best model based on such oracle knowledge is unrealistic.

The difference between the model selected based on the validation results and the test gold standard reflects possibly a difference in data distribution and Ng (2016) would suggest to collect more validation data so that the difference between the validation and test set is kept to a minimum.

5 Analysis

Figure 1 and 2 presents the confusion matrices for the `DCT mini` and `DCT micro` models.

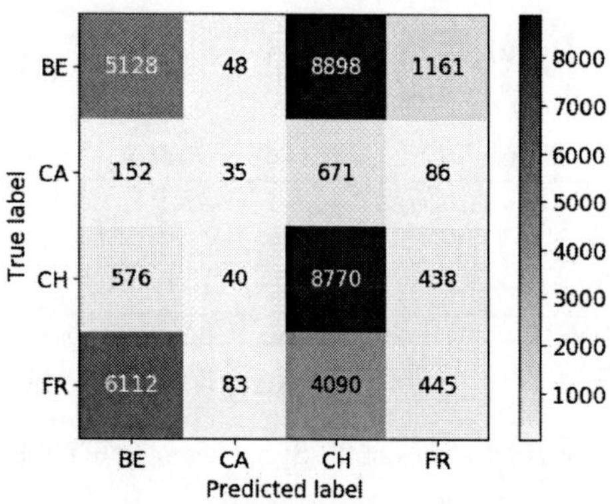

Figure 1: Confusion Matrix for `DCT mini`

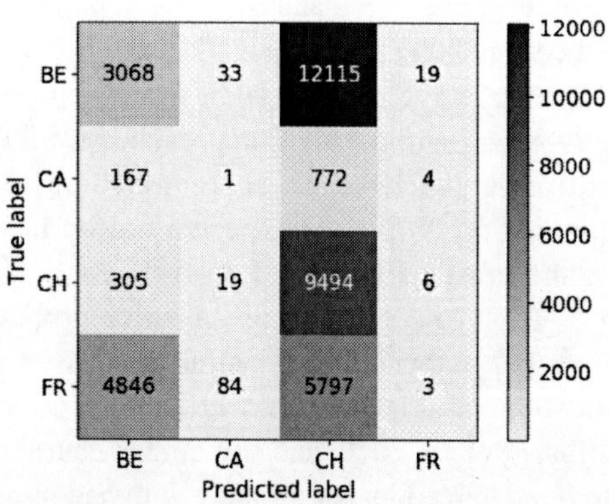

Figure 2: Confusion Matrix for `DCT micro`

For both models, we observe that the:

- `FR` label was commonly misidentified as `BE` or `CH`
- `BE` label was commonly misidentified as `CH`
- true positive rate for the `CA` label is relatively low compared to other labels

Specific to the `DCT mini` model, it has higher false positive rate when wrongly classifying `BE` as `FR` while the `DCT micro` did not present this behavior.

5.1 Label Class Distribution

One possible suspicion for the high false positives on `CH` and `FR` in the test set might be due to the training/validation label distribution. Ideally, a robust language identification should not be affected by the label class distribution of the training and validation data.

But label distribution is not the culprit here, Table 2 gives no evidence of the DCT model biasing label classes that resembles training/validation distribution. This is unlike classical classification models that requires imbalanced data.

	Training	Validation	Test	Predicted
BE	33.93	42.9	41.47	33.26
CA	9.48	0.95	2.57	0.57
CH	39.37	29.13	26.74	62.33
FR	17.22	27.02	29.21	3.85

Table 2: Label Class Distribution of the Training, Validation, Test Data and the Predicted Labels from the `DCT Mini` model.

5.2 The FDI Dataset

If you've read till now, you would have realized that we deliberately avoided in-depth exploratory data analysis before we trained discussed model training and the results. That is because we know that ***there will be issues with any dataset***, whether it is inherent bias added when collecting or cleaning the data.

Hence, our first-pass proof of concept to validate the '*Don't Classify, Translate*' approach is to trust the integrity and the quality of the data and participate in the closed shared task scenario, where only the data provided can be used to train the model.

Now that we established a baseline model (`DCT mini`), compared it to an optimized version and a non-neural baseline and explored the obvious hyperparameter optimization options. We want to dig deeper into the dataset to understand how and when our model fail.

5.3 Uncertain Labels

Unlike a typical classification model where the last layer decides the most salient class label that the input should fall into, the DCT approach has an interesting by-product where it returns an empty string or a hallucinated string.

The following examples are some of the inputs on the FDI test set that `DCT mini` produced an empty label.

- *identifiez-vous*
- *Pour aller plus loin*
- *À lire aussi*
- *Un entretien*
- *Mais que l'on peut...*

There are a total of 744 empty labels produced by `DCT mini` on 22 unique text inputs in the test sets. It is worth noting *identifiez-vous* was repeated 714 times in the test set and *Pour aller plus loin* repeated 9 times.

These are 3 data points in the test set that produced hallucinating string as a label, the first *? ? ? ? ? ?* input appeared 8 times in the test data and the other are singleton occurrences.

- *? ? ? ? ? ?*
- *Quel est le seuil minimum d'acceptation pour que ça fonctionne ?* +
- +

To handle the above empty and hallucination situations, we simply fallback to the `FR` labels for these instances.

Technically, we could have looked at the n-best options produced in our beam search and look for the next best output that fits one of the label. However, leaving this bug/feature as is, we can use it to identify oddities in the training and validation data to improve the data quality.

5.4 Repetition in the Test Data

Academically, it makes sense to deduplicate the test set and report accuracy or F1-scores. Unless a test set is plagued with rampant repetitions, e.g. more than 30% of the test set are made up of repeats; from a user-experience perspective, ***deduplicating do no good to reflect the actual amount of errors a user experience*** when using the tool. It is best to leave the test data as if without deduplication if it is a random sample from the natural distribution of the full dataset.

Hypothetically, if the natural distribution of the input data has certain strings that repeats frequent, a user is more likely to report the error on the language label multiple times than sporadic errors that occurs once or twice. Thus, we view the repeated instances in the test set as a valid phenomenon and provide the following statistics solely to understand which instances are would cause the most user-dissatisfaction. Such scenario is evident in Table 3 where it shows 3 unique test instances repeating more than 100 times results in 4.2% of the test data.

No. of Times Repeated	No. of Unique Instances	% of Data
1	34,292	**93.35**
2	382	2.08
3	20	0.16
4 - 10	11	0.15
22	1	0.06
> 100	3	**4.20**

Table 3: Test Data Instances with Repeated Occurrences

Table 3 presents some statistics of repeated data in the test set. Of the 36,733 instances in the test set, 34,292 of them occurred once and 382 unique instances occurred twice. There are 3 instances that repeated >100 times, we have:

- *identifiez-vous* (714 times)
- *ici pour connaître la suite. déjà abonné ? identifiez-vous* (567 times)
- *déjà abonné ? identifiez-vous* (260 times)

Repeating the same exercise on training and development/validation dataset, Table 4 and 5 raises some alarm with 10-20% of the data repeating >50 times.

No. of Times Repeated	No. of Unique Train Instances	% of Data
1	234,518	**65.36**
2	40,745	22.71
3	1,547	1.29
4	4,97	0.23
5-50	75	0.30
> 50	172	**9.83**

Table 4: Training Data Instances with Repeated Occurrences

No. of Times Repeated	No. of Unique Dev Instances	% of Data
1	12,316	**68.41**
2	426	2.37
3	246	1.37
4	764	4.24
5-50	3298	**18.32**
> 50	482	2.67

Table 5: Dev Data Instances with Repeated Occurrences

Given this knowledge of the repeated instances, the natural experiment to test is to deduplicate and/or remove the instances that >50 times and retrain the model to see if these data irregularities affected the weighted F1 performance of classification task. But that is out of scope of this report.

6 Related Work

While generic language identification seemed solved (McNamee, 2005; Lui et al., 2014; Xia et al., 2010), distinguishing language varieties which are often lower resourced remains a challenge (Fertmann et al., 2014; Tan et al., 2014; Zampieri et al., 2014, 2015). Hence, the language varieties identification task is a staple of the evaluation campaigns hosted by the VarDial workshops (Malmasi et al., 2016; Zampieri et al., 2017, 2018, 2019; Gaman et al., 2020; Chakravarthi et al., 2021). Across the many evaluation campaigns, probabilistic models like naive Bayes have often ranked top on the leaderboard (Bernier-Colborne et al., 2019; Bernier-Colborne and Goutte, 2020; Bernier-Colborne et al., 2021).

7 Conclusion

In this paper, we have described our experiments to reuse encoder-decoder transformer models as a classifier based on the "*Don't Classify, Translate*" idea. Evaluating on the French Dialect Identification (FDI) dataset, we found that a simple naive Bayes model works better than the 6 layers encoder-decoder models and a really small neural model worked even worse. And now, some concluding remarks:

> *The encoder-decoder transformer is a shiny hammer that works fairly well for many NLP/MT tasks. But note, the 'your miles may vary' (YMMV) caution. Also, as a sanity check, a simple non-neural approach is a good baseline.*

References

Noëmi Aepli, Antonios Anastasopoulos, Adrian Chifu, William Domingues, Fahim Faisal, Mihaela Găman, Radu Tudor Ionescu, and Yves Scherrer. 2022. Findings of the VarDial evaluation campaign 2022. In *Proceedings of the Ninth Workshop on NLP for Similar Languages, Varieties and Dialects*, Gyeongju, Republic of Korea. International Committee on Computational Linguistics (ICCL).

Gabriel Bernier-Colborne and Cyril Goutte. 2020. Challenges in neural language identification: Nrc at vardial 2020. In *Proceedings of the 7th Workshop on NLP for Similar Languages, Varieties and Dialects*, pages 273–282.

Gabriel Bernier-Colborne, Cyril Goutte, and Serge Léger. 2019. Improving cuneiform language identification with BERT. In *Proceedings of the Sixth Workshop on NLP for Similar Languages, Varieties and Dialects*, pages 17–25, Ann Arbor, Michigan. Association for Computational Linguistics.

Gabriel Bernier-Colborne, Serge Leger, and Cyril Goutte. 2021. N-gram and neural models for uralic language identification: NRC at VarDial 2021. In *Proceedings of the Eighth Workshop on NLP for Similar Languages, Varieties and Dialects*, pages 128–134, Kiyv, Ukraine. Association for Computational Linguistics.

Bharathi Raja Chakravarthi, Gaman Mihaela, Radu Tudor Ionescu, Heidi Jauhiainen, Tommi Jauhiainen, Krister Lindén, Nikola Ljubešić, Niko Partanen, Ruba Priyadharshini, Christoph Purschke, Eswari Rajagopal, Yves Scherrer, and Marcos Zampieri. 2021. Findings of the VarDial evaluation campaign 2021. In *Proceedings of the Eighth Workshop on NLP for Similar Languages, Varieties and Dialects*, pages 1–11, Kiyv, Ukraine. Association for Computational Linguistics.

Tobias Domhan, Michael Denkowski, David Vilar, Xing Niu, Felix Hieber, and Kenneth Heafield. 2020. The sockeye 2 neural machine translation toolkit at AMTA 2020. In *Proceedings of the 14th Conference of the Association for Machine Translation in the Americas (Volume 1: Research Track)*, pages 110–115, Virtual. Association for Machine Translation in the Americas.

Susanne Fertmann, Guy Emerson, and Liling Tan. 2014. Language identification for low-resource languages. Technical Report for NLP projects for low-resource languages. Saarland, Germany.

Mihaela Gaman, Adrian Gabriel Chifu, William Domingues, and Radu Tudor Ionescu. 2022. FreCDo: A New Corpus for Large-Scale French Cross-Domain Dialect Identification. *(under review)*.

Mihaela Gaman, Dirk Hovy, Radu Tudor Ionescu, Heidi Jauhiainen, Tommi Jauhiainen, Krister Lindén, Nikola Ljubešić, Niko Partanen, Christoph Purschke, Yves Scherrer, and Marcos Zampieri. 2020. A report on the VarDial evaluation campaign 2020. In *Proceedings of the 7th Workshop on NLP for Similar Languages, Varieties and Dialects*, pages 1–14, Barcelona, Spain (Online). International Committee on Computational Linguistics (ICCL).

Yonatan Hadar and Erez Shmueli. 2021. Categorizing items with short and noisy descriptions using ensembled transferred embeddings. *arXiv preprint arXiv:2110.11431*.

Marcin Junczys-Dowmunt, Roman Grundkiewicz, Tomasz Dwojak, Hieu Hoang, Kenneth Heafield, Tom Neckermann, Frank Seide, Ulrich Germann, Alham Fikri Aji, Nikolay Bogoychev, André F. T. Martins, and Alexandra Birch. 2018. Marian: Fast neural machine translation in C++. In *Proceedings of ACL 2018, System Demonstrations*, pages 116–121, Melbourne, Australia. Association for Computational Linguistics.

Maggie Yundi Li, Stanley Kok, and Liling Tan. 2018. Don't classify, translate: Multi-level e-commerce product categorization via machine translation.

Marco Lui, Jey Han Lau, and Timothy Baldwin. 2014. Automatic detection and language identification of multilingual documents. *Transactions of the Association for Computational Linguistics*, 2:27–40.

Shervin Malmasi, Marcos Zampieri, Nikola Ljubešić, Preslav Nakov, Ahmed Ali, and Jörg Tiedemann. 2016. Discriminating between similar languages and Arabic dialect identification: A report on the third DSL shared task. In *Proceedings of the Third Workshop on NLP for Similar Languages, Varieties and Dialects (VarDial3)*, pages 1–14, Osaka, Japan. The COLING 2016 Organizing Committee.

Paul McNamee. 2005. Language identification: A solved problem suitable for undergraduate instruction. *J. Comput. Sci. Coll.*, 20(3):94–101.

Gillin Nat. 2016. Sensible at SemEval-2016 task 11: Neural nonsense mangled in ensemble mess. In *Proceedings of the 10th International Workshop on Semantic Evaluation (SemEval-2016)*, pages 963–968, San Diego, California. Association for Computational Linguistics.

Andrew Ng. 2016. Nuts and bolts of applying deep learning.

Raymond Hendy Susanto, Ohnmar Htun, and Liling Tan. 2019. Sarah's participation in WAT 2019. In *Proceedings of the 6th Workshop on Asian Translation*, pages 152–158, Hong Kong, China. Association for Computational Linguistics.

Liling Tan, Marcos Zampieri, and Jörg Tiedemann. 2014. Merging comparable data sources for the discrimination of similar languages: The dsl corpus collection. In *In Proceedings of The 7th Workshop on Building and Using Comparable Corpora (BUCC*.

Khin Yee Mon Thant and Khin Thandar Nwet. 2020. Comparison of supervised machine learning models for categorizing e-commerce product titles in myanmar text. In *2020 International Conference on Advanced Information Technologies (ICAIT)*, pages 194–199. IEEE.

Ashish Vaswani, Noam Shazeer, Niki Parmar, Jakob Uszkoreit, Llion Jones, Aidan N. Gomez, Łukasz Kaiser, and Illia Polosukhin. 2017. Attention is all you need. In *Proceedings of the 31st International Conference on Neural Information Processing Systems*, NIPS'17, page 6000–6010, Red Hook, NY, USA. Curran Associates Inc.

Fei Xia, Carrie Lewis, and William D. Lewis. 2010. The problems of language identification within hugely multilingual data sets. In *Proceedings of the Seventh International Conference on Language Resources and Evaluation (LREC'10)*, Valletta, Malta. European Language Resources Association (ELRA).

Marcos Zampieri, Shervin Malmasi, Nikola Ljubešić, Preslav Nakov, Ahmed Ali, Jörg Tiedemann, Yves Scherrer, and Noëmi Aepli. 2017. Findings of the VarDial evaluation campaign 2017. In *Proceedings of the Fourth Workshop on NLP for Similar Languages, Varieties and Dialects (VarDial)*, pages 1–15, Valencia, Spain. Association for Computational Linguistics.

Marcos Zampieri, Shervin Malmasi, Preslav Nakov, Ahmed Ali, Suwon Shon, James Glass, Yves Scherrer, Tanja Samardžić, Nikola Ljubešić, Jörg Tiedemann, Chris van der Lee, Stefan Grondelaers, Nelleke Oostdijk, Dirk Speelman, Antal van den Bosch, Ritesh Kumar, Bornini Lahiri, and Mayank Jain. 2018. Language identification and morphosyntactic tagging: The second VarDial evaluation campaign. In *Proceedings of the Fifth Workshop on NLP for Similar Languages, Varieties and Dialects (VarDial 2018)*, pages 1–17, Santa Fe, New Mexico, USA. Association for Computational Linguistics.

Marcos Zampieri, Shervin Malmasi, Yves Scherrer, Tanja Samardžić, Francis Tyers, Miikka Silfverberg, Natalia Klyueva, Tung-Le Pan, Chu-Ren Huang, Radu Tudor Ionescu, Andrei M. Butnaru, and Tommi Jauhiainen. 2019. A report on the third VarDial evaluation campaign. In *Proceedings of the Sixth Workshop on NLP for Similar Languages, Varieties and Dialects*, pages 1–16, Ann Arbor, Michigan. Association for Computational Linguistics.

Marcos Zampieri, Liling Tan, Nikola Ljubešić, and Jörg Tiedemann. 2014. A report on the DSL shared task 2014. In *Proceedings of the First Workshop on Applying NLP Tools to Similar Languages, Varieties and Dialects*, pages 58–67, Dublin, Ireland. Association for Computational Linguistics and Dublin City University.

Marcos Zampieri, Liling Tan, Nikola Ljubešić, Jörg Tiedemann, and Preslav Nakov. 2015. Overview of the DSL shared task 2015. In *Proceedings of the Joint Workshop on Language Technology for Closely Related Languages, Varieties and Dialects*, pages 1–9, Hissar, Bulgaria. Association for Computational Linguistics.

Xuan Zhang and Kevin Duh. 2020. Reproducible and efficient benchmarks for hyperparameter optimization of neural machine translation systems. *Transactions of the Association for Computational Linguistics*, 8:393–408.

The Curious Case of Logistic Regression for Italian Languages and Dialects Identification

Giacomo Camposampiero, **Quynh Anh Nguyen**, and **Francesco Di Stefano**
ETH Zürich University of Milan
{gcamposampie, fdistefano, quynguyen}@student.ethz.ch

Abstract

Automatic Language Identification represents an important task for improving many real-world applications such as opinion mining and machine translation. In the case of closely-related languages such as regional dialects, this task is often challenging. In this paper, we propose an extensive evaluation of different approaches for the identification of Italian dialects and languages, spanning from classical machine learning models to more complex neural architectures and state-of-the-art pre-trained language models. Surprisingly, shallow machine learning models managed to outperform huge pre-trained language models in this specific task. This work was developed in the context of the Identification of Languages and Dialects of Italy (ITDI) task organized at VarDial 2022 Evaluation Campaign. Our best submission managed to achieve a weighted F_1-score of 0.6880, ranking 5th out of 9 final submissions.

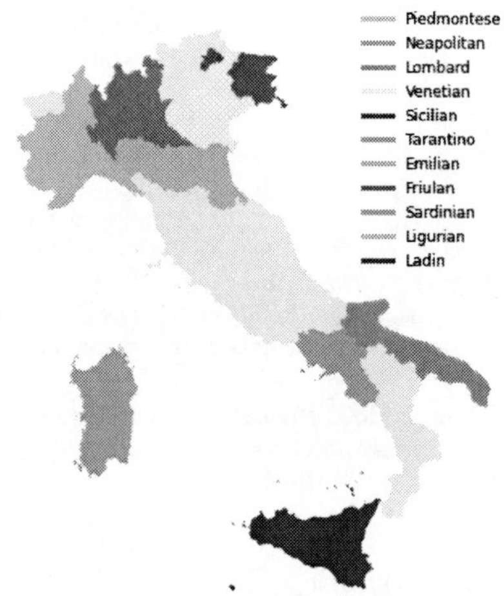

Figure 1: Geographical origin of the Italian dialects and languages studied in the shared task.[1]

1 Introduction

Dialect classification represents a key task in the improvement of many other downstream tasks such as opinion mining and machine translation, where the enrichment of text with geographical information can potentially result in improved performances for real-world applications (Zampieri et al., 2020).

As a result, the interest in the study of language variation has been steadily growing in the last few years, as highlighted by the increasing number of publications and events related to the topic (Zampieri et al., 2014, 2015; Malmasi et al., 2016; Zampieri et al., 2017, 2018, 2019; Gaman et al., 2020; Chakravarthi et al., 2021). However, little has been done so far by researchers in the context of automatic dialect and language recognition for the Italian language.

In this context, the Identification of Languages and Dialects of Italy (ITDI) task of VarDial 2022 Evaluation Campaign (Aepli et al., 2022) aims to bridge this gap, facilitating the development of models capable of properly classifying 11 regional languages and dialects from Italy's mainland and islands. Figure 1 shows the geographical origin of these different dialects and languages.

In this paper, we present the results of an extensive evaluation of three different approaches for the automatic identification of the given dialects. After an introductory literature review (§2), we proceed with a more in-depth discussion on the details of the ITDI task and the dataset provided by the organizers (§3). Then, we introduce the proposed architectures (§4) and the experimental results for each one of them (§5). We also provide some additional analysis of the models on classification errors and feature space visualization (§6). Finally, we include some concluding remarks on the shared tasks and possible limitations and routes for improvement of our work (§7).

Equal contribution.

[1] For a more complete and accurate map, refer to https://en.wikipedia.org/wiki/Languages_of_Italy.

Proceedings of the Ninth Workshop on NLP for Similar Languages, Varieties and Dialects, pages 86–98
October 16, 2022.

2 Related Works

Dialect identification represents a well-known task in the literature, for which the first contributions can be traced back to more than fifty years ago (Mustonen, 1965). An extensive and complete review of the field can be found in (Jauhiainen et al., 2019). However, language identification still represents a non-trivial task in the case of closely-related languages and dialects.

Although deep neural models nowadays yield state of the art performances in many NLP tasks, shallow machine learning models have shown to be still highly competitive in discriminating between similar languages. Some examples are Linear SVM and Naïve Bayes classifiers (Ceolin, 2021; Çöltekin, 2020) and Logistic Regression (Bhargava et al., 2015; Ács et al., 2015).

Also the use of Convolutional Neural Networks is still popular in this type of task. In particular, CNN-based approaches achieved competitive results in both VarDial 2019 Evaluation Campaign (Tudoreanu, 2019) and VarDial 2020 Evaluation Campaign (Rebeja and Cristea, 2020).

The introduction of transformers (Vaswani et al., 2017) has represented a breakthrough in many NLP tasks, and language identification is no exception. Models based on this architecture achieved state-of-the-art performance in many practical applications. A recent example is again VarDial 2020 Evaluation Campaign, where the use of a fine-tuned version of BERT previously trained on three publicly available Romanian corpora (Zaharia et al., 2020) reached a weighted F_1 score of 96.25% on the MOROCO dataset (Butnaru and Ionescu, 2019) in the Romanian vs Moldavian identification task.

However, the literature regarding automatic Italian languages and dialects identification is still relatively underdeveloped. Some recent work has been done to encourage the study of the diachronic evolution of Italian language and the differences between its dialects (Zugarini et al., 2020), but no prior work has focused specifically on contemporary Italian dialects identification.

3 Task and Data Description

3.1 ITDI

ITDI is one of the three tasks proposed as part of the VarDial 2022 Evaluation Campaign.

The language varieties evaluated in this task are 11, both from Northern Italy (Piedmontese, Venetian, Emilian-Romagnol, Ligurian, Friulian, Ladin, and Lombard), Southern Italy (Neapolitan and Tarantino) and Islands (Sardinian and Sicilian). In the following chapters, varieties' names will be abbreviated coherently with (Aepli et al., 2022).

This is the first edition of the task.The task is closed, therefore, participants are not allowed to use external data to train their models (except for off-the-shelf pre-trained language models).

The training dataset is provided by the organizers and consists of 265 016 selected Wikipedia articles from March 1st 2022 dumps, comprehensive of all the 11 varieties evaluated in the task. The development set consists of 6799 annotated sentences that cover only 7 out of the 11 varieties evaluated in the shared tasks (there are no development samples for Emilian, Neapolitan, Ladin, and Tarantino). The test set, on the other hand, consists of 11 090 samples, and covers only 8 out of the 11 varieties (Piedmontese, Sicilian and Sardinian are not represented). The composition of the test set was disclosed only after the end of the competition.

3.2 Data Exploration

Since the training data don't come from a well-known documented dataset, a preliminary exploration has been initially conducted to gain useful insight about them. This investigation highlighted a huge imbalance between classes as shown in Figure 2, since the 3 most represented dialects (Venetian, Piedmontese and Lombard) account for almost three quarters of the articles in the training data. On the other hand, other dialects (such as Friulian, Emilian-Romagnol, and Ligurian) are heavily under-represented.

Hence, imbalanced data seems to represent a major challenge and should be addressed during the development and evaluation of the model.

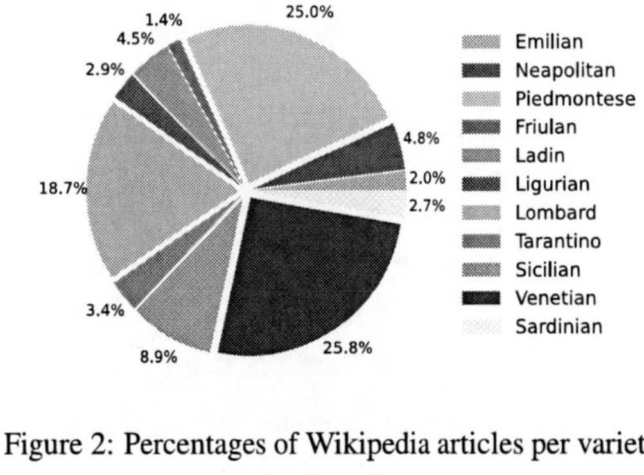

Figure 2: Percentages of Wikipedia articles per variety.

3.3 Pre-Processing of the Wikipedia Dumps

The training data is provided in the form of raw Wikipedia dumps and, as highlighted by the organizers, a careful pre-processing is an important part of the task. In this section, we describe how we extracted and cleaned samples from the raw Wikipedia dumps.

Document extraction The extraction of Wikipedia documents and an initial pre-processing step is performed using WikiExtractor (Attardi, 2015), a Python script that extracts and cleans text from Wikipedia database dumps. The use of this particular tool for extraction was suggested by the organizers of the shared task. However, a careful qualitative analysis of the resulting text samples pointed out the need for more fine-grained processing of training samples.

Document cleaning Firstly, we remove all the HTML tags (e.g.
, &, etc.) and Wikipedia meta information (e.g. contributors, timestamps and comments) that were not successfully filtered out by WikiExtractor. Then, we observe that most of the documents of length < 50 characters are not valuable samples, as they come from documents for which WikiExtractor failed to extract any text at all or from pages that contain simple and repetitive name entity definitions (e.g. small towns or years articles). Hence, we trim them from the training dataset. Moreover, we observe that the training set contains duplicate documents (e.g. Web domain pages in Venetian Wikipedia). Therefore, we remove all the duplicate documents from the dataset.

Sentence splitting Finally, since the task evaluates dialect classification at sentence level, we split all the documents into sentences using the Italian spaCy tokenizer (Honnibal and Montani, 2017). After the splitting, a further filtering is applied to the sentences to trim a huge set of almost-identical sentences from the training data (e.g. sentences about municipalities, cities or years that occur thousand of times and differ only in the entity name). Moreover, we fix some transcription mismatches between training and validation samples (e.g. Venetian Wikipedia articles use the letter "ł" to transcribe particular phonemes, which is, on the other hand, transcribed as a standard "l" in the validation samples).

Pre-processing step	# samples
Original documents	265 016
remove length < 50	244 688
remove duplicates	218 670
sentence split	698 837
sentence cleaning	382 859

Table 1: Number of training samples after each pre-processing step.

Pre-processing results The exact number of samples after each pre-processing step is shown in Table 1, while a representation of the distribution of the input sentences over all the 11 dialects can be found in Figure 3. It can be observed from the latter that the distribution of training samples is slightly more uniform compared to the initial Wikipedia document distribution. Nonetheless, the substantial class imbalance between different languages and dialects persists.

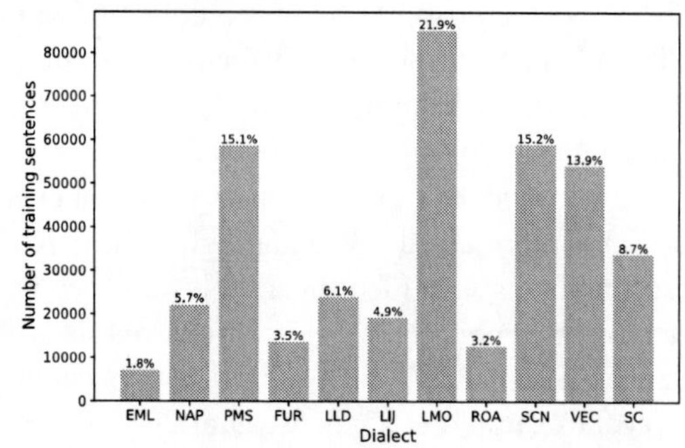

Figure 3: Number of sentences in the training set for each of the eleven dialects included in the task.

4 Methods

4.1 Linear Models

Linear models are still a widely used tool in the context of automatic language identification. We experiment with three different models, namely Linear Support Vector Machines (SVM), Naïve Bayes classifiers (NB) and Logistic Regression (LR). The models are trained on scaled word-level TF-IDF feature vectors. We also experiment with models trained on character-level n-grams TF-IDF, word-level n-grams TF-IDF, or other type of text embedding (e.g. hashing vectorizers) and scaling techniques. Dimensionality-reduction techniques to reduce the initial embedding dimensions are also investigated. All the models that we use in these experiments are off-the-shelf models from the Python library scikit-learn (Pedregosa et al., 2011).

4.2 Convolutional Neural Networks

Convolutional Neural Networks (CNN) are a powerful modular approach for text classification (Zhang et al., 2015). We implemented both word-based and character-based networks. In this section, we introduce the design of the character-level network. Besides replacing an alphabet of characters with a vocabulary of words, the word-level CNN approach is identical. The encoding is performed extracting an alphabet of size m from the training data. Each input sentence is transformed into a sequence of m-sized vectors with fixed length l_0. Any character exceeding length l_0 is ignored, and any character that is not in the alphabet, including blank characters, is encoded as an all-zero vector. In our particular dataset, the alphabet extracted from the training set consists of $m = 989$ characters. We set $l_0 = 60$ and add 0 padding if the sequence is shorter than 60 characters.

Table 7 describes in detail the CNN architecture. Both character-level and word-level networks are 3 layers deep, with 2 convolutional layers and 1 fully-connected layer. ReLU function is then used as an additional step on top of convolution. We choose max-pooling to represent features map to Pooled Feature Map, which helps reducing the number of parameters and prevent overfitting. In the fully-connected step, we combine all input features resulting from the last hidden layer to predict the classes using a softmax function.

4.3 Transformers

The use of transformer-based models has been proved effective even in the context of language identification. In particular, the fine-tuning of large pre-trained language models such as BERT (Devlin et al., 2019) yielded competitive performances in the previous iteration of VarDial Evaluation Campaign (Zaharia et al., 2020). Following this line of work, we experiment with the fine-tuning of six HuggingFace BERT models:

- AlBERTo (Polignano et al., 2019), an Italian uncased $\text{BERT}_{\text{BASE}}$ model pre-trained on Italian tweets.
- dbmdz-cased/uncased (Schweter, 2020), an Italian $\text{BERT}_{\text{BASE}}$ model pre-trained on Italian Wikipedia dump and various texts from the OPUS corpora.
- dbmdz-xxl-cased (Schweter, 2020), an Italian $\text{BERT}_{\text{LARGE}}$ model pre-trained on Italian Wikipedia dump and various texts from the OPUS corpora and OSCAR corpus.
- mrm8488-bert (Romero, 2020), a dbmdz-cased with an additional fine-tuning on Italian SQuAD for Q&A, to measure the impact of additional tuning on downstream tasks.
- multilingual $\text{BERT}_{\text{BASE}}$ (Devlin et al., 2019), pre-trained on a corpora of 102 languages.

For all the encoders, a linear classifier is added on top of the CLS token, and the resulting model is then fine-tuned for two epochs on the identification task. A non-extensive hyper-parameter tuning is performed on the best-scoring model, re-training it with both frozen and non-frozen embeddings and with variable maximum sequence length. The use of class weights to counter class imbalance, as well as different classifier layers, are also investigated.

5 Results and Discussion

5.1 Linear Models

Initially designed and implemented as baseline references, linear models ended up achieving the greatest performances among all the investigated methods. Table 2 shows the results for this category of approaches.

For conciseness, we only report validation scores for models trained on word-level TF-IDF embeddings scaled to zero mean and unit variance. Other embedding (hashing vectorization) and scaling (no scaling, robust scaling) techniques don't show any performance improvement. Projecting the original embeddings to a lower-dimensional features space with Principal Component Analysis also results in an overall performance decay.

Among the implemented models (SVM, NB and LR), LR is the one that achieves the best performance, with a F_1-micro score of 0.8957. Thus, we proceed with an extensive hyper-parameter search for this specific method.

Model	**Embedding**	**F_1-micro**
Linear SVM	tf-idf	0.8308
Naïve Bayes	tf-idf	0.8467
Logistic Regression	tf-idf	0.8957
+ SAG solver		0.9295
+ class weights		**0.9445**
LR ensemble	tf-idf	0.9424

Table 2: Linear model evaluation on the validation set.

We find that the use of SAG solver (Schmidt et al., 2017) and class weights (to counter the training set class imbalance, defined using cross-validation) further increases the validation score, reaching a final F_1-micro of 0.9445. Table 3 shows a more detailed evaluation of the model on single dialects. Finally, we implement an ensemble of LR models trained with different class weights (inversely proportional to class frequency and cross-validated) and random seeds. However, the ensemble doesn't improve the validation score.

Dialect	Precision	Recall	F_1	Support
PMS	0.95	0.99	0.97	1191
FUR	0.99	0.99	0.99	676
LIJ	0.96	0.99	0.98	617
LMO	0.92	0.93	0.92	1231
SCN	0.96	0.96	0.96	1371
VEC	0.95	0.89	0.92	1236
SC	0.93	0.85	0.89	477
acc.			0.94	6799
w. avg	0.95	0.94	0.95	6799

Table 3: Best LR model evaluation on single validation dialects. The last two rows report the overall model accuracy and weighted average of each metric.

We speculate that the great performances achieved by this method depend on the consistent linguistic variety between the evaluated Italian dialects and languages, which allows for a neat separation of the different classes in the feature space induced by TF-IDF. Moreover, an important advantage of LR model might be, surprisingly, its simplicity. The number of parameters learned by the model is relatively small ($\sim$5 million) compared to other investigated models (BERT has 110 million parameters). This might prevent the model from overfitting the training data and improve its ability to generalize to out-domain sentences.

On the other hand, the LR approach shows some intrinsic limitations that are difficult to overcome, namely the impossibility of handling out-of-vocabulary words (OOV) and the missing dialects in the validation set, which might lead to an overfit of the validation dialects.

5.2 CNN

The details of implemented models are provided in Appendix A section with the table 7. By implementing different sets of hyper-parameter, we aim to find a better model architecture and training regime for classifier tasks. Several hyper-parameters, including learning rate, dropout, kernel sizes, batch sizes, embedding size, are taken into consideration in our experiment.

Table 4 shows the classification results of two CNN models over a different number of epochs. The best performance is achieved from the CNN model tokenized at character-level trained over 20 epochs. In general, there is no significant difference between CNN char-level and word-level implementation. On the other hand, the training for the word-level implementation is remarkably more time-expensive compared to the same setting running on the CNN char-level. The computational cost difference between the two approaches might be explained by their different vocabulary size. The vocabulary size of CNN word-level models and CNN character-level models are shown in the table 7 and are respectively 989 and 788, 197 tokens.

The best CNN model achieves a F_1-micro score of 0.8605 on the validation data, showing a significant performance gap compared to linear models results mentioned in §5.1.

We identify two main reasons why Convolutional Neural Network could not perform better than other linear classifiers. Firstly, the noncompetitive result of CNN might be the consequences of how text is embedded. We encode text in character-level/word-level with different embedding sizes. However, a single character, i.e., 1-gram, is the only way to encode the text. Meanwhile, in linear models we encoded texts with different configurations, including word levels, character levels and characters within the boundary of word level. Secondly, CNN might be more complicated than classifier methods to handle our dataset. In general, a powerful model tends to treat simple problems with complicated architecture. This leads to the over-fitting issue, which indicates that our model is too complex for the problem that it is solving. Consequently, the model resulting from CNN performs poorly on the unseen data.

Encoding	Epochs	F_1-micro
char-level	5	0.8421
char-level	10	0.8555
char-level	20	**0.8605**
word-level	5	0.8299
word-level	10	0.8513

Table 4: CNN models evaluation on the validation set.

5.3 Transformers

Table 5 shows the evaluation for the 6 different pre-trained BERT (Devlin et al., 2019) investigated. In general, all models yield similar performances, fluctuating from approximately 0.87 to 0.89 of F_1-micro score, while there is a significant difference in the training time between *dbmdz-xxl-cased* and the others. However, *dbmdz-xxl-cased* achieves the best identification performance, with an F_1-micro score of 89.07%.

In the second phase, we perform a more detailed investigation on the best-scoring model built on *dbmdz-xxl-cased*. Table 8 in Appendix B shows models evaluation with several set of hyperparameters. Class weights, sequence max lengths, and freezing embeddings are investigated.

Concerning class weights, both validation weights used in LR and proportionally-inverse weight are investigated to reduce the class imbalance issue. Yet, both weights slightly decrease model performances. In particular, class weights result in a score decrease of 0.43%.

Then, we observe that freezing the CLS embeddings for the model, i.e. training only the linear classifier and not the stacked encoding layers during the fine-tuning, leads to a significant decrease in the validation score. We hypothesize that, due to the significant difference between Italian language and its dialects, BERT model cannot be used as feature extractor without an additional fine-tuning.

Finally, we observe that increasing the max length of each sentence from 50 to 70 improved the identification score. Setting a sequence's maximum length is important because it decides how much information the model can extract. However, an increased training cost is the direct drawback of this approach. Table 8 shows that the training time increased more than 35%, from 56 minutes to 76 minutes, with the same setup.

Model name	F_1-micro	Train time
AlBERTo	0.8850	0:58:01
dbmdz-cased	0.8813	0:57:33
dbmdz-xxl-cased	**0.8907**	1:45:51
dbmdz-uncased	0.8784	0:57:55
mrm8488-bert	0.8829	0:57:22
multilingual-BERT	0.8711	0:57:23

Table 5: Different pre-trained BERTs evaluation. Training times refer to a 2-epochs training on GPU, in the same settings described in Appendix C.

The visualization of CLS embeddings (described in §6.2) pushed us to further experiment with different classifiers trained on top of them. However, none of the investigated methods (MLPs, bagging and boosting) achieved noticeable improvements on the default linear classifier.

Team	Model	Accuracy	F_1-micro
SUKI	-	0.9053	0.9007
Phlyers	-	0.6817	0.6943
ETHZ	LR	0.6718	**0.6880**
	BERT	0.5759	0.5760
	LR**	0.6952	0.7058

Table 6: Final ITDI shared leaderboard.

5.4 Shared Task Results

The final results of ITDI task are shown in Table 6. In our case, the best submission ranked 5th out of 9 total submissions with an F_1-micro score of 0.6880. This submission was produced using the best LR model from §5.1, trained on both training and validation data together. However, this solution could have been further improved with a better choice of class weights. Inspired by (King and Zeng, 2001), we defined alternative weights as $w_c = \tau/\bar{y}$, where τ is the fraction of class c in the population (here supposed uniform across all the dialects), and $\bar{y}$ is the fraction in the training sample. With this choice of weights, our late submission (**, not ranked) achieved an F_1-micro of 0.7058. Predictions from the best-performing BERT model (described in §5.3) achieved an F_1-micro of 0.5760. The submission produced with the CNN was withdraw from the competition because of a minor bug in the prediction shuffling. Detailed identification scores for every class are included in Appendix D.

For all the models, a huge gap between validation and test score can be clearly observed. This discrepancy can be mainly attributed to two dialects that were not included in the validation set but were evaluated in the test, namely Tarantino and Ladin.

We speculate that Ladin, in particular, caused the greatest decay in our final score. Its low recall, together with the low accuracy registered for Venetian and Lombard, points out a degenerate behaviour of the classifier, which seems to classify most of Ladin samples as one of the other two dialects, hence lowering all the respective F_1 scores. On the other hand, Tarantino was probably intrinsically difficult to discriminate, as all the teams achieved poor performances on its identification.

6 Analysis

6.1 Error Analysis

In this section, we present a more fine-grained analysis of the incorrect predictions for our best-performing model, Logistic Regression.

Firstly, we investigate the most confounded dialects and languages on the development set. The resulting confusion matrix is reported in Figure 4. It is possible to observe how the greatest source of confusion for the models is represented by two pairs of dialect, Lombard-Venetian and Sardinian-Sicilian. In fact, 6.5% of Venetian sentences (81 sentences) are classified as Lombard, and 7.9% of Sardinian sentences (38 sentences) are labeled as Sicilian. This, together with the trade-off between the performances on the exact same two pairs of dialects (observed during the fine-tuning of the model), corroborates the hypothesis of an intrinsic difficulty in the discrimination between the two pairs of dialects. We speculate that this phenomenon might origin in a consistent number of shared lexical features, mainly due to geographical and cultural factors. Furthermore, this behaviour is observed also for CNN and BERT models (as shown in the confusion matrices included in Appendix E), confirming its model-agnostic nature.

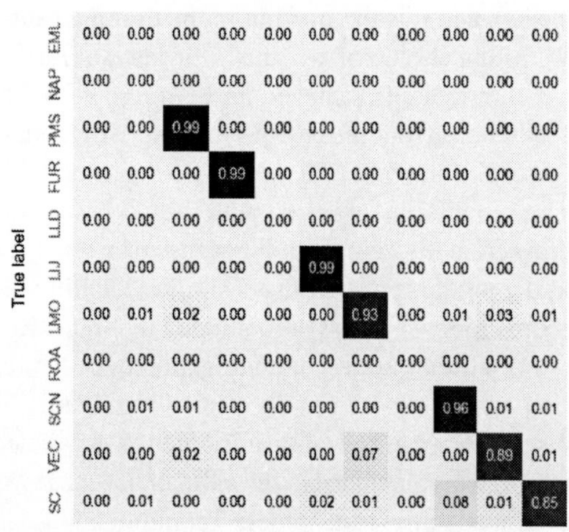

Figure 4: Confusion matrix on the development set predictions for Logistic Regression.

Finally, we leverage the simple and explainable nature of Logistic Regression to investigate which features contribute the most to wrong classifications (which will be referred to as *confounding features*).

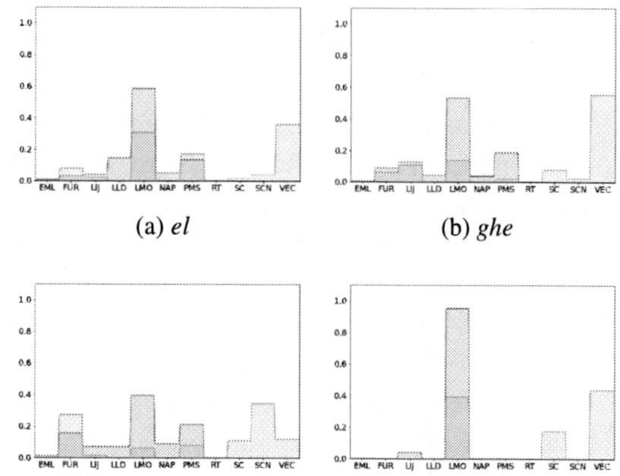

(a) *el* (b) *ghe*

(c) *lu* (d) *perché*

Figure 5: Distribution of some selected confounding features across dialects, both in the training (blue) and validation (orange) sets.

In Multinomial Logistic Regression, for each class y_k the model computes a log-odds ratio $\log p/(1-p)$ (also known as logit(p)) of the probability p that sample X belongs to class y_k as

$$\text{logit}_{y_k}(p) = \beta_{k,0} + \sum_{i=1}^{N} \beta_{k,i} X_i \quad (1)$$

where X is the input vector and β is the learned coefficients vector. Hence, the contribution ψ_k of each feature X_i to the odds that the sample X is classified as y_k equals to

$$\psi_k(X_i) = e^{\beta_i X_i} \quad (2)$$

In our analysis, we extract for each wrongly classified sample all the the confounding features with a contribution to the wrong class $\psi_{wrong} > 1.2$, that is all the features that increased the odds of the wrong class by more than 20%.

As expected, most of these features are either Italian words (for example *no*, *perché*, *non*, *con*, *chi*) or words shared between the confounded dialects (for example *cossa*, *lu*, *me*, *vegnir*). In particular, we further investigate the distribution of these words in the training and validation dataset. The result of this analysis shows a considerable discrepancy in the distributions for most of the studied features, reported for some of them in Figure 5.

We therefore speculate that the difference across in-domain and out-domain vocabulary distribution is one of the main issues that cause misclassification of the model.

6.2 Visualization

To gain additional insights on the different embedding techniques used by the investigated methods, we try to visualize their respective high-dimensional feature spaces. In particular, we exploit two well-known dimensionality-reduction techniques, Principal Component Analysis (Pearson, 1901) and t-distributed Stochastic Neighbor Embedding (t-SNE) (van der Maaten and Hinton, 2008), to obtain 2-dimensional projections of the validation embeddings.

Technique PCA is initially used to project the TF-IDF embeddings to a 1000-dimensional space (preserving 68.71% of the information). Then, t-SNE is applied to these projection to obtain a final two-dimensional visualization. The combination of PCA and t-SNE obtained slightly better visual results compared to their independent application. In the case of CNN and BERT the PCA step is omitted, as the original embeddings (linear layer input for CNN and CLS token for BERT, both extracted from fine-tuned instances of the respective best models) have already a limited number of dimensions 7728 and 768 respectively. The results of these visualizations are presented in Figure 6.

Results In TF-IDF visualization, it's possible to identify one cluster for each dialect (with the exception of Sardinian). The clusters are not well-separated when compared to BERT visualization, but this might be due to the loss of information introduced in the projection from an extremely high-dimensional space (3 orders of magnitude higher than BERT) to the 2-dimensional space.

CNN embeddings are on the other hand chaotic. It is possible to identify some clusters in the projected space, but they are not as clear as for the other two models.

The visualization for BERT embeddings is, on the other hand, particularly meaningful. The clusters for different dialects are clearly outlined. Moreover, it's interesting to observe how the most confused dialects from §6.1 (Lombard-Venetian and Sardinian-Sicilian) effectively show overlapping embeddings in the hyperspace.

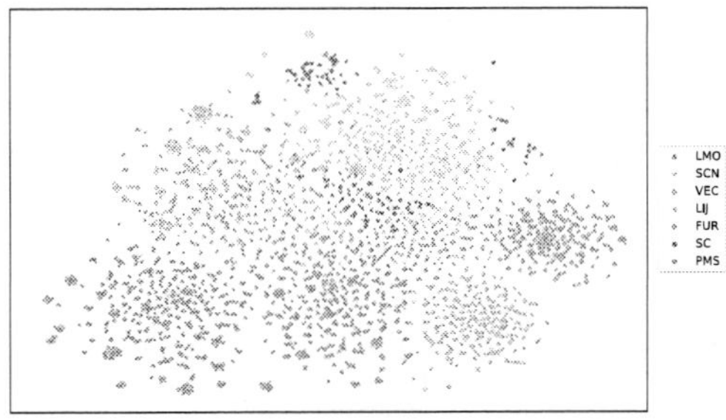

(a) TF-IDF embeddings.

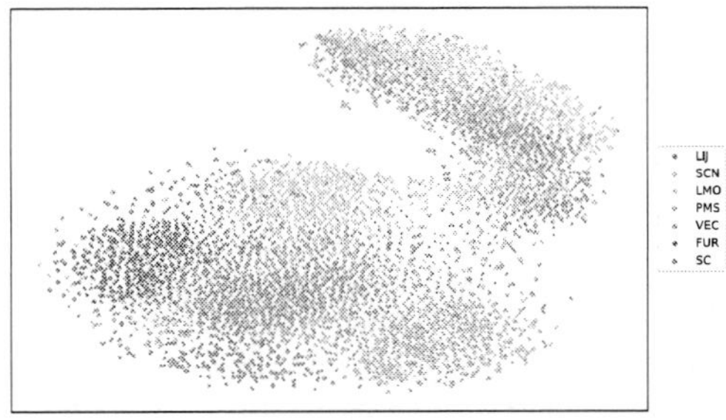

(b) CNN embeddings.

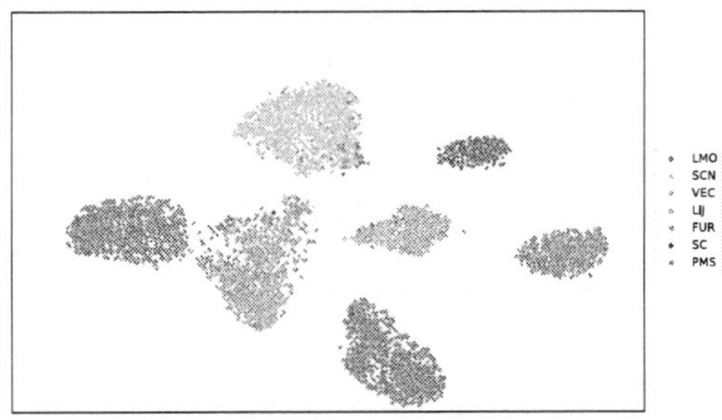

(c) BERT embeddings.

Figure 6: Visualization of the feature space for the different embedding techniques.

7 Conclusion

This paper presented the findings of our team at the Vardial 2022 ITDI shared tasks. The Logistic Regression model achieved the best results, outperforming the other two models and ranking within the top 5 submissions. Although CNN and BERT approaches have not yielded remarkable results, the experiments produced valuable insights. In particular, we observed no notable difference in the model performance of character-based and word-based CNN, of which the vast vocabulary size is more costly in terms of training time. On the other hand, BERT models performed weakly in this cross-domain language identification task, generalising less than linear models.

In the future, models' performances could be increased by calibrating different class weights on a validation set comprehensive of all the dialects and languages, and also a more extensive hyper-parameters fine-tuning for the neural models could be carried out. This could, eventually, increase the cross-domain adaptability of our models.

Acknowledgements

We would like to thanks Professor Mrinmaya Sachan, Alessandro Stolfo, and Shehzaad Dhuliawala for their precious feedback and suggestions on this work.

Additional Resources

The code from our experiments can be found on GitHub [2], while a deployed demo of our model can be found on Herokuapp [3].

References

Judit Ács, László Grad-Gyenge, and Thiago Bruno Rodrigues de Rezende Oliveira. 2015. A two-level classifier for discriminating similar languages. In *Proceedings of the Joint Workshop on Language Technology for Closely Related Languages, Varieties and Dialects*, pages 73–77, Hissar, Bulgaria. Association for Computational Linguistics.

Noëmi Aepli, Antonios Anastasopoulos, Adrian Chifu, William Domingues, Fahim Faisal, Mihaela Găman, Radu Tudor Ionescu, and Yves Scherrer. 2022. Findings of the VarDial evaluation campaign 2022. In *Proceedings of the Ninth Workshop on NLP for Similar Languages, Varieties and Dialects*, Gyeongju, Republic of Korea. International Committee on Computational Linguistics (ICCL).

Giuseppe Attardi. 2015. Wikiextractor. `https://github.com/attardi/wikiextractor`.

Rupal Bhargava, Yashvardhan Sharma, Shubham Sharma, and Abhinav Baid. 2015. Query labelling for indic languages using a hybrid approach. In *Post Proceedings of the Workshops at the 7th Forum for Information Retrieval Evaluation, Gandhinagar, India, December 4-6, 2015*, volume 1587 of *CEUR Workshop Proceedings*, pages 40–42. CEUR-WS.org.

Andrei Butnaru and Radu Tudor Ionescu. 2019. MOROCO: The Moldavian and Romanian dialectal corpus. In *Proceedings of the 57th Annual Meeting of the Association for Computational Linguistics*, pages 688–698, Florence, Italy. Association for Computational Linguistics.

Andrea Ceolin. 2021. Comparing the performance of CNNs and shallow models for language identification. In *Proceedings of the Eighth Workshop on NLP for Similar Languages, Varieties and Dialects*, pages 102–112, Kiyv, Ukraine. Association for Computational Linguistics.

Bharathi Raja Chakravarthi, Gaman Mihaela, Radu Tudor Ionescu, Heidi Jauhiainen, Tommi Jauhiainen, Krister Lindén, Nikola Ljubešić, Niko Partanen, Ruba Priyadharshini, Christoph Purschke, Eswari Rajagopal, Yves Scherrer, and Marcos Zampieri. 2021. Findings of the VarDial evaluation campaign 2021. In *Proceedings of the Eighth Workshop on NLP for Similar Languages, Varieties and Dialects*, pages 1–11, Kiyv, Ukraine. Association for Computational Linguistics.

Çağrı Çöltekin. 2020. Dialect identification under domain shift: Experiments with discriminating Romanian and Moldavian. In *Proceedings of the 7th Workshop on NLP for Similar Languages, Varieties and Dialects*, pages 186–192, Barcelona, Spain (Online). International Committee on Computational Linguistics (ICCL).

Jacob Devlin, Ming-Wei Chang, Kenton Lee, and Kristina Toutanova. 2019. BERT: Pre-training of deep bidirectional transformers for language understanding. In *Proceedings of the 2019 Conference of the North American Chapter of the Association for Computational Linguistics: Human Language Technologies, Volume 1 (Long and Short Papers)*, pages 4171–4186, Minneapolis, Minnesota. Association for Computational Linguistics.

Mihaela Gaman, Dirk Hovy, Radu Tudor Ionescu, Heidi Jauhiainen, Tommi Jauhiainen, Krister Lindén, Nikola Ljubešić, Niko Partanen, Christoph Purschke, Yves Scherrer, and Marcos Zampieri. 2020. A report on the VarDial evaluation campaign 2020. In *Proceedings of the 7th Workshop on NLP for Similar Languages, Varieties and Dialects*, pages 1–14, Barcelona, Spain (Online). International Committee on Computational Linguistics (ICCL).

Matthew Honnibal and Ines Montani. 2017. spaCy 2: Natural language understanding with Bloom embeddings, convolutional neural networks and incremental parsing. To appear.

Tommi Jauhiainen, Marco Lui, Marcos Zampieri, Timothy Baldwin, and Krister Lindén. 2019. Automatic language identification in texts: A survey. *J. Artif. Int. Res.*, 65(1):675–682.

Gary King and Langche Zeng. 2001. Logistic regression in rare events data. *Political Analysis*, 9:137–163.

Shervin Malmasi, Marcos Zampieri, Nikola Ljubešić, Preslav Nakov, Ahmed Ali, and Jörg Tiedemann. 2016. Discriminating between similar languages and Arabic dialect identification: A report on the third DSL shared task. In *Proceedings of the Third Workshop on NLP for Similar Languages, Varieties and Dialects (VarDial3)*, pages 1–14, Osaka, Japan. The COLING 2016 Organizing Committee.

Seppo Mustonen. 1965. Multiple discriminant analysis in linguistic problems. *Statistical Methods in Linguistics*, 4:37–44.

Karl Pearson. 1901. Liii. on lines and planes of closest fit to systems of points in space. *The London,*

[2]https://github.com/giacomocamposampiero/italian-dialects-identification

[3]https://itdiethz.herokuapp.com

Edinburgh, and Dublin Philosophical Magazine and Journal of Science, 2(11):559–572.

F. Pedregosa, G. Varoquaux, A. Gramfort, V. Michel, B. Thirion, O. Grisel, M. Blondel, P. Prettenhofer, R. Weiss, V. Dubourg, J. Vanderplas, A. Passos, D. Cournapeau, M. Brucher, M. Perrot, and E. Duchesnay. 2011. Scikit-learn: Machine learning in Python. *Journal of Machine Learning Research*, 12:2825–2830.

Marco Polignano, Pierpaolo Basile, Marco de Gemmis, Giovanni Semeraro, and Valerio Basile. 2019. AlBERTo: Italian BERT Language Understanding Model for NLP Challenging Tasks Based on Tweets. In *Proceedings of the Sixth Italian Conference on Computational Linguistics (CLiC-it 2019)*, volume 2481. CEUR.

Petru Rebeja and Dan Cristea. 2020. A dual-encoding system for dialect classification. In *VARDIAL*.

Manuel Romero. 2020. Italian bert fine-tuned on squad.

Mark Schmidt, Nicolas Le Roux, and Francis Bach. 2017. Minimizing finite sums with the stochastic average gradient. *Mathematical Programming*, 162(1):83–112.

Stefan Schweter. 2020. Italian bert and electra models.

Diana Tudoreanu. 2019. DTeam @ VarDial 2019: Ensemble based on skip-gram and triplet loss neural networks for Moldavian vs. Romanian cross-dialect topic identification. In *Proceedings of the Sixth Workshop on NLP for Similar Languages, Varieties and Dialects*, pages 202–208, Ann Arbor, Michigan. Association for Computational Linguistics.

Laurens van der Maaten and Geoffrey Hinton. 2008. Visualizing data using t-sne. *Journal of Machine Learning Research*, 9(86):2579–2605.

Ashish Vaswani, Noam Shazeer, Niki Parmar, Jakob Uszkoreit, Llion Jones, Aidan N Gomez, Ł ukasz Kaiser, and Illia Polosukhin. 2017. Attention is all you need. In *Advances in Neural Information Processing Systems*, volume 30. Curran Associates, Inc.

George-Eduard Zaharia, Andrei-Marius Avram, Dumitru-Clementin Cercel, and Traian Rebedea. 2020. Exploring the power of Romanian BERT for dialect identification. In *Proceedings of the 7th Workshop on NLP for Similar Languages, Varieties and Dialects*, pages 232–241, Barcelona, Spain (Online). International Committee on Computational Linguistics (ICCL).

Marcos Zampieri, Shervin Malmasi, Nikola Ljubešić, Preslav Nakov, Ahmed Ali, Jörg Tiedemann, Yves Scherrer, and Noëmi Aepli. 2017. Findings of the VarDial evaluation campaign 2017. In *Proceedings of the Fourth Workshop on NLP for Similar Languages, Varieties and Dialects (VarDial)*, pages 1–15, Valencia, Spain. Association for Computational Linguistics.

Marcos Zampieri, Shervin Malmasi, Preslav Nakov, Ahmed Ali, Suwon Shon, James Glass, Yves Scherrer, Tanja Samardžić, Nikola Ljubešić, Jörg Tiedemann, Chris van der Lee, Stefan Grondelaers, Nelleke Oostdijk, Dirk Speelman, Antal van den Bosch, Ritesh Kumar, Bornini Lahiri, and Mayank Jain. 2018. Language identification and morphosyntactic tagging: The second VarDial evaluation campaign. In *Proceedings of the Fifth Workshop on NLP for Similar Languages, Varieties and Dialects (VarDial 2018)*, pages 1–17, Santa Fe, New Mexico, USA. Association for Computational Linguistics.

Marcos Zampieri, Shervin Malmasi, Yves Scherrer, Tanja Samardžić, Francis Tyers, Miikka Silfverberg, Natalia Klyueva, Tung-Le Pan, Chu-Ren Huang, Radu Tudor Ionescu, Andrei M. Butnaru, and Tommi Jauhiainen. 2019. A report on the third VarDial evaluation campaign. In *Proceedings of the Sixth Workshop on NLP for Similar Languages, Varieties and Dialects*, pages 1–16, Ann Arbor, Michigan. Association for Computational Linguistics.

Marcos Zampieri, Preslav Nakov, and Yves Scherrer. 2020. Natural language processing for similar languages, varieties, and dialects: A survey. *Natural Language Engineering*, 26(6):595–612.

Marcos Zampieri, Liling Tan, Nikola Ljubešić, and Jörg Tiedemann. 2014. A report on the DSL shared task 2014. In *Proceedings of the First Workshop on Applying NLP Tools to Similar Languages, Varieties and Dialects*, pages 58–67, Dublin, Ireland. Association for Computational Linguistics and Dublin City University.

Marcos Zampieri, Liling Tan, Nikola Ljubešić, Jörg Tiedemann, and Preslav Nakov. 2015. Overview of the DSL shared task 2015. In *Proceedings of the Joint Workshop on Language Technology for Closely Related Languages, Varieties and Dialects*, pages 1–9, Hissar, Bulgaria. Association for Computational Linguistics.

Xiang Zhang, Junbo Zhao, and Yann LeCun. 2015. Character-level convolutional networks for text classification.

Andrea Zugarini, Matteo Tiezzi, and Marco Maggini. 2020. Vulgaris: Analysis of a corpus for middle-age varieties of italian language. *CoRR*, abs/2010.05993.

Appendix A CNN Model Summary

In this Appendix section, we provide a more detailed insight on the CNN model structure. Table 7 reports the summary of both character-level and word-level networks.

Tokenization	CNN Model Summary
Character level	(embeddings): Embedding(989, 512) (conv2d): Conv2d(1, 16, kernel_size=(3, 3), stride=(2, 1), padding=(1, 0)) (max_pool2d): MaxPool2d(kernel_size=(6, 12), stride=(2, 1), padding=(1, 0), dilation=1, ceil_mode=False) (conv2d_2): Conv2d(16, 16, kernel_size=(6, 6), stride=(2, 1), padding=(1, 0)) (max_pool2d_2): MaxPool2d(kernel_size=(6, 12), stride=(2, 1), padding=(1, 0), dilation=1, ceil_mode=False) (linear): Linear(in_features=7728, out_features=12, bias=True)
Word level	(embeddings): Embedding(788197, 512) (conv2d): Conv2d(1, 16, kernel_size=(3, 3), stride=(2, 1), padding=(1, 0)) (max_pool2d): MaxPool2d(kernel_size=(6, 12), stride=(2, 1), padding=(1, 0), dilation=1, ceil_mode=False) (conv2d_2): Conv2d(16, 16, kernel_size=(6, 6), stride=(2, 1), padding=(1, 0)) (max_pool2d_2): MaxPool2d(kernel_size=(6, 12), stride=(2, 1), padding=(1, 0), dilation=1, ceil_mode=False) (linear): Linear(in_features=7728, out_features=12, bias=True)

Table 7: CNN Model Summary

Appendix B Evaluation of BERT dbmdz-xxl-cased

In this Appendix section, we provide the evaluation results for the best-scoring BERT model, dbmdz-xxl-case, with several set of hyper-parameters. Results are shown in Table 8.

Weights	Embedding	Max length	F_1-micro	Training time
No weights	trainable	50	0.8907	1:45:51
LogReg cross-validated weights	frozen	50	0.2023	0:17:00
LogReg cross-validated weights	trainable	50	0.8866	0:56:00
LogReg cross-validated weights	trainable	70	**0.8931**	1:16:47
Inverse weights	trainable	50	0.8907	0:55:59

Table 8: Experiments with dbmdz-xxl-cased BERT

Appendix C Run-time Efficiency

In this Appendix section, we present a simple evaluation on the profiled run-time efficiency of the proposed models. The Logistic Regression model is trained locally on CPU (with 8 concurrent workers), with an Apple M1 @ 3.2 GHz and 16GB memory. On the other hand, the neural models (CNN and BERT) were trained on Google Colab Nvidia K80 @ 0.82GHz and 12GB memory. The training for LR required 73s, extremely less than to 2-epochs BERT (6351s) and 20-epochs CNN (6480s).

The inference times were elapsed from models loaded in Google Colab, with a Intel(R) Xeon(R) CPU @ 2.20GHz and 13GB of memory. Inference on the test set (11087 samples) took 0.45s for LR, 1.37s for CNN and 11.87s for BERT.

Appendix D Shared Task Submission Results in Detail

In this Appendix section, we report the detail test evaluation results for Logistic Regression (Table 9), improved Logistic Regression (Table 10) and BERT (Table 11) submissions.

Dialect	Precision	Recall	F_1-micro	Support
EML	0.9721	0.7176	0.8257	825
FUR	0.942	0.969	0.9553	1323
LIJ	0.9226	0.8203	0.8685	2282
LLD	0.9362	0.26	0.407	2200
LMO	0.5365	0.9608	0.6885	689
NAP	0.8758	0.7034	0.7802	2026
TAR	0.6047	0.1725	0.2684	603
VEC	0.377	0.8244	0.5174	1139
weighted average	0.8254	0.6718	0.6880	11087

Table 9: LR test results for single languages and dialects.

Dial.	Prec.	Rec.	F_1-micro	Supp.
EML	0.9455	0.7782	0.8537	825
FUR	0.8945	0.9743	0.9327	1323
LIJ	0.8569	0.8554	0.8561	2282
LLD	0.9312	0.3568	0.5159	2200
LMO	0.4687	0.9681	0.6316	689
NAP	0.8364	0.7621	0.7975	2026
TAR	0.4833	0.1924	0.2752	603
VEC	0.4313	0.6260	0.5107	1139
w. avg	0.7908	0.6952	0.7058	11087

Table 10: Improved LR test results for single languages and dialects.

Dial.	Prec.	Rec.	F_1-micro	Supp.
EML	0.9489	0.7661	0.8478	825
FUR	0.9542	0.9448	0.9495	1323
LIJ	0.9081	0.7533	0.8235	2282
LLD	0.9727	0.0486	0.0926	2200
LMO	0.5833	0.9753	0.7300	689
NAP	0.8830	0.4654	0.6096	2026
TAR	0.7455	0.0680	0.1246	603
VEC	0.3176	0.8964	0.4690	1139
w. avg	0.8352	0.5759	0.576	11087

Table 11: Improved LR test results for single languages and dialects (late submission, not ranked).

Appendix E Confusion Matrices for CNN and BERT Models.

In this Appendix section, we include the confusion matrices for CNN and BERT predictions on the development set (Figure 7).

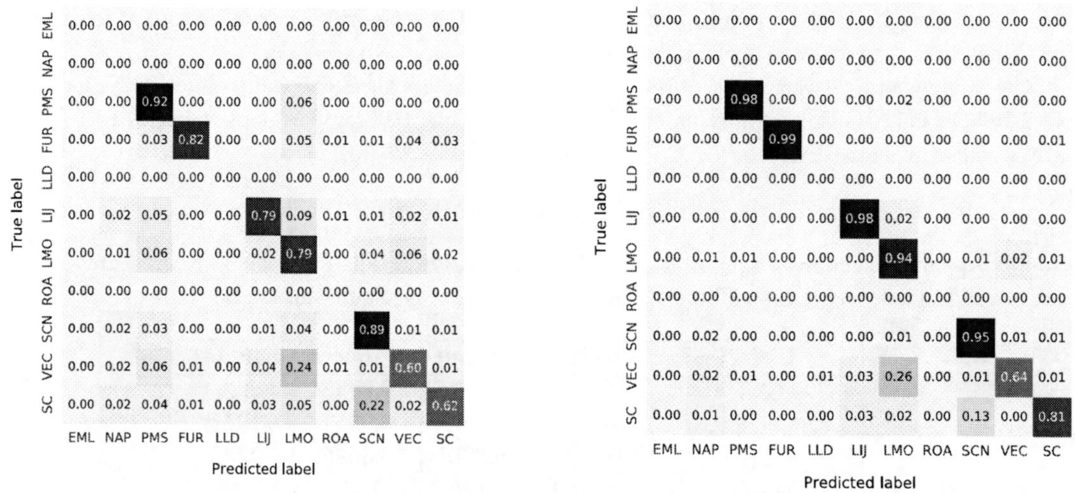

Figure 7: CNN (left) and BERT (right) confusion matrices.

Neural Networks for Cross-domain Language Identification. Phlyers @Vardial 2022

Andrea Ceolin
Università di Modena e Reggio Emilia
ceolin@unimore.it

Abstract

We present our contribution to the Identification of Languages and Dialects of Italy shared task (ITDI) proposed in the VarDial Evaluation Campaign 2022 (Aepli et al., 2022), which asked participants to automatically identify the language of a text associated to one of the language varieties of Italy. The method that yielded the best results in our experiments was a Deep Feedforward Neural Network (DNN) trained on character ngram counts, which provided a better performance compared to Naïve Bayes methods and Convolutional Neural Networks (CNN). The system was among the best methods proposed for the ITDI shared task. The analysis of the results suggests that simple DNNs could be more efficient than CNNs to perform language identification of close varieties.

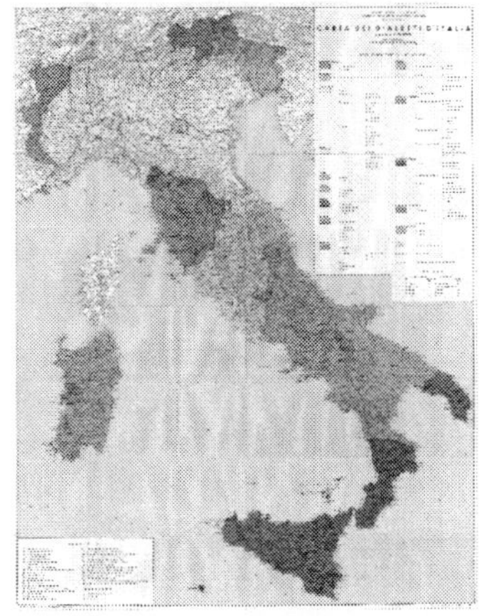

Figure 1: A map of the language varieties of Italy, from Pellegrini (1977).

1 Introduction

In this paper, we present the submissions of Team Phlyers to the Identification of Languages and Dialects of Italy (ITDI) shared task of the VarDial Evaluation Campaign 2022 (Aepli et al., 2022). The campaign is part of a conference series, the Workshop on NLP for Similar Languages, Varieties and Dialects (VarDial), which has reached its ninth edition, six of which have included several shared tasks (Zampieri et al., 2017, 2018, 2019; Găman et al., 2020; Chakravarthi et al., 2021; Aepli et al., 2022). The shared tasks involve the categorization of text documents according to their language variety, typically across different domains. Language identification has received attention in the literature because it is important in the context of machine translation and categorization of social media posts, and several approaches to perform it have been proposed (House and Neuburg, 1977; Dunning, 1994; Bergsma et al., 2012; Lui and Baldwin, 2014; Zubiaga et al., 2016; Jauhiainen et al., 2019c). Most of the VarDial shared tasks invite participants to develop language identification systems in contexts characterized by minimal diversification of the languages involved and low-resource settings, often with lack of data for the domain of interest.

In the next sections, we briefly describe our submissions for the ITDI shared task.[1]

2 ITDI

The ITDI task involves the classification of sentences from eleven different language varieties from Italy. Five of these varieties - Piedmontese (pms), Lombard (lmo), Ligurian (lij), Emilian-Romagnol (eml), Venetian (vec) - are part of a Northern group composed of Gallo-Italic and Venetan varieties; they are represented in yellow in the *Carta dei Dialetti Italiani*, the reference map drawn by Pellegrini (1977) using a set of isoglosses that define the boundaries of certain morpho-phonological properties. Two of the varieties, Neapolitan (nap) and Tarantino (roa-tara), are part of the Southern group, in pink. Sicilian (scn)

[1] The material developed for this work is available at https://github.com/AndreaCeolin/VarDial2022.

Proceedings of the Ninth Workshop on NLP for Similar Languages, Varieties and Dialects, pages 99–108
October 16, 2022. ©2022 Association for Computational Linguistics

is the only representative of the Extreme Southern group, in purple. Friulian (fur) and Ladin (lld) are part of the Northeastern Rhaeto-Romance group, although Pellegrini keeps them separate (in orange and dark green). Finally, Sardinian (sc) is represented in brown.

Training data is provided in the form of Wikipedia dumps containing a total of 233K sentences, while evaluation data is provided in the form of approximately 7K short sentences for seven out of the eleven languages. The test set contains sentences from a subset of the given language varieties, and the classifier is evaluated on sentence level.

An inspection of the development data clearly shows that the sentences are not taken from Wikipedia articles, but from other sources, like literary texts or folktales (see Table 1 for some examples). The sentences in the test dataset also appear to be clearly different from the kind of sentences one expects to find in Wikipedia articles, and we assume that they were taken from domains similar to those used to collect the development sentences.

The fact that the training and validation/testing data come from different domains implies that the task is essentially a cross-domain classification task.

3 Methods

The state-of-the-art methods for language identification are typically inspired by Support Vector Machines (SVM) models (Goutte et al., 2014; Çöltekin and Rama, 2017; Medvedeva et al., 2017; Kreutz and Daelemans, 2018; Benites de Azevedo e Souza et al., 2018; Wu et al., 2019; Çöltekin, 2020) and multinomial Naïve Bayes (NB) models (Barbaresi, 2016; Clematide and Makarov, 2017; Jauhiainen et al., 2019a, 2020; Ceolin and Zhang, 2020; Jauhiainen et al., 2021b), that are trained on features derived from word and character ngrams.

Deep learning methods have also been successfully applied to language identification tasks (Cianflone and Kosseim, 2016; Jaech et al., 2016; Butnaru and Ionescu, 2019; Hu et al., 2019; Tudoreanu, 2019), and in particular several of the most recent VarDial shared tasks have been addressed using transformer models (Bernier-Colborne et al., 2019; Popa and Stefănescu, 2020; Scherrer and Ljubešić, 2020; Zaharia et al., 2020; Jauhiainen et al., 2021b; Zaharia et al., 2021).

While last year we decided to use Convolutional Neural Networks (CNNs) to address the shared tasks (Ceolin, 2021), this year we decided to focus on Deep Feedforward Neural Networks (DNNs), since they represent an alternative approach to language identification.

The reason for this shift of focus is that while CNNs have been the most popular neural architecture used for language identification (Zhang et al., 2015; Conneau et al., 2016; Kim et al., 2016; Jaech et al., 2016), following their success in tasks like image classification and sequence processing, language identification is quite different from such tasks.

While in domains like image classification and sequence processing hard-coding features is not straightforward, in language identification the cues for discriminating among classes are usually words or orthographic/morpheme sequences, which can be directly extracted and used as input features for a simple DNN in the form of word and character ngrams of different size. A CNN instead performs feature extraction indirectly, using fixed-size filters applied to input sequences that have to be of the same length (which is rarely the case for texts), and therefore is less flexible.[2]

For these reasons, comparing these two different approaches can be informative to decide whether CNNs provide any advantage over regular DNNs for language identification.

3.1 DNN

The DNN we used has two hidden layers of size 50, and is trained on a term-frequency matrix of 20K character ngrams in the window [1-5] derived from the training sentences.[3] The DNN is trained with a learning rate of 0.0001 and a batch size of 4 for 20 epochs. The number of parameters is ≈1M. The hyper-parameters and the size of the network were manually selected based on the performance on the evaluation set across different runs. The architecture is visualized in Figure 2.

3.2 CNN

The CNN has two 1-D convolutional layers, one with 256 filters and one with 128 filters, both of size 3 with stride 1, each followed by a max pool layer

[2] Google's LID system, CLD3 (https://github.com/google/cld3), also uses a DNN trained on character ngrams rather than a CNN.

[3] The term-frequency matrix has been extracted using the CountVectorizer method in *sklearn*.

Dataset	Label	Text	Source
train	vec	El Yucatán el ze uno dei 31 Stati del Mèsego, situà inte el sud-est del teritòrio, inte ła parte nord de l'omònema penìzoła. El confina verso nord col Golfo del Mèsego, verso est col Stato de Quintana Roo e verso sud-òvest col Stato de Campeche.	vec.wikipedia.org, "Yucatán"
train	scn	Heaven For Everyone è na canzuni scritta ra Roger Taylor e pubbricatu nto 1988 da li The Cross comu singulu trattu ra l'album Shove It, ru stissu annu.	scn.wikipedia.org, "Heaven For Everyone"
dev	vec	Da seno a mi me par Che no ghe sia rason de barufar	Iliad (version by Luigi de Giorgi)
dev	scn	e Mirimì chi aiutava nnâ mandria na picuredda a fighiari, lassau l'opira a mezzu e si misi a curriri chî manu ntê capiddi, non sapennu chi fari	Storia di Pietracucca (Francesco Lanza)

Table 1: Example sentences from the training and evaluation data. We can see that while the training data contains Wikipedia articles which look like direct translations from other languages, the evaluation data contains sentences from other sources, like poetry or short stories.

(with a window of size 3). Then, it is followed by a fully connected layer of size 50, and is trained with a learning rate of 0.0001 and a batch size of 4 for 20 epochs. The number of parameters is ≈250K. The hyper-parameters and the size of the network were manually selected based on the performance on the evaluation set across different runs. The architecture is visualized in Figure 3. Each input sentences was truncated at 160 characters.

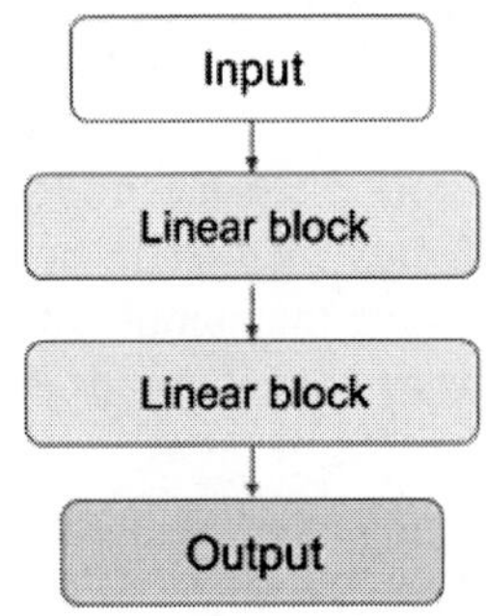

Figure 2: This is the architecture of the DNN model trained for the task. Learning rate: 0.0001, Batch: 4, Epochs: 20. Each hidden layer has size=50.

3.3 NB

We also decided to use a NB system as a baseline. The system is trained on the same term-frequency matrix of character ngrams that was used to train the DNN, with alpha=1.

All models were run on Google Colab, with 1 GPU, using the *sklearn* and *tensorflow* libraries.

4 Evaluation

This section summarizes our contributions to the ITDI shared task and the evaluation of our models.

4.1 In-domain Classification

One of the main challenges of the ITDI shared task was to find a proper way to evaluate the performance of the classifiers given that the evaluation set and the test set were not expected to contain the same languages. In a first experiment, we tried a simple in-domain classification task, using only the ≈7K sentences in the evaluation dataset for the seven languages represented in it (henceforth, 'gold' languages) divided in training/test sets using a 80:20 split. We applied minimum normalization: the text was converted to lowercase and numbers and punctuation were removed, with the exception

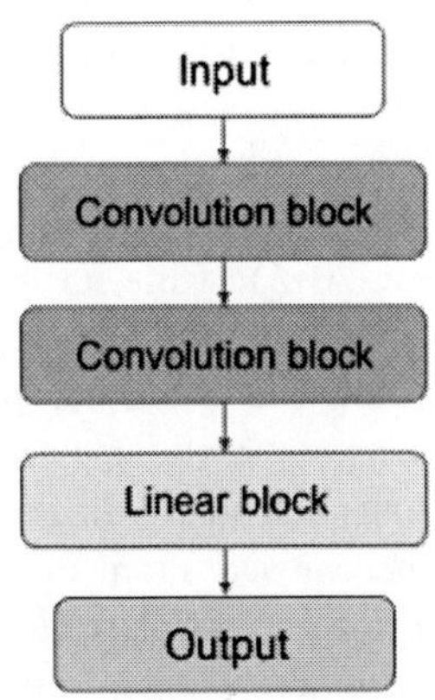

Figure 3: This is the architecture of the CNN model trained for the task. Learning rate: 0.0001, Batch: 4, Epochs: 20. The first convolutional layer has 256 filters of size 3x1, while the second one has 128 of them. Stride: 1. Each layer is followed by a max pool layer, with a window of size 3x1. The fully connected layer has size=50.

Model	Micro F_1 score	Macro F_1 score
DNN	0.994	0.994
Naïve Bayes	0.983	0.984
CNN + data aug. (10ep.)	0.982	0.983
CNN	0.977	0.978

Table 2: Performance of the models on the evaluation set, in-domain classification. The DNN is the model that yields the best performance when using the evaluation set for both training and testing.

Model	Micro F_1 score	Macro F_1 score
Naïve Bayes	0.861	0.554
DNN	0.791	0.520
CNN	0.718	0.471

Table 3: Performance of the models on the evaluation set, cross-domain classification. The Naïve Bayes system is the model that yields the best performance when using the training set for training, and the evaluation set for testing.

of "'", that in these varieties can represent elision of vowels or syllables, and thus is informative. As we can see from Table 2, all models yielded very good results, with the DNN performing best.

We also tried to improve the performance of the CNN by augmenting the training data. Two copies of each sentence were added to the training set with their words shuffled, following the strategy described in Ceolin (2021). Indeed, the strategy allows the network to reach convergence in just 10 epochs and slightly increase its accuracy.[4] Interestingly, increasing the number of parameters of the CNN or the number of epochs did not have the same effect.

These results suggest that the 'gold' languages are well distinguished, and that the amount of sentences in the evaluation set is sufficient to train a robust classifier, assuming that the sentences in the evaluation and test sets belong to the same domain.

4.2 Cross-domain Classification

The second experiment we attempted was a cross-domain classification task. For training, we used a balanced sample of 20K sentences from the 233K training sentences extracted from the Wikipedia dumps using the script recommended by the organizers (Attardi, 2015), while for testing we used the 7K evaluation sentences.[5] In this case, a heavier normalization was required, since the texts contained roman numerals, several proper names of cities/regions, and many different hyperlinks, which had to be removed. From Table 3, we can see that the performance dropped significantly, especially for the neural networks. In particular, many of the predictions (up to 10%, depending on the model and the run) contain one of the four languages which are not represented in the evaluation set (henceforth, 'silver' languages), and so the macro F_1 score is quite low.[6]

4.3 Combining Cross-domain and In-domain Classification

Since the cross-domain classification task turned out to be much harder than the in-domain task, we decided to run a third experiment that was similar to the first one, which relied on the evaluation set for both training and testing. However, after dividing the evaluation set into training/testing sets using a 80:20 split, we augmented the training set using the sentences from the Wikipedia dumps for the four 'silver' languages, in order to cover all languages in the training phase, and we retrained the models. The results are in Table 4.

In this setting, the performance is much better, which means that using the in-domain sentences from the evaluation set instead of the Wikipedia sentences (whenever possible) has a positive effect on the systems. In particular, the improvement in the macro F_1 score is caused by the fact that these systems are more conservative when it comes to the four 'silver' languages: only 1% of the test sentences are assigned to a label that is not part of the evaluation set in all models.

In particular, the DNN and NB systems turned out to be more reliable than the CNNs, both the regular one and the one trained with data augmentation. Interestingly, data augmentation had a clear positive effect on the CNN model (2% for the micro and 9% for the macro F_1 score), but it was still not sufficient to make the CNN reach the accuracy of the other systems.[7]

[4] We explained this behavior with the fact that this prevents the network from focusing on character sequences at word boundaries, i.e. involving space characters in the middle (Ceolin, 2021), which are not informative and can lead to overfitting.

[5] The only reason why we used a subset of the data was to avoid RAM issues. However, we noticed that using more training data did not have any noticeable effect on the results.

[6] In this case we did not try to augment the data for the CNN because the operation was not legitimate, given our access to more training data.

[7] We note that these effects could have been overestimated because, contrary to the in-domain experiment, variation in text length was higher with Wikipedia articles, and so shuffling sentences had the effect of exposing the network to words that

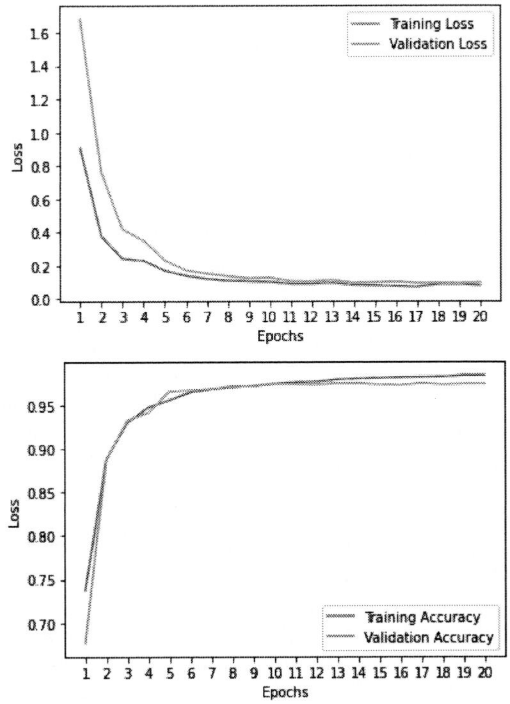

Figure 4: Evaluation of the DNN model on a training set composed of sentences from both the evaluation set (for the seven 'gold' languages) and the Wikipedia dumps (for the four 'silver' languages). Training and validation loss converge after 10 epochs and then decrease together. Accuracy improves up to the 13th/14th epoch, and then stays constant.

For these reasons, we decided to select the DNN as the model of choice for this task. In particular, its high precision, that was highlighted from the results of the in-domain experiment, gives us the option of using some of the sentences from the test set for which the network makes a confident prediction to augment the training data, a form of language model adaptation (Jauhiainen et al., 2018a,b, 2019b), as is explained in the next section. See Figure 4 for the loss and accuracy plots obtained during the evaluation of the DNN.

4.4 Predictions

Table 5 contains the predictions for the 11K sentences in the test set, made by the DNN model which was trained on the evaluation set for the seven 'gold' languages and on the Wikipedia sentences for the four 'silver' languages (in bold).

The most represented among the 'silver' languages is Neapolitan (nap), which is the second most common predicted label. This suggests that the language is present in the test set.

Model	Micro F_1 score	Macro F_1 score
DNN	0.978	0.761
Naïve Bayes	0.974	0.757
CNN + data aug. (10ep.)	0.951	0.740
CNN	0.929	0.651

Table 4: Performance of the models on the evaluation set, final model.

Label	Labels
vec	3127
nap	1519
scn	1365
fur	1325
lmo	1014
lld	751
eml	700
lij	585
sc	562
roa-tara	79
pms	63

Table 5: Predictions of the DNN for the test dataset. 'Silver' languages in bold.

Ladin (lld) and Emilian-Romagnol (eml) are predicted to each represent about 6-7% of the sentences, a number which is not far from the number of sentences we expect to find a priori, especially given that we might expect 'silver' languages to be underpredicted.

The situation with the last 'silver' language, Tarantino (roa-tara) is tricky: the language appears to be quite rare in the test set (0.7%), and an examination of the logit scores associated with the predictions (Figure 5) revealed that Tarantino was the language whose average confidence was the lowest. All the other languages were associated with many more predictions and higher logit scores.

On the other end, Piedmontese (pms), a 'gold' language for which we have several sentences in the evaluation set, is also rare as a prediction, with an occurrence of 0.6%, which is compatible with the ratio of out-of-sample predictions detected in the evaluation experiments.

For these reasons, we decided to remove both Tarantino and Piedmontese, and re-train the classifier to predict only the remaining nine languages.

5 Results

For our first submission, we simply re-trained the DNN excluding Piedmontese and Tarantino, and submitted the predictions on the test set obtained

would have otherwise been truncated. Truncation could thus be the main reason why CNNs underperform in this setting.

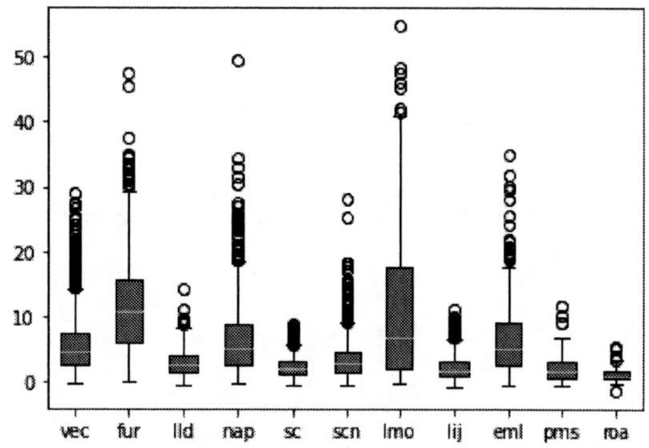

Figure 5: Logit scores associated to each prediction made by our DNN, divided per class.

Team	Model	Weighted F_1 score
SUKI	NB + language adaptation	0.901
Baseline	SVM Char-ngram TFIDF	0.773
Phlyers	**DNN**	**0.694**
ETHZ	Logistic Regression	0.688
Baseline	SVM Unigram TFIDF	0.490
ETHZ	BERT	0.576
Baseline	FastText	0.132

Table 6: Performance of the models on the evaluation of the ITDI task.

in this way. The second and third submission were similar, but we re-trained the network changing the way in which the 'silver' languages were represented: instead of the Wikipedia sentences, we used the label/sentences from the test set for which the predicted label was associated with a high likelihood, following a language model adaptation strategy similar to the one proposed by Jauhiainen et al. (2019b). The main difference is that instead of adding the new predictions, we used them to directly replace the training data for the 'silver' languages, with the aim of obtaining a better representation. We used different likelihood threshold to filter the predictions (>0.90 and >0.95, after transforming the logits into probabilities). On average, the number of predictions per class that were included was quite high, between 75-80%, which seemed a good balance in the trade-off between number of sentences and confidence associated with them.

The overall results of the ITDI shared task are summarized in Table 6.

The best system by far was the SUKI system (Jauhiainen et al., 2021a), a Naïve Bayes-like classifier which performs language adaptation. One of the baselines provided by the organizers, a SVM trained on character ngrams, provided the second

Label	Real	Predicted	F_1 score
vec	1139	1642	0.64
nap	2026	2296	0.78
scn	0	1003	0
fur	1323	1283	0.96
lmo	689	921	0.84
lld	2200	1937	0.85
eml	825	746	0.91
lij	2282	626	0.40
sc	0	636	0
roa-tara	603	0	0

Table 7: Predictions of the third submission, a DNN model trained on the evaluation set augmented with the test sentences that, according to the basic DNN model, belonged to the classes not represented in the evaluation set with probability >0.95.

Label	Sub-1	Sub-2	Sub-3
vec	1646 (0.63)	1205 (0.60)	1642 (0.64)
nap	2787 (0.73)	3229 (0.71)	2296 (0.78)
scn	638 (0)	654 (0)	1003 (0)
fur	1248 (0.96)	1299 (0.94)	1283 (0.96)
lmo	816 (0.89)	711 (0.93)	921 (0.84)
lld	2060 (0.86)	2513 (0.86)	1937 (0.85)
eml	1083 (0.80)	964 (0.86)	746 (0.91)
lij	459 (0.32)	268 (0.20)	626 (0.40)
sc	353 (0)	247 (0)	636 (0)
all	0.66	0.64	**0.69**

Table 8: Output of the models on the evaluation of our ITDI task submissions.

best result, with an F_1 score of 0.773. Our best submission, the third one, completes the podium with an F_1 score of 0.694.

The organizers provided us with the results per class, in Table 7. It is apparent that our system overpredicted texts written in Sicilian (scn) and Sardinian (sc), which were actually absent from the data, and underpredicted texts written in Ligurian (lij) and in Tarantino (roa-tara), which was actually present in the test set, contrary to what we were expecting.

A comparison of the predictions of our three submissions, in Table 8, shows that the last submission led to improvements across the board, with one clear exception (Lombard, 'lmo') and a minor one (Ladin, 'lld'). This suggests that language adaptation had a positive impact on the system. However, it also led to the increase of sentences associated with the two languages absent from the test set, which had the effect of countering any substantial improvement, since their presence necessarily ended up hurting the performance of the other classes.

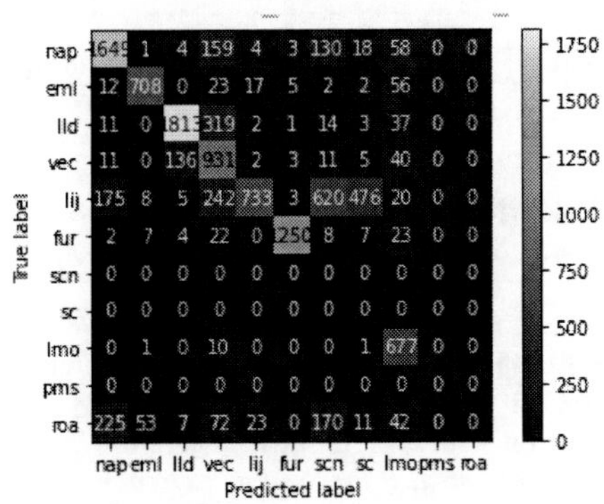

Figure 6: Confusion matrix with the predicted and the gold labels for our third submission.

6 Discussion

Comparing our class results with those of the other teams, the main weakness of our approach turned out not to be the underprediction of Tarantino (roa-tara), with which all the systems struggled, but that of Ligurian ('lij'), which was heavily weighted in the evaluation of the systems, since it was the most common language. An inspection of our evaluation results showed that Ligurian was not among the languages for which we were expecting underprediction. Moreover, Ligurian is a Gallo-Italic language like Lombard and Emilian-Romagnol, but both languages were associated with high F_1 scores in testing, and therefore cannot be responsible for this misclassification.

Since the organizers provided us with the gold labels, we were able to further investigate the behavior of our model by examining the confusion matrix (Figure 6). Some of the patterns were expected: most of the Tarantino (roa-tara) sentences were classified as Neapolitan (nap) or Sicilian (scn), the other two Southern varieties of the sample, and many of the predictions involving Venetian (vec) were instead sentences from Ladin (lld), which is spoken in the same region.

One pattern is instead very peculiar. Sicilian (scn) and Sardinian (sc) were the main responsible for the underprediction of Ligurian (lij), a result which was unexpected, given that the three languages belong to distinct groups, they were all represented in the evaluation set, and were well discriminated in the evaluation phase.

From a linguistic viewpoint, this outcome has an explanation: while Ligurian is a Gallo-Italic language, even classical works like the *Carta dei Dialetti Italiani* by Pellegrini (1977) noticed that there are at least two broad phenomena that the language shares with varieties spoken far from the Gallo-Italic area: the preservation of many word-final vowels, including -u, and the palatalization of [pl] and [bl] clusters. This means that even though Ligurian is clearly a Northern Italy language, an analysis limited to some of its phonological sequences or its morphology could well mistake it for languages spoken outside of the area.

In particular, the first phenomenon was the main responsible for the mistakes in this specific case. Table 9 shows some sentences that were misclassified, from the Ligurian version of Carlo Collodi's *The adventures of Pinocchio*, and in each of them we see morphemes which are typically associated with Southern varieties like Neapolitan and Sicilian and with Sardinian.

It is worth mentioning that the author of the translation published a second version of the text in which the orthographic conventions are different, and *u* is replaced by *o*, which is the case also in the sentences of the evaluation dataset. This variation in orthographic conventions explains why this ambiguity did not emerge in our evaluation phase. There are two reasons why the ambiguity could have affected our results more than those of the other teams. First, in our preprocessing we did not remove proper names from the test sentences because in the evaluation phase they did not seem to affect the results, but clearly having a name like *Pinocchiu* being strongly associated with Southern varieties (the only varieties in which the sequence *cchiu* was present in the training data) heavily affected the performance of our classifier. Second, our classifier was not able to learn that the letter *æ* was unambiguously associated with Northern varieties (only Ligurian and Emilian-Romagnol had it), a cue that should have corrected the mistake.

7 Conclusion

While in some of the previous VarDial evaluation campaigns neural networks yielded the best performance in language identification tasks, (Tudoreanu, 2019; Bernier-Colborne et al., 2019), it was not the case with this shared task, where traditional shallow models like Naïve Bayes and Support Vector Machines performed better, and the DNN model we devised failed to capture important cues like the presence of *æ* in the text.

Even though we were not able to present neural models that reach state-of-the-art performance, we

Target	Prediction	Text	Source
lij	nap	dumandò **u** Pinoc**chiu** cun anscêtæ e aff**annu**	Pinocchio (version by Cino Peripateta)
lij	sc	E ti rendime a mæ, e **femmu** paxe	Pinocchio (version by Cino Peripateta)
lij	scn	Mi suin mariun**ettu**	Pinocchio (version by Cino Peripateta)

Table 9: Sample of sentences written in Ligurian that were misclassified. The phonological sequences/morphemes that are strongly associated with other language varieties (Neapolitan, Sicilian, and Sardinian) are in bold.

still argue that this work makes two contributions.

First, data augmentation has proven to be an effective way to improve the performance of neural networks when the data is limited, a point that we also made last year (Ceolin, 2021) and which has been confirmed throughout the experiments conducted here. Data augmentation has had limited application in NLP (Coulombe, 2018; Kobayashi, 2018; Wei and Zou, 2019), but our experiments suggest that it can play an important role in adapting neural models to the task of language identification in low-resource settings.

Second, DNNs turned out to be more efficient than CNNs to handle language identification. They do not suffer from overfitting in the same way that CNNs do (Ceolin, 2021), they are more flexible, and they yield a better performance.

We hope that our results will encourage the exploration of neural architectures for low-resource language identification and more research in the automatic classification of languages varieties in Italy.

References

Noëmi Aepli, Antonios Anastasopoulos, Adrian Chifu, William Domingues, Fahim Faisal, Mihaela Găman, Radu Tudor Ionescu, and Yves Scherrer. 2022. Findings of the VarDial evaluation campaign 2022. In *Proceedings of the Ninth Workshop on NLP for Similar Languages, Varieties and Dialects*, Gyeongju, Republic of Korea.

Giuseppe Attardi. 2015. Wikiextractor. `https://github.com/attardi/wikiextractor`.

Adrien Barbaresi. 2016. An Unsupervised Morphological Criterion for Discriminating Similar Languages. In *Proceedings of the Third Workshop on NLP for Similar Languages, Varieties and Dialects*, pages 212–220, Osaka, Japan.

Shane Bergsma, Paul McNamee, Mossaab Bagdouri, Clayton Fink, and Theresa Wilson. 2012. Language identification for creating language-specific Twitter collections. In *Proceedings of the Second Workshop on Language in Social Media*, pages 65–74, Montréal, Canada.

Gabriel Bernier-Colborne, Cyril Goutte, and Serge Léger. 2019. Improving cuneiform language identification with BERT. In *Proceedings of the Sixth Workshop on NLP for Similar Languages, Varieties and Dialects*, pages 17–25, Minneapolis, USA.

Andrei M. Butnaru and Radu Tudor Ionescu. 2019. MOROCO: The Moldavian and Romanian Dialectal Corpus. In *Proceedings of ACL 2019*, pages 688–698.

Andrea Ceolin. 2021. Comparing the performance of CNNs and shallow models for language identification. In *Proceedings of the Eighth Workshop on NLP for Similar Languages, Varieties and Dialects*, pages 102–112, Kiyv, Ukraine.

Andrea Ceolin and Hong Zhang. 2020. Discriminating between standard Romanian and Moldavian tweets using filtered character ngrams. In *Proceedings of the Seventh Workshop on NLP for Similar Languages, Varieties and Dialects*, pages 265–272, Barcelona, Spain.

Bharathi Raja Chakravarthi, Mihaela Găman, Radu Tudor Ionescu, Heidi Jauhiainen, Tommi Jauhiainen, Krister Lindén, Nikola Ljubešić, Niko Partanen, Ruba Priyadharshini, Christoph Purschke, Eswari Rajagopal, Yves Scherrer, and Marcos Zampieri. 2021. Findings of the VarDial Evaluation Campaign 2021. In *Proceedings of the Eighth Workshop on NLP for Similar Languages, Varieties and Dialects*, pages 1–11, Kiyv, Ukraine.

Andre Cianflone and Leila Kosseim. 2016. N-gram and Neural Language Models for Discriminating Similar Languages. In *Proceedings of the Third Workshop on NLP for Similar Languages, Varieties and Dialects*, pages 243–250, Osaka, Japan.

Simon Clematide and Peter Makarov. 2017. CLUZH at VarDial GDI 2017: Testing a Variety of Machine Learning Tools for the Classification of Swiss German Dialects. In *Proceedings of the Fourth Workshop on NLP for Similar Languages, Varieties and Dialects*, pages 170–177, Valencia, Spain.

Çağrı Çöltekin. 2020. Dialect identification under domain shift: Experiments with discriminating Romanian and Moldavian. In *Proceedings of the Seventh Workshop on NLP for Similar Languages, Varieties and Dialects*, pages 186–192, Barcelona, Spain.

Çağrı Çöltekin and Taraka Rama. 2017. Tübingen system in VarDial 2017 shared task: experiments with language identification and cross-lingual parsing. In

Proceedings of the Fourth Workshop on NLP for Similar Languages, Varieties and Dialects, pages 146–155, Valencia, Spain.

Alexis Conneau, Holger Schwenk, Loïc Barrault, and Yann Lecun. 2016. Very deep convolutional networks for text classification. *arXiv preprint arXiv:1606.01781*.

Claude Coulombe. 2018. Text data augmentation made simple by leveraging NLP Cloud APIs. *arXiv preprint arXiv:1812.04718*.

Ted Dunning. 1994. *Statistical identification of language*. Computing Research Laboratory, New Mexico State University Las Cruces, NM, USA.

Cyril Goutte, Serge Léger, and Marine Carpuat. 2014. The NRC System for Discriminating Similar Languages. In *Proceedings of the First Workshop on Applying NLP Tools to Similar Languages, Varieties and Dialects*, pages 139–145, Dublin, Ireland.

Mihaela Găman, Dirk Hovy, Radu Tudor Ionescu, Heidi Jauhiainen, Tommi Jauhiainen, Krister Lindén, Nikola Ljubešić, Niko Partanen, Christoph Purschke, Yves Scherrer, and Marcos Zampieri. 2020. A Report on the VarDial Evaluation Campaign 2020. In *Proceedings of the Seventh Workshop on NLP for Similar Languages, Varieties and Dialects*, pages 1–14, Barcelona, Spain.

Arthur S House and Edward P Neuburg. 1977. Toward automatic identification of the language of an utterance. I. Preliminary methodological considerations. *The Journal of the Acoustical Society of America*, 62(3):708–713.

Hai Hu, Wen Li, He Zhou, Zuoyu Tian, Yiwen Zhang, and Liang Zou. 2019. Ensemble Methods to Distinguish Mainland and Taiwan Chinese. In *Proceedings of the Sixth Workshop on NLP for Similar Languages, Varieties and Dialects*, pages 165–171, Minneapolis, USA.

Aaron Jaech, George Mulcaire, Mari Ostendorf, and Noah A Smith. 2016. A neural model for language identification in code-switched tweets. In *Proceedings of The Second Workshop on Computational Approaches to Code Switching*, pages 60–64, Austin, USA.

Tommi Jauhiainen, Heidi Jauhiainen, and Krister Linden. 2018a. HeLI-based experiments in Swiss German dialect identification. In *Proceedings of the Fifth Workshop on NLP for Similar Languages, Varieties and Dialects*, pages 254–262, Santa Fe, USA.

Tommi Jauhiainen, Heidi Jauhiainen, and Krister Lindén. 2018b. Iterative language model adaptation for Indo-Aryan language identification. In *Proceedings of the Fifth Workshop on NLP for Similar Languages, Varieties and Dialects*, pages 66–75, Santa Fe, USA.

Tommi Jauhiainen, Heidi Jauhiainen, and Krister Lindén. 2019a. Discriminating between Mandarin Chinese and Swiss-German varieties using adaptive language models. In *Proceedings of the Sixth Workshop on NLP for Similar Languages, Varieties and Dialects*, pages 178–187, Minneapolis, USA.

Tommi Jauhiainen, Heidi Jauhiainen, and Krister Lindén. 2020. Experiments in language variety geolocation and dialect identification. In *Proceedings of the Seventh Workshop on NLP for Similar Languages, Varieties and Dialects*, pages 220–231, Barcelona, Spain.

Tommi Jauhiainen, Heidi Jauhiainen, and Krister Lindén. 2021a. Naive Bayes-based Experiments in Romanian Dialect Identification. In *Proceedings of the Eighth Workshop on NLP for Similar Languages, Varieties and Dialects*, pages 76–83, Kiyv, Ukraine.

Tommi Jauhiainen, Krister Lindén, and Heidi Jauhiainen. 2019b. Language model adaptation for language and dialect identification of text. *Natural Language Engineering*, 25(5):561–583.

Tommi Jauhiainen, Marco Lui, Marcos Zampieri, Timothy Baldwin, and Krister Lindén. 2019c. Automatic language identification in texts: A survey. *Journal of Artificial Intelligence Research*, 65:675–782.

Tommi Jauhiainen, Tharindu Ranasinghe, and Marcos Zampieri. 2021b. Comparing approaches to Dravidian language identification. In *Proceedings of the Eighth Workshop on NLP for Similar Languages, Varieties and Dialects*, pages 120–127, Kiyv, Ukraine.

Yoon Kim, Yacine Jernite, David Sontag, and Alexander M Rush. 2016. Character-aware neural language models. In *Thirtieth AAAI conference on artificial intelligence*, Phoenix, USA.

Sosuke Kobayashi. 2018. Contextual augmentation: Data augmentation by words with paradigmatic relations. In *Proceedings of the 2018 Conference of the North American Chapter of the Association for Computational Linguistics: Human Language Technologies, Volume 2 (Short Papers)*, pages 452–457, New Orleans, Louisiana.

Tim Kreutz and Walter Daelemans. 2018. Exploring classifier combinations for language variety identification. In *Proceedings of the Fifth Workshop on NLP for Similar Languages, Varieties and Dialects*, pages 191–198, Santa Fe, USA.

Marco Lui and Timothy Baldwin. 2014. Accurate language identification of Twitter messages. In *Proceedings of the 5th workshop on language analysis for social media (LASM)*, pages 17–25, Gothenburg, Sweden.

Maria Medvedeva, Martin Kroon, and Barbara Plank. 2017. When sparse traditional models outperform dense neural networks: the curious case of discriminating between similar languages. In *Proceedings of the Fourth Workshop on NLP for Similar Languages, Varieties and Dialects*, pages 156–163, Valencia, Spain.

Giovan Battista Pellegrini. 1977. *Carta dei dialetti d'Italia*. Pisa: Pacini.

Cristian Popa and Vlad Stefănescu. 2020. Applying multilingual and monolingual transformer-based models for dialect identification. In *Proceedings of the Seventh Workshop on NLP for Similar Languages, Varieties and Dialects*, pages 193–201, Barcelona, Spain.

Yves Scherrer and Nikola Ljubešić. 2020. HeLju@ VarDial 2020: Social media variety geolocation with BERT models. In *Proceedings of the Seventh Workshop on NLP for Similar Languages, Varieties and Dialects*, pages 202–211, Barcelona, Spain.

Fernando Benites de Azevedo e Souza, Ralf Grubenmann, Pius von Däniken, Dirk Von Gruenigen, Jan Milan Deriu, and Mark Cieliebak. 2018. Twist bytes: German dialect identification with data mining optimization. In *Proceedings of the Fifth Workshop on NLP for Similar Languages, Varieties and Dialects*, pages 218–227, Santa Fe, USA.

Diana Tudoreanu. 2019. DTeam@ VarDial 2019: Ensemble based on skip-gram and triplet loss neural networks for Moldavian vs. Romanian cross-dialect topic identification. In *Proceedings of the Sixth Workshop on NLP for Similar Languages, Varieties and Dialects*, pages 202–208, Minneapolis, USA.

Jason Wei and Kai Zou. 2019. EDA: Easy data augmentation techniques for boosting performance on text classification tasks. In *Proceedings of the 2019 Conference on Empirical Methods in Natural Language Processing and the 9th International Joint Conference on Natural Language Processing (EMNLP-IJCNLP)*, pages 6382–6388, Hong Kong, China.

Nianheng Wu, Eric DeMattos, Kwok Him So, Pin-zhen Chen, and Çağrı Çöltekin. 2019. Language discrimination and transfer learning for similar languages: experiments with feature combinations and adaptation. In *Proceedings of the Sixth Workshop on NLP for Similar Languages, Varieties and Dialects*, pages 54–63, Minneapolis, USA.

George-Eduard Zaharia, Andrei-Marius Avram, Dumitru-Clementin Cercel, and Traian Rebedea. 2020. Exploring the power of Romanian BERT for dialect identification. In *Proceedings of the Seventh Workshop on NLP for Similar Languages, Varieties and Dialects*, pages 232–241, Barcelona, Spain.

George-Eduard Zaharia, Andrei-Marius Avram, Dumitru-Clementin Cercel, and Traian Rebedea. 2021. Dialect identification through adversarial learning and knowledge distillation on Romanian BERT. In *Proceedings of the Eighth Workshop on NLP for Similar Languages, Varieties and Dialects*, pages 113–119, Kiyv, Ukraine.

Marcos Zampieri, Shervin Malmasi, Nikola Ljubešić, Preslav Nakov, Ahmed Ali, Jörg Tiedemann, Yves Scherrer, and Noëmi Aepli. 2017. Findings of the VarDial Evaluation Campaign 2017. In *Proceedings of the Fourth Workshop on NLP for Similar Languages, Varieties and Dialects*, pages 1–15, Valencia, Spain.

Marcos Zampieri, Shervin Malmasi, Preslav Nakov, Ahmed Ali, Suwon Shuon, James Glass, Yves Scherrer, Tanja Samardžić, Nikola Ljubešić, Jörg Tiedemann, Chris van der Lee, Stefan Grondelaers, Nelleke Oostdijk, Antal van den Bosch, Ritesh Kumar, Bornini Lahiri, and Mayank Jain. 2018. Language Identification and Morphosyntactic Tagging: The Second VarDial Evaluation Campaign. In *Proceedings of the Fifth Workshop on NLP for Similar Languages, Varieties and Dialects*, pages 1–17, Santa Fe, USA.

Marcos Zampieri, Shervin Malmasi, Yves Scherrer, Tanja Samardžić, Francis Tyers, Miikka Silfverberg, Natalia Klyueva, Tung-Le Pan, Chu-Ren Huang, Radu Tudor Ionescu, Andrei Butnaru, and Tommi Jauhiainen. 2019. A Report on the Third VarDial Evaluation Campaign. In *Proceedings of the Sixth Workshop on NLP for Similar Languages, Varieties and Dialects*, pages 1–16, Minneapolis, USA.

Xiang Zhang, Junbo Zhao, and Yann LeCun. 2015. Character-level convolutional networks for text classification. In *Advances in neural information processing systems*, pages 649–657.

Arkaitz Zubiaga, Inaki San Vicente, Pablo Gamallo, José Ramom Pichel, Inaki Alegria, Nora Aranberri, Aitzol Ezeiza, and Víctor Fresno. 2016. TweetLID: a benchmark for tweet language identification. *Language Resources and Evaluation*, 50(4):729–766.

Transfer Learning Improves French Cross-Domain Dialect Identification: NRC @ VarDial 2022

Gabriel Bernier-Colborne and **Serge Léger** and **Cyril Goutte**
National Research Council Canada
{Gabriel.Bernier-Colborne | Serge.Leger | Cyril.Goutte}@nrc-cnrc.gc.ca

Abstract

We describe the systems developed by the National Research Council Canada for the French Cross-Domain Dialect Identification shared task at the 2022 VarDial evaluation campaign. We evaluated two different approaches to this task: SVM and probabilistic classifiers exploiting n-grams as features, and trained from scratch on the data provided; and a pre-trained French language model, CamemBERT, that we fine-tuned on the dialect identification task. The latter method turned out to improve the macro-F1 score on the test set from 0.344 to 0.430 (25% increase), which indicates that transfer learning can be helpful for dialect identification.

1 Introduction

This paper describes the NRC team's submissions to the French Cross-Domain Dialect Identification (FDI) task that was organized as part of the evaluation campaign at VarDial 2022.

For this task, participants had to "train a model on news samples collected from a set of publication sources and evaluate it on news samples collected from a different set of publication sources. Not only the sources are different, but also the topics. Therefore, participants have to build a model for a cross-domain 4-way classification by dialect task, in which a classification model is required to discriminate between the French (FR), Swiss (CH), Belgian (BE) and Canadian (CA) dialects across different news samples."[1]

Our main motivation to participate in this shared task was that it would allow us to compare fine-tuning of a pre-trained neural language model to n-gram based methods trained from scratch, which have been successful at discriminating between similar languages (DSL) in the past. This was not possible in many shared tasks on DSL in the past, at least not since transfer learning became a common approach to various NLP tasks, with the advent of models such as BERT (Devlin et al., 2019), GPT (Radford et al., 2018), etc. So we took this opportunity to investigate whether DSL is also an area where transfer learning can improve accuracy.

We submitted three runs each to the closed and open tracks of the FDI shared task. Our closed submissions ended up achieving the highest scores in that track, and we were the only team to submit to the open track. Our open submissions outperformed the baselines computed by Gaman et al. (2022) as well as our closed submissions, which indicates that transfer learning can be helpful for discriminating between similar languages, at least when a domain shift is present.

2 Related Work

Thorough surveys of research on language identification are provided by Jauhiainen et al. (2019) and Zampieri et al. (2020).

Language identification is one of the few tasks in natural language processing where deep learning methods have yet to provide convincing gains in accuracy, at least in the context of shared tasks. Jauhiainen et al. (2019) pointed out that linear SVMs exploiting character n-grams as features have been highly successful in shared tasks on language identification.

The winning submission by the NRC team to the Cuneiform Language Identification task at VarDial 2019 (Bernier-Colborne et al., 2019), which involved seven language varieties written in Cuneiform script, was the first time a neural system was ranked first on a language identification shared task (Zampieri et al., 2019). This system was a character-based BERT model trained from scratch.

However, we also submitted both n-gram models and deep learning models to the Uralic Language Identification (ULI) shared task at VarDial

[1] https://sites.google.com/view/vardial-2022/shared-tasks

Proceedings of the Ninth Workshop on NLP for Similar Languages, Varieties and Dialects, pages 109–118
October 16, 2022. ©2022 Association for Computational Linguistics

2021 (Bernier-Colborne et al., 2021; Chakravarthi et al., 2021), and in that case, our best n-gram models outperformed our best BERT models.

These results cast doubt on whether a deep neural network can reliably produce the best results in settings more representative of real-world applications of language identification, as the ULI task involved a total of 179 languages, including pairs of very similar languages. They suggested that the simpler, n-gram based approach was still a very strong baseline.

Note that all our previous shared task participations that involved deep learning were in a closed setting, so no pre-trained models were allowed. This has usually been the case for shared tasks on language identification in our experience. However, transfer learning has been used for language identification outside of shared tasks (Caswell et al., 2020, inter alia).

3 Data and Task Definition

The FDI task (Aepli et al., 2022) requires participating systems to predict the French language variety used in a sample of text. The set of four language varieties that the systems must learn to discriminate are the national varieties used in France, Belgium, Switzerland, and Canada.

The evaluation metrics for this shared task were not specified, so we chose to focus on macro-averaged F1-score, which is commonly used for language identification and DSL tasks.

This shared task featured both open and closed tracks. For the closed track, participants were not allowed to use pre-trained language models or any external data to train their models. This is the usual setting for DSL shared tasks in our experience. For the open track, external resources such as unlabelled corpora, lexicons, and pre-trained language models were allowed, but no additional labelled data could be used. Thus, this shared task provided us a unique opportunity to evaluate transfer learning on a DSL shared task.

Gaman et al. (2022) describe the corpus they developed for this task, which they named FreCDo (for French Cross-Domain [dialect identification]). This corpus contains 413,522 text samples collected from public news websites. The CA class is under-represented in the dataset, as fewer open sources were available. As we will show below, the presence of duplicates makes this class imbalance even greater.

Efforts were carried out to eliminate potential biases related to factors such as topic and writing style. This was done by using separate sets of publication sources and search keywords to compile the training, validation (aka development), and test sets. The keywords represent general topics that are not specific to any of the four countries involved. The keywords were: "guerre" ("war") and "Ukraine" for the training set; "Russie" ("Russia") and "États-Unis" ("United States") for the development set; and "réchauffement climatique" ("global warming") and "Covid" for the test set. Note that there is likely more topical similarity between the training and development set, than between either and the test set, so the development set may not be a good estimator of test accuracy, which is confirmed by our experiments below.

Furthermore, named entities were identified using spaCy[2] and replaced with the special token "NE", again in order to remove biases related to topic or country.

The training, development and test sets contain 358,787, 18,002, and 36,733 samples respectively. Each text sample is a paragraph containing up to three sentences.

Gaman et al. (2022) also evaluated three baseline systems on this corpus and concluded that it is a difficult task. Their baseline models were able to outperform a naive baseline that always selects the most frequent class, but macro-averaged F1 scores did not exceed 0.4.

It turns out that one of those baselines was a fine-tuned CamemBERT model, which is the model that we used for the open track, although we were not aware of this before submitting our runs. That baseline produced the best results, and the runs we submitted outperformed this baseline by a few points (in terms of macro-F1). This may be due to differences in hyperparameter settings, or to the fact that we used the development set along with the training set to fine-tune the model. Whether this was done by Gaman et al. (2022) is not specified, so we would tend to assume it was not.

They also evaluated SVM and XGBoost models based on the text encodings produced by a fine-tuned CamemBERT model, but the best results were achieved by CamemBERT itself. Their results were much better on Belgian and Swiss French than on the other two varieties.

[2]`https://spacy.io`

3.1 Data Analysis

Gaman et al. (2022) analyzed the most discriminative features of the CamemBERT model, by manually inspecting "a few correctly classified samples [and analysing] the features for which CamemBERT has given high scores." They concluded that "there are quite a few noticeable dialectal patterns learned by the model," such as numerals only used in Belgian French and a currency only used in Switzerland.

We carried out some analysis on this dataset before starting to develop our systems. Looking at text lengths showed that the training set contains both very short texts, containing a single character, and very long texts, containing up to 18,218 characters, although the text samples are supposed to contain only up to three sentences. Here is a small part of the longest training text: "<NE> Gardiens : <NE> <NE> (<NE> <NE>), <NE> <NE> (<NE>), <NE> <NE> (<NE>) Défenseurs : <NE> <NE> (<NE> <NE>), <NE> <NE> (<NE>), <NE> <NE> (<NE> <NE>), <NE> <NE> (<NE>), <NE> <NE> (<NE> <NE>), <NE> <NE> (<NE> <NE>), <NE> <NE> (<NE> <NE>), <NE> <NE> (Leeds), <NE> <NE> (<NE> <NE>) <NE> : Ilkay Gündogan (<NE> <NE>) [...]" Such training texts may inflate the importance of the NE word feature.

An example of the shortest texts contains only the character "»" (closing quote in French), which appears 372 times in the training set, in three different classes.

These two examples show several potential sources of noise, besides the presence of very long or short texts.

- Large number of NE tokens. Indeed, "NE" is the most frequent word in the training, development, and test sets.
- Duplicates within classes.
- Duplicates across classes (i.e. ambiguous examples).

We looked into the issue of duplicates, and found a large number of them. In the training data, 43,007 unique texts appear more than once in the same class, and 70 belong to more than one class. In the development data, those counts are 897 and 2 respectively.

Applying deduplication (within classes, not across) reduces the number of examples in the training set from 358,787 to 277,565 (and from 18,002 to 13,216 for the dev set). The class that suffers most from this is CA, for which the training set size shrinks from 34,003 to only 169 unique texts after applying simple deduplication (see Table 1 for full stats). This creates a huge imbalance between CA and the other classes in terms of the training set size. And even within these 169 remaining texts, we found 36 that contained either of these two boilerplate patterns:

Class	# before dedup	# after dedup
BE	121,746	113,487
CA	34,003	169
CH	141,261	107,982
FR	61,777	55,927

Table 1: Number of training samples before and after deduplication.

- "Nous utilisons les témoins de navigation (cookies) afin d'opérer et d'améliorer nos services ainsi qu'à des fins publicitaires. Le respect de votre vie privée est important pour nous." This appears in 6631 training examples for CA (as well as 1-3 times in the other classes)
- "Si vous n'êtes pas à l'aise avec l'utilisation de ces informations, NE NE vos paramètres avant de poursuivre votre visite." This also appears in 6631 CA training examples. Also note that the two words that were detected as NE here are "veuillez" and "revoir", which are not named entity mentions. So noisy NER may be another source of errors.

Because of all the duplicates we observed, we decided to try applying deduplication (within classes) to the training data. Also, since we observed boilerplate even after deduplication, we decided to apply it after splitting the training data into sentences, using the sentence splitter in Portage Text Processing (Larkin et al., 2022). We also optionally applied word tokenization (again using Portage Text Processing) and removal of redundant NE tokens (see Section 4.1) – these preprocessing steps were also applied to the development and test data, but sentence splitting and deduplication were only applied to the training data. Applying this preprocessing to the training data reduces the average text length by more than half, and increases the number of training samples from 358,787 to around 700,000, depending on the version. In the original training set, there were 43,007 unique texts that had duplicates within a single class, and 70 unique texts that had duplicates in multiple classes. In the preprocessed versions, no unique texts have duplicates within a single class, but around 1700 unique texts have more than one label. Note that we did not try removing these ambiguous training examples from the training data, but this might be worth investigating.

We also checked for duplicates between the training, development, and test sets (i.e. data leakage). 146 of 18,002 development texts are also in the training set, as well as 29 of 36,733 test texts, and 6 test texts are also in the development set. Given these small numbers, using a heuristic to ensure that these texts have the same label as in training did not seem worthwhile.

Another potential source of noise is the presence of many non-Latin characters, including right-to-left scripts and many emoji. We might want to discard such characters to avoid overfitting, but we did not explore this.

4 Methodology

In this section we will explain how we processed the data and trained the models that we used for our submissions to the FDI task.

4.1 Data Processing

We produced four different pre-processed versions of the data by optionally applying word tokenization or removal of redundant NE tokens. In the case of the training set, before applying these pre-processing steps, we applied sentence splitting followed by deduplication within classes. We did not apply this to development or test data (and we did not check the impact of this mismatch between the training and evaluation data, e.g. by sentence-splitting the evaluation data and aggregating the predictions over the sentences of each example).

To remove redundant NEs, we simply replace consecutive NE tokens with a single token. Note that we converted the "NE" token to "<NE>", so that it would not be split into multiple tokens by our word tokenizer. Also note that CamemBERT's subword tokenizer split the "<NE>" into three tokens: "<", "NE", and ">".

We chose not to fold the data for cross-validation, because this is a cross-domain task, so simply using the training and development sets as is should provide a better estimator of test accuracy.

4.2 Models Tested

We tested various models for the open and closed tracks of this shared task, which we describe below.

4.2.1 Closed Track

For the closed track, we tested multi-class support vector machine (SVM) classifiers, as well as a probabilistic classifier (Gaussier et al., 2002), that we call ProbCat. This classifier is similar to multinomial Naive Bayes except that it does not assume that all features in a given text are generated from a single class. It has been used in the past to obtain state-of-the-art results on language identification tasks (Goutte and Léger, 2016). For more details on this classification algorithm, refer to Goutte et al. (2014, Sec. 2.2).

To train these models, we tested a variety of character n-gram and word n-gram features. Features were weighted with a variant of tf-idf, and texts were always converted to lower-case before extracting the features.

Note that training a multi-class SVM classifier involves calibrating the predicted probabilities of single-class classifiers, which are trained to distinguish a specific class from all other classes combined (i.e. one-vs-all training). Part of the training data must be held out for this calibration step. We chose to hold out 10% of the training set (using stratified sampling to ensure the classes are sampled proportionally) for calibration purposes. We did this for both model selection (on the development set) and our final submissions (on the test set), as we wanted to use the whole dev set for held-out evaluation during model selection and for training our final models. As for ProbCat, it does not require calibration, so no training data was held out in that case.

We tested two additional methods to improve accuracy: pseudo-labelling of test cases and ensembling. In the first case, we used a model's predictions on the development set (or test set, once we had selected the models we wanted to submit) as pseudo-labels, added these examples to the training data, and trained a model on this augmented training set before evaluating the model on the development (or test) set. We ended up training a ProbCat model on the pseudo-labels produced by SVM models, as model selection experiments indicated this worked better than training an SVM on its own pseudo-labels (which is commonly known as "self-training").

As for ensembling, we use a plurality vote approach, so we simply take the most frequently predicted class for each text sample. To select the models included in the ensemble, we conducted a brute force search among a set of candidate models and greedily added the model that improved the ensemble's score the most at each step, then selected one of the ensembles that achieved the best scores overall.

Note that pseudo-labelling was only used in the closed track. We experimented with ensembling in the open track as well as in the closed track, but we selected the models included in the open ensemble arbitrarily, not based on a systematic search.

4.2.2 Open Track

For the open track, we fine-tuned a pre-trained CamemBERT model (Martin et al., 2020), which uses the RoBERTa architecture and training procedure (Liu et al., 2019). More, specifically, we downloaded the `camembert-base` checkpoint from HuggingFace's repository of pre-trained models.[3] This model has 110 million parameters, and was pre-trained on the French portion of the OSCAR corpus (Ortiz Suárez et al., 2019; Ortiz Suárez et al., 2020; Abadji et al., 2021), which contains 138 GB of unlabelled French text. We fine-tuned this model on the FreCDo training data using the AdamW optimizer (Loshchilov and Hutter, 2019) with a learning rate of 5×10^{-5}.

These settings are similar to those used by Gaman et al. (2022) for their CamemBERT baseline, except that we used smaller batch sizes (8 or 16 rather than 32), fewer epochs (3 or 5 instead of 30), and we only fine-tuned the last one or two layers of the encoder, along with the classification head, which is randomly initialized. This requires less compute and the results we observed on the development set were better, possibly due to less forgetting or easier optimisation. Also, Gaman et al. (2022) used average pooling of the token encodings as input to the classification head, whereas we used the encoding of the "<s>" token (equivalent to "[CLS]" in BERT) that is prepended to the token sequence, which is the default used by RoBERTa's classification head.[4]

[3] https://huggingface.co/camembert-base

[4] https://github.com/huggingface/transformers/blob/v4.20.1/src/transformers/models/roberta/modeling_roberta.py#L1435

CamemBERT comes with a subword tokenizer based on the Byte Pair Encoding (BPE) algorithm (Sennrich et al., 2016) implemented in SentencePiece.[5] The tokenizer produces a maximum of 512 tokens, as this is the maximum input length of the model. Longer sequences are truncated to the maximum length. This is a rare occurrence in the FDI dataset: if we tokenize the raw (untokenized) data provided, we obtain the maximum number of tokens for 107 training texts, 1 development text, and 22 test texts. Note that if we apply word tokenization or removal of redundant NE tokens to the texts, these numbers are slightly different.

When processing each mini-batch, the sequences are padded to the maximum sequence length in that batch – this reduces the amount of computation compared to padding everything to the maximum input length of 512 tokens. The vocabulary of the pre-trained tokenizer contains 32K sub-word tokens, plus 5 special tokens (beginning and end of text, padding, out-of-vocabulary, and mask).

Note that we also tested FastText (Joulin et al., 2017) with pre-trained word embeddings,[6] but this was not used for our final submissions in the open track. Our best development scores with FastText were slightly lower than those achieved with an SVM trained from scratch, and quite a bit lower than a fine-tuned CamemBERT, so we decided to focus on the latter for the open track.

Finally, it is worth mentioning that we did not test any methods specifically designed to deal with domain/topic shift, as we decided to focus on comparing transfer learning to vanilla supervised learning.

4.3 Model Selection Experiments

To select models for the closed track, we tested different feature sets on different pre-processed versions of the datasets, and computed the macro-F1 score on the development set. We also tested pseudo-labelling the development set. The main findings of our model selection experiments can be summarized as follows:

- SVM generally produced higher scores than ProbCat (even though 10% of the training data was held out for calibration in the case of SVM models).

[5] https://github.com/google/sentencepiece

[6] https://fasttext.cc/docs/en/crawl-vectors.html

- We tried various combinations of character n-grams (with $n \in \{3,4\}$) and word n-grams (with $n \in \{1,2\}$), and the highest scores were achieved by using only word bi-grams. Note that this is somewhat unusual for a language identification task, where it has often been observed that character n-grams produce the best results.
- We tried filtering out very short texts from the training data, but scores did not improve.
- Pseudo-labelling did not improve the SVM's scores. However, we accidentally trained a ProbCat model on data that had been pseudo-labelled by an SVM, and observed that the ProbCat model did better than the SVM trained only on the training set.
- The SVM models never predicted the CA class. ProbCat sometimes predicted it, but was generally wrong.

We inspected the most discriminative (positive) features of ProbCat and SVM models using only word bigrams as features. For ProbCat they were:

- BE: "à jour", "jour le", "- mis", "mis à", """", a", """" <ne>", "<ne> le", ": """, "<ne> (<ne>)", "<ne>. """
- CA: "— une", "vos paramètres", "paramètres avant", "poursuivre votre", "votre visite.", "la hausse", "citation de", "une citation", "avec l'utilisation", "l'aise avec"
- CH: ": «", "<ne> est", "premier ministre", "la «", "<ne> –", "[. . . ", "la guerre", ". . .]", "« la", "de <ne>."
- FR: "<ne> -", "», a", "<ne> /", "/ <ne>", "par <ne>", "[<ne>", "— <ne>", "« <ne>", "<ne>]", "- le"

And for SVM, the top 10 features with the highest weights were:

- BE: """", a", "<ne>. """, "<ne>. """, "juin 2013", "son appréciation", """", a-t-il", "revenues sur", "horrible "",", "53 voix,", "pouvoir, ni,"
- CA: "journalistes en", "à lire", "sentiment dévastateur.", "source :", "du widget.", "photo :", "incendie fait", "<ne> tremblay", "la correction.", "collaboration d'<ne>."
- CH: "seraient vus", "suspects des", "rayonnement de", "droits que", "activement à", "métier est", "<ne> tira", "armé pourrait", "grandes foules", "outre, le"
- FR: "a lire", ""a lire", "les fesses", "charges nucléaires.", "angleterre -", "mémoires à", "— <ne>", "« défendrait", "mécanisation de", "signalés par"

This (admittedly limited) exploration of discriminative features does not reveal many obvious dialectal markers, but we can observe some boilerplate patterns, such as "mis à jour le..." for BE when using ProbCat, or "à lire aussi :" for FR when using the SVM.

As for CamemBERT, we did an ad hoc search for the best settings of a few hyperparameters. Our main findings can be summarized as follows:

- Fine-tuning only the last 1 or 2 layers of the 12-layer encoder provided better results than full fine-tuning. It also reduced the computation required, and the runtime of our experiments.
- Results on the four different pre-processed versions of the dataset were similar. Word tokenization had little impact. Removing redundant NEs tended to improve scores slightly. Lower-casing was not beneficial.
- The best scores were generally achieved within five epochs (we tested up to 10). Our three best models, which we used for our final submissions, were trained for either 3 or 5 epochs.
- Batch size had little impact, but 8 worked slightly better than 16 in general.
- Various learning rate schedules were tested, and provided similar results.
- Weighting the loss to penalize the CA class more heavily did not improve results.
- Filtering out very short texts from the training data had very little impact.

Based on these model selection experiments, we decided to submit the following 6 runs:

- Closed 1: Majority vote ensemble of five multi-class SVMs trained on the concatenation of the training and development data, using different data processing and feature sets.

The differences between the models involve: whether word tokenization was applied to the input; whether we removed redundant NE tokens from the input; whether training data was filtered using a minimum text length threshold; and the n-grams used as features. Three of the models used only word bigrams as features, and the two others used word unigrams and bigrams, as well as character trigrams and 4-grams. To select the models, we carried out a greedy search among a dozen SVM models, and used results on the development set to select the best subset of models.

- Closed 2: ProbCat trained on the concatenation of the training and development data, as well as the pseudo-labelled test data, where the test labels are those predicted by the SVM ensemble used for our first run. The feature set used by this classifier includes only word bigrams.

- Closed 3: Our best multi-class SVM classifier according to results on the development data. It was trained on the concatenation of the training and development data, using only word bi-grams as features.

- Open 1: Majority vote ensemble of three pretrained CamemBERT models, which were fine-tuned on the concatenation of the training and development data. Model selection was based on their scores on the development data, but the number of models included in the ensemble was arbitrary. The differences between the three models involve the batch size (8 or 16), the learning rate schedule (linear decay or constant) and the number of encoder layers that were fine-tuned (either just the last layer, or the last two layers).

- Open 2: Our best single CamemBERT model according to results on the development data, fine-tuned on the concatenation of the training and development data. This model was fine-tuned using a batch size of 8 and a constant learning rate for 3 epochs. Only the last two layers of the encoder were fine-tuned.

- Open 3: Our second-best single CamemBERT model according to results on the development data, fine-tuned on the concatenation of the training and development data. This model was fine-tuned using a batch size of 16 for 5 epochs with linear decay of the learning rate. Only the last two layers of the encoder were fine-tuned.

The development scores of the 6 models we decided to submit are shown in Table 2.

Run	MacroF1
Closed 1	0.4816
Closed 2	0.4858
Closed 3	0.4747
Open 1	0.5556
Open 2	0.5506
Open 3	0.5497

Table 2: Scores of our 6 runs on the development set.

After producing our runs on the test set, we computed the pairwise overlap between the 6 lists of predicted labels, and observed the following:

- The maximum agreement between open and closed models was only 65%.

- Even our two single CamemBERT models (open runs 2 and 3) had pretty low agreement, at 78%.

- The highest overlap, at 96%, was between the SVM ensemble and the ProbCat model trained using the pseudo-labels of the SVM ensemble (i.e. closed runs 1 and 2 respectively).

5 Results on Test Set

The official scores of our 6 runs on the test set are shown in Table 3. The scores that ended up being computed by the organizers were: macro-averaged F1 score, weighted F1 score, and micro-averaged F1 score (i.e. accuracy).

Run	MacroF1	WeightedF1	MicroF1
Closed 1	0.3266	0.4333	0.4642
Closed 2	0.3437	0.4581	0.4936
Closed 3	0.3149	0.4188	0.4530
Open 1	0.4299	0.5121	0.5243
Open 2	0.4108	0.4977	0.5067
Open 3	0.4145	0.4910	0.4936

Table 3: Scores of our 6 runs on the test set.

These results show that, in the closed track, the SVM ensemble did better than a single SVM, and ProbCat with pseudo-labelling did best overall.

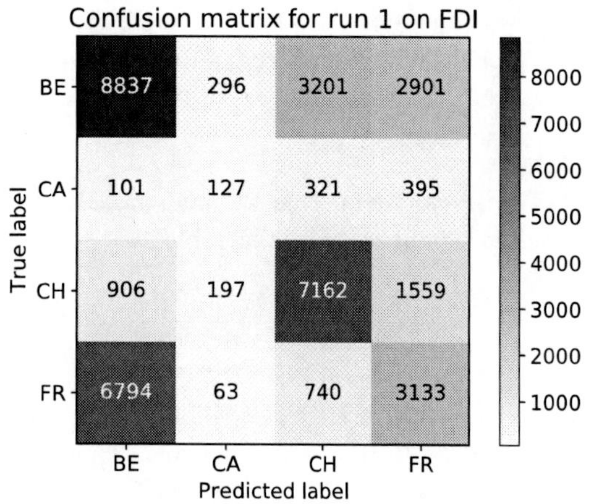

Figure 1: Confusion matrix of our best run on the test set.

This corroborated our findings on the development set, although the scores are lower, perhaps because of a larger domain shift. In the open track, the ensemble (run 1) did better than our best two individual models as expected, but our second-best model (run 3) ended up doing slightly better than our best model (run 2).

Three teams ended up submitting runs in the closed track (two or three runs each), and our three runs achieved the highest scores on the test set. We were the only team who participated in the open track, so we can only compare our results to the baselines computed by the organizers (Gaman et al., 2022). Our best open run, i.e. the ensemble of 3 fine-tuned CamemBERT models, achieved a higher macro-F1 score than the highest baseline score, which was 0.3967. This was also achieved by fine-tuning a CamemBERT model, but with different hyperparameter settings and data processing (and probably not including the development data for training). That model scored 0.4784 on the development set, whereas our run 1 model (but trained only on the training set, during model selection) scored 0.5556.

Looking at the confusion matrices of each of our runs, we observed that our open runs did quite a bit better on the CA class, getting up to 157 cases right (run 3), whereas the closed runs all got a single CA case right. The confusion matrix of our best run on the test set is shown in Fig. 1.

To get a fuller picture of the results, we investigated various potential sources of errors.

First, we looked at the class-wise F1 scores of open run 1 and how they relate to the class frequency distribution of the training data, and observed an obvious correlation between the two. Table 4 shows that the two most frequent classes in the (deduplicated) training data are also the two classes for which F1 is highest, i.e. BE and CH, and the least frequent class by far, CA, has the lowest score. Imbalanced training data is often challenging for machine learning models, and our only attempt at addressing this, by weighting the loss function when fine-tuning CamemBERT, was unsuccessful.

Class	TrainFreq	F1
BE	0.4008	0.555
CA	0.0005	0.156
CH	0.4002	0.674
FR	0.1985	0.335

Table 4: Class-wise relative frequencies in the deduplicated training set and F1 scores on the test set

Another factor that can impact the accuracy of language identification systems is the length of texts. To investigate this, we binned the test examples by length (after removing redundant NE tokens) into 10 bins of approximately equal sizes, and computed the macro-F1 and accuracy for each bin, using the predictions of our best model (open run 1). The results, shown in Table 5, indicate that macro-F1 tends to increase as texts get longer. The trend for overall accuracy (regardless of class) is less clear.

# Chars	N	Macro-F1	Accuracy
4-110	3758	0.344	0.554
111-189	3624	0.369	0.487
190-235	3656	0.389	0.508
236-275	3693	0.419	0.534
276-314	3698	0.411	0.511
315-356	3690	0.411	0.513
357-406	3627	0.445	0.522
407-471	3675	0.446	0.528
472-571	3653	0.422	0.516
572-4946	3659	0.463	0.569

Table 5: Scores with respect to text length

We also checked whether test cases that were also present in the training data had the same label, and whether our best model (open run 1) got them right. The examples we inspected included the following:

- The example "? ? ? ? ? ?" appears 8 times

in the test set, always labelled BE. Yet, in training, it was labelled FR. For some reason, our model predicts CH.

- The example "NE" appears 4 times in the test set, 3 times as BE, and once as FR. Our model predicted BE, so it was right 3 times. In the training data, it appeared in 3 classes: BE, CH, and FR.

- The example "Pour aller plus loin" was labelled CH in the training data, and predicted as such, but labelled CA in the test data.

We also inspected the examples where our 6 submissions disagreed the most, and found several examples containing boilerplate such as "Vous avez lu 29 des 432 mots de cet article", on which all 4 possible classes were among the predictions of our 6 systems. This boilerplate pattern is also present in a lot of the most likely CA examples in the test set according to our best CamemBERT model, although it generally does not belong to the CA class in the training or test data. We can not provide an explanation for this, but perhaps the lack of diversity of CA examples in the training data is the cause, as well as the frequency of such boilerplate in all classes.

One possible reason for the superior performance of CamemBERT is its subword tokenizer. We tokenized the dataset, then trained SVM and ProbCat models on the CamemBERT tokens, using token n-grams (with n between 1 and an upper bound that we raised up to 5) as features. None of the model fared better using CamemBERT tokens, so the superior performance of CamemBERT must be attributable to its pre-trained token embeddings and encoder weights.

To explore how CamemBERT's performance might be improved, we checked how many out-of-vocabulary tokens, which are represented by "<unk>", are produced by CamemBERT's tokenizer on the test set. Less than 1% of test examples (342) contain any "<unk>" tokens, so this is probably not an important source of errors, and expanding the vocabulary of the CamemBERT tokenizer and model seems unlikely to lead to significant gains.

On the whole, the analysis presented in this section seems to say more about the properties of the data than it does about the behaviour of our models, and does not point to any obvious means to improve predictive accuracy, as far as we can tell.

6 Conclusion

For the French Cross-Domain Dialect Identification shared task at the 2022 VarDial evaluation campaign, the NRC team evaluated two different approaches: SVM and probabilistic classifiers using n-gram features and trained from scratch on the data provided; and a pre-trained CamemBERT model fine-tuned on that data. The latter increased the macro-averaged F1 score on the test set from 0.344 to 0.430 (25% increase). This indicates that transfer learning can be helpful for dialect identification, and provides clear evidence that neural models can be effective at such tasks, at least when they are pre-trained on large amounts of unlabelled text.

Acknowledgements

We would like to thank the organizers for developing and running this shared task.

References

Julien Abadji, Pedro Javier Ortiz Suárez, Laurent Romary, and Benoît Sagot. 2021. Ungoliant: An optimized pipeline for the generation of a very large-scale multilingual web corpus. In *Proceedings of the Workshop on Challenges in the Management of Large Corpora (CMLC-9) 2021. Limerick, 12 July 2021 (Online-Event)*, pages 1 – 9, Mannheim. Leibniz-Institut für Deutsche Sprache.

Noëmi Aepli, Antonios Anastasopoulos, Adrian Chifu, William Domingues, Fahim Faisal, Mihaela Găman, Radu Tudor Ionescu, and Yves Scherrer. 2022. Findings of the VarDial evaluation campaign 2022. In *Proceedings of the Ninth Workshop on NLP for Similar Languages, Varieties and Dialects*, Gyeongju, Republic of Korea. International Committee on Computational Linguistics (ICCL).

Gabriel Bernier-Colborne, Cyril Goutte, and Serge Léger. 2019. Improving cuneiform language identification with BERT. In *Proceedings of the Sixth Workshop on NLP for Similar Languages, Varieties and Dialects*, pages 17–25, Ann Arbor, Michigan. Association for Computational Linguistics.

Gabriel Bernier-Colborne, Serge Leger, and Cyril Goutte. 2021. N-gram and neural models for uralic language identification: NRC at VarDial 2021. In *Proceedings of the Eighth Workshop on NLP for Similar Languages, Varieties and Dialects*, pages 128–134, Kiyv, Ukraine. Association for Computational Linguistics.

Isaac Caswell, Theresa Breiner, Daan van Esch, and Ankur Bapna. 2020. Language ID in the wild: Unexpected challenges on the path to a thousand-language web text corpus. In *Proceedings of the 28th International Conference on Computational Linguistics*, pages 6588–6608, Barcelona, Spain (Online). International Committee on Computational Linguistics.

Bharathi Raja Chakravarthi, Mihaela Găman, Radu Tudor Ionescu, Heidi Jauhiainen, Tommi Jauhiainen, Krister Lindén, Nikola Ljubešić, Niko Partanen, Ruba Priyadharshini, Christoph Purschke, Eswari Rajagopal, Yves Scherrer, and Marcos Zampieri. 2021. Findings of the VarDial Evaluation Campaign 2021. In *Proceedings of the Eighth Workshop on NLP for Similar Languages, Varieties and Dialects (VarDial)*.

Jacob Devlin, Ming-Wei Chang, Kenton Lee, and Kristina Toutanova. 2019. BERT: Pre-training of deep bidirectional transformers for language understanding. In *Proceedings of the 2019 Conference of the North American Chapter of the Association for Computational Linguistics: Human Language Technologies, Volume 1 (Long and Short Papers)*, pages 4171–4186, Minneapolis, Minnesota. Association for Computational Linguistics.

Mihaela Gaman, Adrian Gabriel Chifu, William Domingues, and Radu Tudor Ionescu. 2022. FreCDo: A New Corpus for Large-Scale French Cross-Domain Dialect Identification. *(under review)*.

Eric Gaussier, Cyril Goutte, Kris Popat, and Francine Chen. 2002. A hierarchical model for clustering and categorising documents. In *Proceedings of the 24th BCS-IRSG European Colloquium on IR Research: Advances in Information Retrieval*, pages 229–247. Springer-Verlag.

Cyril Goutte and Serge Léger. 2016. Advances in Ngram-based Discrimination of Similar Languages. In *Proceedings of the Third Workshop on NLP for Similar Languages, Varieties and Dialects (VarDial3)*, pages 178–184, Osaka, Japan.

Cyril Goutte, Serge Léger, and Marine Carpuat. 2014. The NRC system for discriminating similar languages. In *Proceedings of the First Workshop on Applying NLP Tools to Similar Languages, Varieties and Dialects (VarDial)*, pages 139–145, Dublin, Ireland.

Tommi Jauhiainen, Marco Lui, Marcos Zampieri, Timothy Baldwin, and Krister Lindén. 2019. Automatic Language Identification in Texts: A Survey. *Journal of Artificial Intelligence Research*, 65:675–782.

Armand Joulin, Edouard Grave, Piotr Bojanowski, and Tomas Mikolov. 2017. Bag of tricks for efficient text classification. In *Proceedings of the 15th Conference of the European Chapter of the Association for Computational Linguistics: Volume 2, Short Papers*, pages 427–431, Valencia, Spain. Association for Computational Linguistics.

Samuel Larkin, Eric Joanis, Darlene Stewart, Michel Simard, George Foster, Nicola Ueffing, and Aaron Tikuisis. 2022. Portage Text Processing.

Yinhan Liu, Myle Ott, Naman Goyal, Jingfei Du, Mandar Joshi, Danqi Chen, Omer Levy, Mike Lewis, Luke Zettlemoyer, and Veselin Stoyanov. 2019. RoBERTa: A robustly optimized BERT pretraining approach.

Ilya Loshchilov and Frank Hutter. 2019. Decoupled weight decay regularization. In *International Conference on Learning Representations*.

Louis Martin, Benjamin Muller, Pedro Javier Ortiz Suárez, Yoann Dupont, Laurent Romary, Éric de la Clergerie, Djamé Seddah, and Benoît Sagot. 2020. CamemBERT: a tasty French language model. In *Proceedings of the 58th Annual Meeting of the Association for Computational Linguistics*, pages 7203–7219, Online. Association for Computational Linguistics.

Pedro Javier Ortiz Suárez, Laurent Romary, and Benoît Sagot. 2020. A monolingual approach to contextualized word embeddings for mid-resource languages. In *Proceedings of the 58th Annual Meeting of the Association for Computational Linguistics*, pages 1703–1714, Online. Association for Computational Linguistics.

Pedro Javier Ortiz Suárez, Benoît Sagot, and Laurent Romary. 2019. Asynchronous pipelines for processing huge corpora on medium to low resource infrastructures. In *Proceedings of the Workshop on Challenges in the Management of Large Corpora (CMLC-7) 2019. Cardiff, 22nd July 2019*, pages 9 – 16, Mannheim. Leibniz-Institut für Deutsche Sprache.

Alec Radford, Karthik Narasimhan, Tim Salimans, and Ilya Sutskever. 2018. Improving language understanding by generative pre-training.

Rico Sennrich, Barry Haddow, and Alexandra Birch. 2016. Neural machine translation of rare words with subword units. In *Proceedings of the 54th Annual Meeting of the Association for Computational Linguistics (Volume 1: Long Papers)*, pages 1715–1725, Berlin, Germany. Association for Computational Linguistics.

Marcos Zampieri, Shervin Malmasi, Yves Scherrer, Tanja Samardžić, Francis Tyers, Miikka Silfverberg, Natalia Klyueva, Tung-Le Pan, Chu-Ren Huang, Radu Tudor Ionescu, Andrei Butnaru, and Tommi Jauhiainen. 2019. A Report on the Third VarDial Evaluation Campaign. In *Proceedings of the Sixth Workshop on NLP for Similar Languages, Varieties and Dialects (VarDial)*. Association for Computational Linguistics.

Marcos Zampieri, Preslav Nakov, and Yves Scherrer. 2020. Natural language processing for similar languages, varieties, and dialects: A survey. *Natural Language Engineering*, 26(6):595–612.

Italian Language and Dialect Identification and Regional French Variety Detection using Adaptive Naive Bayes

Tommi Jauhiainen, Heidi Jauhiainen, Krister Lindén
Department of Digital Humanities, University of Helsinki, Finland
tommi.jauhiainen@helsinki.fi

Abstract

This article describes the language identification approach used by the SUKI team in the Identification of Languages and Dialects of Italy and the French Cross-Domain Dialect Identification shared tasks organized as part of the VarDial workshop 2022. We describe some experiments and the preprocessing techniques we used for the training data in preparation for the shared task submissions, which are also discussed. Our Naive Bayes-based adaptive system reached the first position in Italian language identification and came second in the French variety identification task.

1 Introduction

Language identification (LI) of digital text still poses difficulties for text classification methods when performed in more complex situations (Jauhiainen et al., 2019d). One of the problematic contexts is the closeness of the languages to be identified. In this article, we tackle the problem of close language identification for languages or dialects traditionally used in Italy and distinguishing between regional French varieties used in Europe and Canada. The research and experiments were conducted while participating in the language identification shared tasks organized in connection with the ninth edition of the VarDial workshop for NLP for similar languages, varieties, and dialects (Aepli et al., 2022). The French Cross-Domain Dialect Identification (FDI) and the Identification of Languages and Dialects of Italy (ITDI) shared tasks were organized for the first time. However, they were following a long line of VarDial-related LI shared tasks from the Discriminating Between Similar languages (DSL) tasks in 2014–2017 (Zampieri et al., 2014, 2015; Malmasi et al., 2016; Zampieri et al., 2017) to newer, more specialized ones such as Romanian Dialect Identification (RDI) and Uralic Language Identification (ULI) in 2020 and 2021 (Gaman et al., 2020; Chakravarthi et al., 2021).

The ITDI shared task focused on 11 living Romance languages or dialects: Emiliano-Romagnolo (*eml*), Friulian (*fur*), Ladin (*lld*), Ligurian (*lij*), Lombard (*lmo*), Neapolitan (*nap*), Piemontese (*pms*), Sardinian (*srd*), Sicilian (*scn*), Tarantino (considered a dialect of Neapolitan by ISO 639-3), and Venetian (*vec*). The shared task was a closed one; hence, no other data besides that indicated and provided by the organizers were to be used. The organizers also stated that the test set would contain only a subset of the 11 languages.

The FDI shared task featured four regional varieties of written French from news sites in France, Belgium, Switzerland, and Canada. The organizers of the task provided all the data.

In Section 2, we present previous work on language identification of the languages that are the targets of these two shared tasks. In Section 3, we describe the data provided and allowed in the tasks, and, in Section 4, we present our method. Our experiments and the preprocessing done to the training data are explained in Section 5. In Section 6, we present and discuss the results of the submitted runs.

2 Previous Work

To our knowledge, there is no previous LI research focusing specifically on the languages of Italy. However, previous language identification-related research has featured the rare Romance languages that make up the ITDI repertoire. Emiliano-Romagnolo, Friulian, and Sardinian were part of the 372 languages featured in the research by Rodrigues (2012). Benedetto et al. (2002) automatically created a phylogenetic-like tree for languages based on more than 50 versions of the Universal Declaration of Human Rights, including the Friulian and the Sardinian editions. Lombard, Piemontese, Sicilian, and Venetian were featured in the ex-

Proceedings of the Ninth Workshop on NLP for Similar Languages, Varieties and Dialects, pages 119–129
October 16, 2022.

periments leading to the development of the HeLI-method (Jauhiainen, 2010; Jauhiainen et al., 2016). Lombard, Neapolitan, Piemontese, Sicilian, and Venetian were included in the LI experiments conducted by Majliš (2011). King and Abney (2013) and King (2015) investigated word-level language identification in multilingual documents, including mixed Lombard - English, among other combinations. Bernier-Colborne et al. (2021) mention the Lombard - Italian pair as one of the top 10 most frequently confused pairs in the ULI-178 track of the Uralic Language Identification shared task. The ULI-178 track was a general language identification task between 178 languages, among them Lombard, Piemontese, Sardinian, Sicilian, and Venetian (Jauhiainen et al., 2020b). Neapolitan, Piemontese, and Sicilian were part of the ALTW 2010 multilingual language identification shared task dataset (Baldwin and Lui, 2010). Caswell et al. (2020) investigated language identification in the context of web crawling and mention Neapolitan, Sicilian, and Venetian as part of the lowest-resource languages in their research. All the languages of the task except Lombard were included in the language identifier featuring more than 900 languages developed by Brown (2012, 2013). Also, Lombard was added to his version with more than 1300 languages (Brown, 2014).[1] Emiliano-Romagnolo, Lombard, Neapolitan, Piemontese, Sicilian, and Venetian are part of the repertoire of the FastText off-the-shelf language identifier[2] and Lombard, Piemontese, Sardinian, and Sicilian are included in the HeLI-OTS off-the-shelf language identifier (Jauhiainen et al., 2022).[3]

Distinguishing between French regional varieties from France and Canada was part of the overall aims in the 2016 and 2017 editions of the Discriminating between Similar Languages (DSL) shared tasks (Malmasi et al., 2016; Zampieri et al., 2017).[4] The 2016 edition of the DSL was won by the *tubasfs* team using SVM and character n-grams from one to seven (Çöltekin and Rama, 2016). They managed to achieve 95.8% recall for the Canadian variety and 94.0% recall for the French variety. In 2016, we came second with a HeLI method-based identifier using words and character n-grams from one to six (Jauhiainen et al., 2016). The DSL 2017, the last one of its kind, was won by the *CECL* team using SVM with character n-grams from one to four in the first stage to detect the language group and another SVM with a variety of features in addition to character n-grams such as POS tag n-grams, the proportion of capitalized letters and punctuation marks to detect the language within the group (Bestgen, 2017).

[1] https://sourceforge.net/projects/la-strings/files/

[2] https://fasttext.cc/docs/en/language-identification.html

[3] https://doi.org/10.5281/zenodo.4780897

[4] http://ttg.uni-saarland.de/resources/DSLCC/

3 Data

3.1 ITDI

In the ITDI, the participants were allowed to train their systems using the Wikipedia dumps for the 11 languages or dialects featured in the shared task. Additionally, it was possible to use the dump of the Italian language Wikipedia. All featured languages or dialects have their version of the Wikipedia online encyclopedia written in their respective language or dialect. The ISO 639-3 identifier *eml* for Emilian-Romagnol is considered deprecated as the language has been split into separate Emilian (*egl*) and Romagnol (*rgn*) languages, but Wikipedia is still shared between both languages.[5] The Sardinian, *srd*, is considered a macrolanguage in ISO 639-3, containing four separate Sardinian languages. It is possible that the Wikipedias for the *eml* and *srd* contain articles written in those separate languages. However, we did not investigate this possibility further. We did not utilize the Italian Wikipedia in any way in the experiments. The list of languages and dialects, their ISO 639-3 codes, tags used in the shared task, and the identities of their Wikipedia dumps can be seen in Table 1.

In contrast to the training data, the material for system development was provided directly by the shared task organizers. It came in one text file containing 6,799 lines which seemed to be single sentences preceded by the shared task tags. The development set included only a subset of seven of the 11 languages. The shared task participants had been informed that the test set would also be a subset of the 11 languages, but the number and identity of the missing languages were not indicated. The languages and the amount of development data for each of them can be seen in Table 2. The test set contained 11,090 lines in unknown languages or dialects.

[5] https://eml.wikipedia.org/wiki/Lèngua_emigliàna-rumagnôla

Language/Dialect	ISO 639-3	ST tag	Dump name with date	.bz2 size
Emiliano-Romagnolo	*eml*	**EML**	emlwiki-20220301	9.3 MB
Friulian	*fur*	**FUR**	furwiki-20220301	2.5 MB
Ladin	*lld*	**LLD**	lldwiki-20220301	2.8 MB
Ligurian	*lij*	**LIJ**	lijwiki-20220301	6.6 MB
Lombard	*lmo*	**LMO**	lmowiki-20220301	25 MB
Neapolitan	*nap*	**NAP**	napwiki-20220301	5.4 MB
Piemontese	*pms*	**PMS**	pmswiki-20220301	14 MB
Sardinian	*srd*	**SC**	scwiki-20220301	7.2 MB
Sicilian	*scn*	**SCN**	scnwiki-20220301	12 MB
Tarantino	*nap*	**ROA_TARA**	roa_tarawiki-20220301	6.4 MB
Venetian	*vec*	**VEC**	vecwiki-20220301	27 MB

Table 1: The Wikipedia dumps used in the ITDI shared task.

ST tag	lines
EML	0
FUR	676
LLD	0
LIJ	617
LMO	1,231
NAP	0
PMS	1,191
SC	477
SCN	1,371
ROA_TARA	0
VEC	1,236

Table 2: The number of lines of each language in the development set of the ITDI shared task.

3.2 FDI

In the FDI, the participants were provided with training and development data for four regional varieties of French from France, Belgium, Switzerland, and Canada (Gaman et al., 2022). The data had been extracted from news websites in these countries using country-independent query words. A named entity recognizer (NER) Spacy had been run on the data, and all the detected entities had been changed to $\$NE\$$ in order to remove country-specific bias. The data is divided into paragraphs of three sentences or less. The amount of data for the different varieties is not balanced, as seen in Table 3. According to the data compilers, it was not easy to get Canadian material as most news sites in the country are subscription-based (Gaman et al., 2022).

In both the training and the development sets, the lines seem not to have been randomized. When we tested combining consecutive lines, they seemed to make up complete news articles or web pages. However, we expected the test set not to repeat this pattern.

4 Method

We used the same system we had developed for and used in the winning submission of the 2021 edition of Romanian Dialect Identification (Jauhiainen et al., 2021).[6] The system uses a Naive Bayes-based method using the observed relative frequencies of multiple-size character n-grams as probabilities. We first used the method as a baseline for the Cuneiform Language Identification (CLI) shared task (Jauhiainen et al., 2019a) and later with adaptive language models (Jauhiainen et al., 2019c) to win the Discriminating between the Mainland and Taiwan variation of Mandarin Chinese (DMT) (Jauhiainen et al., 2019b) and the RDI 2021 (Jauhiainen et al., 2021) shared tasks. The Naive Bayes type method adds together logarithms of the relative frequencies of character *n*-gram combinations f_i in the training data C_g as defined in Equation 1:

$$R(g, M) = -lg_{10} \prod_{i=1}^{\ell_{MF}} v_{C_g}(f_i) = \sum_{i=1}^{\ell_{MF}} -lg_{10}(v_{C_g}(f_i)) \quad (1)$$

where ℓ_{MF} is the number of individual features in the mystery text M to be identified and f_i is M's ith feature. The relative frequency, $v_{C_g}(f)$, is calculated as in Equation 2:

$$v_{C_g}(f) = \begin{cases} \frac{c(C_g, f)}{\ell_{C_g^F}}, \text{ if } c(C_g, f) > 0 \\ \frac{1}{\ell_{C_g^F}} pm, \text{ otherwise} \end{cases} \quad (2)$$

[6]The implementation of the language identifier used to produce the best results for the ITDI shared task is available from GitHub at `https://github.com/tosaja/TunPRF`.

Variety	Code	#lines	#tokens	Tokens per line	#NE
France	FR	61,777	4,224,301	68	587,138
Belgium	BE	121,746	7,241,609	59	1,104,562
Switzerland	CH	141,261	8,494,657	60	1,112,525
Canada	CA	34,003	1,694,760	50	184,083

Table 3: The training and development datasets sizes for the FDI shared task.

where $c(C_g, f)$ is the count of feature f in the training corpus C_g of the language g. $\ell_{C_g^F}$ is the length of the corpus C_g when it has been transformed into a collection of features F, e.g., features of the same type as f. The pm is the penalty modifier, which is optimized using the development data.

The system uses an adaptation technique to learn from the test data (Jauhiainen et al., 2019c). There is also a possibility to perform iterative adaptation, in which the test data is processed several times from the beginning of the adaptation process.

The exact range of the used character n-grams is optimized using the development data. After optimizing the basic method, the parameters for the adaptive version are determined. In the adaptation technique, the test data is first identified with the basic method, and a confidence score is calculated for each identified instance. The confidence score is the difference between the scores of the best and the second-best language. The test instances are sorted according to the confidence scores and then divided into a certain number of splits. The number of splits is determined using the development data. The character n-gram frequency information from the most confident split is added to the respective language models, and the rest of the material is re-identified with the adapted models. Then the rest of the material is again sorted and divided into equally sized splits, and the information from the most confident split is added to the models and the rest re-identified. The previous process is repeated until all the material is added to the language models.

In the iterative version, the adaptation process is restarted from the beginning. The number of possible iterations is also determined using the development set.

5 Experiments

This section presents the details of the experiments and various preprocessing techniques we used when participating in the shared tasks.

5.1 ITDI

The organizers of the Identification of Languages and Dialects of Italy shared task provided a script that could be used to generate a .json file from the .bz2 files downloaded from Wikipedia. Instead of using the script, we created plain text versions of the dumps using the command:

```
-m wikiextractor.WikiExtractor
xxxwiki-20220301- ... .bz2 -o xxx_texts
```

The training data extracted this way contained 1.91 million lines, some extended text passages, and some just short headings, names, or even empty lines. The first thing we did was to remove duplicate lines within each language or dialect. This deduplication procedure reduced the size of the training data to 0.93 million lines.

As the next step, we removed the lines containing wiki markup, which we found by using the following regular expressions:

```
&lt;comment&gt;.*&lt;/comment&gt;
&lt;contributor&gt;
&lt;/contributor&gt;
&lt;format&gt;.*&lt;/format&gt;
&lt;ip&gt;.*&lt;/ip&gt;
&lt;minor /&gt;
&lt;model&gt;.*&lt;/model&gt;
&lt;ns.*/ns&gt;
&lt;parentid&gt;.*&lt;/parentid&gt;
&lt;revision&gt;
&lt;timestamp&gt;.*&lt;/timestamp&gt;
&lt;username&gt;.*&lt;/username&gt;
```

We also removed all lines with a tab character followed by a lowercase letter and unified the numbers so that all number characters were changed to "1". Then, we again removed duplicate lines which left us with 880,000 lines. At this point, we took an inventory of the number of lines for each language and dialect (Table 4).

At each stage, we had tested the performance of our Naive Bayes-based system on the development data. At this stage, the Lombard language had the worst precision with 83.2%, and we decided to try and clean its training data to improve its precision. As it seemed that, in general, shorter lines were of lower quality than longer ones, we removed all Lombard lines with less than 14 characters from

ST tag	# lines
EML	16,425
FUR	18,040
LLD	31,524
LIJ	38,645
LMO	185,116
NAP	34,327
PMS	208,485
SC	41,169
SCN	95,693
ROA_TARA	36,818
VEC	173,452

Table 4: The number of lines for each language or dialect in the ITDI training data after unifying the number characters.

the training corpus. We also did further cleaning of the wiki markup for all languages by removing lines using the following regular expressions:

```
&lt;/math&gt;
&lt;/[pP]oem&gt;
&lt;/small&gt;
&lt;references&gt;
&lt;/html&gt;
&lt;/includeonly&gt;&lt;/onlyinclude&gt;
&lt;/table&gt;
&lt;?php
&lt;BR C.* &gt;
#redirect
```

We removed all lines that did not include lowercase ASCII characters and the remaining “<” and “br>” tags. Once more, we removed any possible duplicate lines. Our efforts to improve the precision of LMO were in vain, as it dropped from 83.2% to 83.0%. However, the micro F1 over all the languages remained the same, 92.7, so we kept the changes.

At this stage, the Venetian language had the worst recall of all the languages, 75.6%. While taking a look at the erroneously identified sentences, we noticed that, in fact, part of the Venetian Wikipedia used a slightly different orthography than the development data. The Wikipedia dumps contained the “ł” and “Ł” characters, whereas only “l” and “L” were present in the development data. We used a simple regular expression to change the training data to correspond with the development data. This unification of orthographies improved the recall of Venetian from 75.6% to 79.1% and the precision of Lombard from 83.0% to 85.6%. The overall micro F1 also increased slightly from 92.7 to 93.3.

One phenomenon we were aware of due to our previous experiences using Wikipedia dumps as training material was that some of the smaller Wikipedias might contain relatively large parts automatically generated from a database. In particular, the pages describing the French municipalities are usually generated using templates. These template-based articles were also found as part of the Venetian Wikipedia: out of the 173,091 Venetian lines, 33,701 were automatically generated information about French communes. We removed the lines using the following regular expression to detect them:

```
egrep -v 'el xe on comun de.*abitanti del
departemento.*in Fransa\.'
```

The recall of Venetian increased from 79,1% to 84,0%, and at the same time, the precision of Lombard rose from 85.6% to 88.2%.

Venetian still had the lowest individual F1 score, 89.9. We aimed to increase further the quality of the training set by first removing all lines which did not have a word beginning with a lowercase ASCII letter and then removing all the 2,983 lines explaining roman numbers such as:

```
El 11 (LXIII en numeri romani) el xe ...
El 11 (LXIV en numeri romani) el xe ...
El 11 (LXIX in numeri romani) el xe ...
El 11 (LXV en numeri romani) el xe ...
```

Additionally, in a similar manner to the French towns, we removed the municipalities of Italy listed in the Venetian Wikipedia. These cleaning operations resulted in a slight increase of the F1 to 90.3. The overall micro F1 had by now risen from 93.3 to 94.2.

Further cleaning, e.g., removing lines describing the Spanish towns in the Venetian Wikipedia and removing all lines containing specific additional wiki markup, did not improve the overall F1 score. As further preprocessing seemed less fruitful, we started experimenting with the adaptive version of the Naive Bayes identifier, with which evaluating new versions of the training corpora would take much longer.

We tested the adaptive version with 128, 256, and 512 splits. Additionally, we tested with 128 splits and two iterations. They all returned the same micro F1 of 96.2, which was higher than the score of 94.2, which was attained without adaptation.[7]

[7]If time allowed, one would begin finding the optimal number of splits from two and then double the number of splits every iteration as we did with FDI (see Table 6). Due to time constraints, for ITDI, we skipped the first ones. If 128 splits had produced better results than 256 splits, we would

In the end, we opted to continue using 512 splits with only one adaptation round.

Afterward, we still decided to continue training corpora cleaning and removed additional template-generated text from Lombard training data. Additionally, we removed from all languages those lines that did not include a space character followed by a lowercase ASCII alphabetical character, e.g., those that did not have a word starting with a lowercase letter. These modifications did not improve the results, but we still decided to use them as we considered the training data to be in better shape.

As stated by the organizers and indicated by the languages missing from the development set, the test data would not include all the languages in the training data. Furthermore, we were unsure what measure would be used to evaluate the submissions. These facts led us to prepare one submission in preparation for the measure being macro F1. Also, we hoped that leaving out unnecessary languages might help to boost the performance of the remaining languages. We have previously developed a method for language set identification (Jauhiainen et al., 2015) and used it while collecting rare Uralic languages from the internet (Jauhiainen et al., 2020a). However, instead of using our language set identification method, we devised a simple thresholding method to leave out the most probable unnecessary languages using the development set as a guideline. Based on the development set, we surmised that it would be safe to remove from the repertoire those languages that, after all lines had been identified once, had been assigned fewer lines than 10% of the average number of lines for each language.

5.2 FDI

In the French Cross-Domain Dialect Identification shared task, the training data seemed to be of better quality than in the ITDI, and when perusing it, we did not notice any need for extensive preprocessing. We started with optimizing the parameters for the Naive Bayes identifier. Our first optimization run gave the best result, a micro F1 of 0.646, with just character six-grams, which were the maximum size for n-grams on that run.

We noticed that the training data for some language varieties contained a large amount of repetition, as seen in Table 5. Especially the Canadian variety training corpus consisted of identical lines

have experimented with 64 splits and continued reducing the number of splits as long as the results improved.

Code	#lines	#unique lines
FR	61,777	55,927
BE	121,746	113,487
CH	141,261	107,982
CA	34,003	169

Table 5: The number of lines in the FDI training data before and after removing duplicates.

repeated hundreds of times. Even the rarest lines in that corpus are repeated 55 times.

We did the same initial optimization run with the deduplicated training data and ended up with a micro F1 of 0.634. The score was slightly worse than before deduplication, so we continued experimenting with the original training set. We also tested lowercasing the training data and the mystery texts, which gave lower micro F1 scores with both original and deduplicated datasets. Further optimization with higher order n-grams led us to use only character eight-grams and the penalty modifier of 1.26, which gave a micro F1 score of 0.675 on the development data. We then optimized with the deduplicated training data, which resulted in eight grams and a penalty modifier of 1.73, giving a micro F1 of 0.659, which was again lower than without deduplication. Next, we experimented with removing the named entity tags from the training and the development data, which again resulted in a slightly lower micro F1 of 0.659.

So far, we had used the micro F1 as our guideline when optimizing the system even though we were aware that the macro F1 would be used to rank the official submissions. The reason for using micro F1 was that our optimization system did not produce correct macro F1 scores, which we fixed at this stage. The macro F1 corresponding to micro F1 of 0.675 was 0.495. We then proceeded to experiment with the adaptive version of the identifier.

We evaluated several combinations of the number of splits and iteration rounds as seen in Table 6. In the end, we used the character eight-grams, the penalty modifier of 1.26, 128 splits, and three iterations, giving us a macro F1 of 0.553 and a micro F1 of 0.745 on the development set.

As a last experiment, we decided to try to unify the numbers in a similar way we did with the ITDI data using the non-adaptive version of the system. Unifying the numbers increased the macro F1 from 0.495 to 0.498 and the micro F1 from 0.675 to 0.681. Due to limited time, we could not run the

# splits	# iterations	Macro F1	Micro F1
2	4	0.510	0.698
4	4	0.523	0.713
8	4	0.537	0.729
16	4	0.550	0.742
32	3	0.552	0.744
64	3-4	0.5526	0.7450
128	3-4	**0.5529**	**0.7454**
256	3-4	0.5527	0.7451
512	3-4	0.5525	0.7449
1024	3-4	0.5524	0.7447

Table 6: Optimizing adaptation parameters with the FDI training and development data. The best scores are bolded.

adaptive version on development data. As unifying improved the results, we decided to unify the numbers with the adaptive version for the actual submissions.

6 Results

In this section, we describe the results of the submitted runs and the conclusions we can derive from them.

6.1 ITDI

We submitted three sets of predictions for the ITDI task. The main difference between the submissions was the data used to train the identifier. All the submissions used character n-grams from three to eight with a penalty modifier of 2.1. The number of splits in adaptation was set to 512, and iterative adaptation was not used. We added a space character to the beginning and the end of the text to be identified so that our identifier would recognize the beginning of the first word and the end of the last word.

The first submission used combined training and development data, and the second just the training data. The third system combined the training and development data but without the data for Piemontese and Sardinian, which were discarded in the language set identification phase due to having less than the threshold amount of instances. The weighted average F1 score for all of our three submissions was quite similar and on a completely different level from the results of the best submissions of the two other participating teams, as seen in Table 7. The best baseline provided by the organizers was closer to our results than those of the other teams but still substantially behind them.

Team	Submission	Wgt. F1	Mac. F1
SUKI	2	0.9007	0.6729
SUKI	1	0.8983	0.6714
SUKI	3	0.8982	0.7458
Org.	Baseline	0.7726	0.5193
Phlyers	3	0.6943	0.5379
ETHZ	3	0.6880	0.4828

Table 7: The results of the ITDI shared task with the best baseline.

Without further experiments, it is difficult to say whether the distance to the other teams is due to differences in preprocessing Wikipedia or to using adaptive language models. The results on the language/dialect level can be seen in Table 8. The worst performing language of the languages present in the test set was the Neapolitan dialect Tarantino.

6.2 FDI

All our submissions to the FDI shared task used character eight grams with a penalty modifier of 1.26. The number of splits in adaptation was set to 128, and three iterations of adaptation to the test data were used. As in the ITDI task, the difference between the submissions comes from the data used for training. The first submission uses the training data, the second uses the development data, and the third uses a combination of both.

In contrast to the ITDI, the FDI shared task was ranked using the macro F1 score. The macro F1 score of our best submission, 0.266, was far behind the 0.344 of the winning NRC team. However, the results of the NRC team were still clearly lower than that of the best baseline, CamemBERT (Gaman et al., 2022), as seen in Table 9.

Table 10 is a confusion matrix for our third and best run. The contrast to our second run in Table 11 is dramatic. In the third run, only 28 lines were identified as the Canadian variety as opposed to the 15,518 lines identified as the Swiss variety. In the second run, 6,188 lines were identified as the Canadian variety and only 28 as the Swiss variety. It seems that the choice of training data is mostly responsible for these great differences.

The difference between our results on the development data vs. the test data is quite significant compared to similar results reported by the organizers (Gaman et al., 2022). Table 12 shows how our Macro F1 drops over 50% from development

Language	Precision	Recall	F1 score	Lines in test
EML	0.8916	0.9273	0.9091	825
FUR	0.9969	0.9781	0.9874	1,323
LIJ	0.9831	0.9947	0.9889	2,282
LLD	0.9971	0.9268	0.9607	2,200
LMO	0.8991	0.9826	0.9390	689
NAP	0.8927	0.887	0.8898	2,026
ROA_TARA	0.7532	0.0962	0.1706	603
SC	0	0	0	0
SCN	0	0	0	0
VEC	0.7929	0.9982	0.8838	1,139

Table 8: Per language results for our best submission on the ITDI shared task.

Team	Submission	Macro F1	Weighted F1	Micro F1
CamemBERT	baseline	0.3967	-	0.5584
NRC	2	0.3437	0.4581	0.4936
SUKI	3	0.2661	0.3422	0.3918
DontClassify	1	0.2627	0.3236	0.3914
SUKI	1	0.2603	0.3439	0.3984
SUKI	2	0.1383	0.1958	0.2339

Table 9: The results of the FDI shared task.

	BE	CA	CH	FR	Recall	Precision	F1 score
BE	7,252	1	7,119	863	47.6%	39.4%	43.1
CA	97	16	574	257	1.7%	57.1%	3.3
CH	2,148	1	6,570	1,105	66.9%	42.3%	51.9
FR	8,912	10	1,255	553	5.2%	19.9%	8.2

Table 10: The confusion matrix for our third and best submission at the FDI shared task, with the recall, precision, and the F1 score for each variety.

	BE	CA	CH	FR	Recall	Precision	F1 score
BE	7,262	5,220	5	2,748	47.7%	31.3%	37.8
CA	717	162	2	63	17.2%	2.6%	4.5
CH	5,940	568	7	3,309	0.1%	25.0%	0.1
FR	9,317	238	14	1,161	10.8%	15.9%	12.9

Table 11: The confusion matrix for our second submission at the FDI shared task, with the recall, precision, and the F1 score for each variety.

to testing, whereas the drop for the best baseline is less than 20%. After the shared tasks, we created a version of our Naive Bayes system, which automatically determines the best parameters using the development set. Using the new implementation, we conducted some further experiments with the language annotated test data, and now it is clear that the optimal character n-gram range for the test data differs significantly from that of the development data. The optimal character range for the test data seems to be from four to seven characters, whereas it is from eight to eight for the development data. With the optimal character n-gram range, the NB identifier gets a macro F1 score of 0.3539 without language model adaptation. This score would be more comparable with the scores of the winning NRC submission. However, the real issue was the language model adaptation which lowered the results considerably. On the one hand, even using just the character eight-grams without adaptation gives the macro F1 score of 0.3306 on the test data, and on the other hand, using character n-grams from four to seven, the optimal range, with adaptation results in macro F1 score of 0.2628.

Acknowledgements

The research was conducted within the Language Identification of Speech and Text project funded by the Finnish Research Impact Foundation from its Tandem Industry Academia funding in cooperation with Lingsoft.

References

Noëmi Aepli, Antonios Anastasopoulos, Adrian Chifu, William Domingues, Fahim Faisal, Mihaela Găman, Radu Tudor Ionescu, and Yves Scherrer. 2022. Findings of the VarDial evaluation campaign 2022. In *Proceedings of the Ninth Workshop on NLP for Similar Languages, Varieties and Dialects*, Gyeongju, Republic of Korea.

Timothy Baldwin and Marco Lui. 2010. Multilingual language identification: ALTW 2010 shared task data. In *Proceedings of the Australasian Language Technology Association Workshop 2010*, pages 4–7, Melbourne, Australia.

Dario Benedetto, Emanuele Caglioti, and Vittorio Loreto. 2002. Language Trees and Zipping. *Physical Review Letters*, 88(4).

Gabriel Bernier-Colborne, Serge Leger, and Cyril Goutte. 2021. N-gram and Neural Models for Uralic Language Identification: NRC at VarDial 2021. In *Proceedings of the Eighth Workshop on NLP for Similar Languages, Varieties and Dialects*, pages 128–134, Kyiv, Ukraine. Association for Computational Linguistics.

Yves Bestgen. 2017. Improving the character ngram model for the DSL task with BM25 weighting and less frequently used feature sets. In *Proceedings of the Fourth Workshop on NLP for Similar Languages, Varieties and Dialects (VarDial)*, pages 115–123, Valencia, Spain. Association for Computational Linguistics.

Ralf Brown. 2014. Non-linear Mapping for Improved Identification of 1300+ Languages. In *Proceedings of the 2014 Conference on Empirical Methods in Natural Language Processing (EMNLP)*, pages 627–632, Doha, Qatar. Association for Computational Linguistics.

Ralf D. Brown. 2012. Finding and Identifying Text in 900+ Languages. *Digital Investigation*, 9:S34–S43.

Ralf D. Brown. 2013. Selecting and Weighting N-grams to Identify 1100 Languages. In *Proceedings of the 16th International Conference on Text, Speech and Dialogue (TSD 2013)*, pages 475–483, Plzeň, Czech Republic.

Isaac Caswell, Theresa Breiner, Daan van Esch, and Ankur Bapna. 2020. Language ID in the wild: Unexpected challenges on the path to a thousand-language web text corpus. In *Proceedings of the 28th International Conference on Computational Linguistics*, pages 6588–6608, Barcelona, Spain (Online). International Committee on Computational Linguistics.

Bharathi Raja Chakravarthi, Mihaela Gaman, Radu Tudor Ionescu, Heidi Jauhiainen, Tommi Jauhiainen, Krister Lindén, Nikola Ljubešić, Niko Partanen, Ruba Priyadharshini, Christoph Purschke, Eswari Rajagopal, Yves Scherrer, and Marcos Zampieri. 2021. Findings of the VarDial evaluation campaign 2021. In *Proceedings of the Eighth Workshop on NLP for Similar Languages, Varieties and Dialects*, pages 1–11, Kyiv, Ukraine. Association for Computational Linguistics.

Çağrı Çöltekin and Taraka Rama. 2016. Discriminating Similar Languages: Experiments with Linear SVMs and Neural Networks. In *Proceedings of the Third Workshop on NLP for Similar Languages, Varieties and Dialects*, pages 15–24, Osaka, Japan.

Mihaela Gaman, Adrian Gabriel Chifu, William Domingues, and Radu Tudor Ionescu. 2022. FreCDo: A New Corpus for Large-Scale French Cross-Domain Dialect Identification. *(under review)*.

Mihaela Gaman, Dirk Hovy, Radu Tudor Ionescu, Heidi Jauhiainen, Tommi Jauhiainen, Krister Lindén, Nikola Ljubešić, Niko Partanen, Christoph Purschke, Yves Scherrer, and Marcos Zampieri. 2020. A Report on the VarDial Evaluation Campaign 2020. In *Proceedings of the 7th Workshop on NLP for Similar Languages, Varieties and Dialects*, pages 1–14,

System	Source data	Target data	Macro F1	Micro F1
CamemBERT	Training	Development	0.4784	0.7352
CamemBERT	Training	Testing	0.3967	0.5584
Adaptive NB	Training	Development	0.5529	0.7454
Adaptive NB	Training + Development	Testing	0.2661	0.3918
Adaptive NB	Training	Testing	0.2603	0.3984

Table 12: Comparison between the baseline results and our best submission.

Barcelona, Spain (Online). International Committee on Computational Linguistics (ICCL).

Heidi Jauhiainen, Tommi Jauhiainen, and Krister Lindén. 2020a. Building Web Corpora for Minority Languages. In *Proceedings of the 12th Web as Corpus Workshop*, pages 23–32, Marseille, France. European Language Resources Association.

Tommi Jauhiainen. 2010. Tekstin kielen automaattinen tunnistaminen. Master's thesis, University of Helsinki, Helsinki.

Tommi Jauhiainen, Heidi Jauhiainen, Tero Alstola, and Krister Lindén. 2019a. Language and Dialect Identification of Cuneiform Texts. In *Proceedings of the Sixth Workshop on NLP for Similar Languages, Varieties and Dialects*, pages 89–98, Ann Arbor, Michigan. Association for Computational Linguistics.

Tommi Jauhiainen, Heidi Jauhiainen, and Krister Lindén. 2019b. Discriminating between Mandarin Chinese and Swiss-German varieties using adaptive language models. In *Proceedings of the Sixth Workshop on NLP for Similar Languages, Varieties and Dialects*, pages 178–187, Ann Arbor, Michigan. Association for Computational Linguistics.

Tommi Jauhiainen, Heidi Jauhiainen, and Krister Lindén. 2021. Naive Bayes-based experiments in Romanian dialect identification. In *Proceedings of the Eighth Workshop on NLP for Similar Languages, Varieties and Dialects*, pages 76–83, Kyiv, Ukraine. Association for Computational Linguistics.

Tommi Jauhiainen, Heidi Jauhiainen, and Krister Lindén. 2022. HeLI-OTS, off-the-shelf language identifier for text. In *Proceedings of the 13th Conference on Language Resources and Evaluation*, pages 3912–3922, Marseille, France. European Language Resources Association.

Tommi Jauhiainen, Heidi Jauhiainen, Niko Partanen, and Krister Lindén. 2020b. Uralic language identification (ULI) 2020 shared task dataset and the wanca 2017 corpora. In *Proceedings of the 7th Workshop on NLP for Similar Languages, Varieties and Dialects*, pages 173–185, Barcelona, Spain (Online). International Committee on Computational Linguistics (ICCL).

Tommi Jauhiainen, Krister Lindén, and Heidi Jauhiainen. 2015. Language Set Identification in Noisy Synthetic Multilingual Documents. In *Proceedings of the Computational Linguistics and Intelligent Text Processing 16th International Conference (CICLing 2015)*, pages 633–643, Cairo, Egypt.

Tommi Jauhiainen, Krister Lindén, and Heidi Jauhiainen. 2016. HeLI, a word-based backoff method for language identification. In *Proceedings of the Third Workshop on NLP for Similar Languages, Varieties and Dialects (VarDial3)*, pages 153–162, Osaka, Japan. The COLING 2016 Organizing Committee.

Tommi Jauhiainen, Krister Lindén, and Heidi Jauhiainen. 2019c. Language model adaptation for language and dialect identification of text. *Natural Language Engineering*, 25(5):561–583.

Tommi Jauhiainen, Marco Lui, Marcos Zampieri, Timothy Baldwin, and Krister Lindén. 2019d. Automatic Language Identification in Texts: A Survey. *Journal of Artificial Intelligence Research*, 65:675–782.

Ben King and Steven Abney. 2013. Labeling the Languages of Words in Mixed-Language Documents using Weakly Supervised Methods. In *Proceedings of the 2013 Conference of the North American Chapter of the Association for Computational Linguistics: Human Language Technologies*, pages 1110–1119, Atlanta, USA.

Benjamin Philip King. 2015. *Practical Natural Language Processing for Low-Resource Languages.* Ph.D. thesis.

Martin Majliš. 2011. Large Multilingual Corpus. Master's thesis, Charles University in Prague, Prague.

Shervin Malmasi, Marcos Zampieri, Nikola Ljubešić, Preslav Nakov, Ahmed Ali, and Jörg Tiedemann. 2016. Discriminating between similar languages and Arabic dialect identification: A report on the third DSL shared task. In *Proceedings of the Third Workshop on NLP for Similar Languages, Varieties and Dialects (VarDial3)*, pages 1–14, Osaka, Japan. The COLING 2016 Organizing Committee.

Paul Rodrigues. 2012. *Processing Highly Variant Language Using Incremental Model Selection.* Ph.D. thesis, Indiana University.

Marcos Zampieri, Shervin Malmasi, Nikola Ljubešić, Preslav Nakov, Ahmed Ali, Jörg Tiedemann, Yves Scherrer, and Noëmi Aepli. 2017. Findings of the VarDial evaluation campaign 2017. In *Proceedings of the Fourth Workshop on NLP for Similar Languages, Varieties and Dialects (VarDial)*, pages 1–15, Valencia, Spain. Association for Computational Linguistics.

Marcos Zampieri, Liling Tan, Nikola Ljubešić, and Jörg Tiedemann. 2014. A report on the DSL shared task 2014. In *Proceedings of the First Workshop on Applying NLP Tools to Similar Languages, Varieties and Dialects*, pages 58–67, Dublin, Ireland. Association for Computational Linguistics and Dublin City University.

Marcos Zampieri, Liling Tan, Nikola Ljubešić, Jörg Tiedemann, and Preslav Nakov. 2015. Overview of the DSL shared task 2015. In *Proceedings of the Joint Workshop on Language Technology for Closely Related Languages, Varieties and Dialects*, pages 1–9, Hissar, Bulgaria. Association for Computational Linguistics.

Author Index

Association for Computational Linguistics
209 N. Eighth Street
Stroudsburg, Pennsylvania 18360

ISBN 978-1-7138-6199-7

CURRAN ASSOCIATES INC.
proceedings
.com